The Overflowing of Friendship

The Overflowing of Friendship

*Love between Men and the Creation
of the American Republic*

RICHARD GODBEER

The Johns Hopkins University Press

Baltimore

© 2009 The Johns Hopkins University Press
All rights reserved. Published 2009
Printed in the United States of America on acid-free paper
9 8 7 6 5 4 3 2 1

The Johns Hopkins University Press
2715 North Charles Street
Baltimore, Maryland 21218-4363
www.press.jhu.edu

Library of Congress Cataloging-in-Publication Data
Godbeer, Richard.
    The overflowing of friendship : love between men and the creation of the American
Republic / Richard Godbeer.
        p.   cm.
    Includes bibliographical references and index.
    ISBN-13: 978-0-8018-9120-5 (hardcover : alk. paper)
    ISBN-10: 0-8018-9120-5 (hardcover : alk. paper)
    1. Men—United States—History—18th century. 2. Male friendship—United States—
History—18th century. 3. United States—Social life and customs—History—18th
century. I. Title.
    HQ1090.3.G63 2009
    305.310973′09033—dc22   2008021044

A catalog record for this book is available from the British Library.

For Andrew and Piotr

CONTENTS

ACKNOWLEDGMENTS

I began work on *The Overflowing of Friendship* a few years before leaving Southern California and have finished it almost four years after moving to Miami. Both the University of California at Riverside and the University of Miami have supported this project in important ways. In particular, I would like to express my appreciation to the Center for Ideas and Society at UCR and especially its director, Emory Elliott, for a resident fellowship in the spring quarter of 2003 and a research grant in 2003–2004; I hope that Emory knows how much his support and encouragement meant to me throughout my years at UCR. I am also thankful for funding from the Academic Senate at UCR to support the initial stages of my research for this project. The Interlibrary Loan staff at the Tomas Rivera Library were tireless in their efforts to locate and procure many of the printed sources used in this book; I remember Janet and her wonderful colleagues with much gratitude and affection. Since arriving at the University of Miami, I have rapidly accumulated debts of gratitude to the staff of the Richter Library, especially its director, William Walker, whose decision to acquire for the library digital versions of the Early American Imprints and Early American Newspapers collections made a dramatic difference to the final phase of my research; Bill is a remarkable colleague and friend. I am also very grateful for research support from the Dean of Arts and Sciences and the Department of History, which enabled me to complete the project in a timely fashion.

As with previous projects, my visits to archival collections have left me indebted to many curators and librarians for their time, expertise, and good cheer. I am grateful to the staff at the Library of Congress; the Massachusetts Historical Society; the Boston Athenaeum; the American Antiquarian Society; Yale University Library's Department of Manuscripts and Archives; the Historical Society of Pennsylvania; the Library Company of Philadelphia; the Quaker Collection at Haverford College Library; the New York Historical Society; the Firestone Rare Books and Manuscripts Library at Princeton University; the Maryland Historical Society; the Library of Virginia; the Virginia Historical Society; the Rare Book, Manuscript, and Special Collections Library at Duke University; and the Southern Historical Collection in the Wilson Library at University of North Carolina, Chapel Hill, for their kind assistance. I also want to thank Michael Bernath, Wendy Lucas Castro, Thomas Foster, Wendy Gamber, Christine Heyrman, Mary Lindemann, Elizabeth Reis, and Ashli White for sharing material and citations. But my greatest debt in this regard is to literary scholar Caleb Crain, who alerted me to the survival of the first volume of John Mifflin's journal and provided me with a copy of the manuscript; my sincere thanks also to the private owner of this journal for allowing Caleb and me to use it.

During the years since I started work on this volume, I have been asked many thought-provoking questions at conferences and other venues where I have given papers relating to the project. A panel on "Cultivating Emotion in the Early Republic" at an annual meeting of the Society for Historians of the Early American Republic and a roundtable on "Historicizing Gender in Early America" at an annual meeting of the Organization of American Historians proved particularly valuable. My thanks to all of these questioners and to those who organized, chaired, and gave formal comments at these gatherings. My colleagues in the Early Modern Gender Reading Group at UM read part of one chapter and gave me invaluable feedback. And then there is Jim Downs, who encouraged me in his own inimitable way to embrace more forthrightly the multilayered possibilities of my material.

Last year several friends and colleagues kindly agreed to read a draft of the entire manuscript. Whatever its faults, this book is certainly much stronger as a result of their comments and suggestions. Catherine Allgor, Jeanne Boydston, Wendy Lucas Castro, Mary Lindemann, Anthony Rotundo, Guido Ruggiero, Sheila Skemp, Ashli White, and Donald Yacovone have all left their mark on the pages that follow. Three of my graduate students—Lauren Lane, Simonetta Marin, and James Smith—also read the manuscript and prompted me to rethink the exposition of my argument at a key moment in the book's evolution. Three of my readers—Mary Lindemann, Guido Ruggiero, and Ashli White—are fellow early modernists in the Department of History at the University of Miami; that I find myself so happy there is due in no small part to the intellectual community that they provide, to say nothing of their zany humor and appreciation for good food. A few years ago, when I met Jeanne Boydston for the first time, we began a conversation about the meaning of gender in the eighteenth century that proved invaluable as I wrote and rewrote several key passages of this book; no one who is lucky enough to know Jeanne will be surprised to read that her comments on the manuscript were as generous and supportive as they were incisive and challenging. In addition, I want to single out Tony Rotundo and Donald Yacovone, in part for their generous reading of my manuscript but also and perhaps especially, for their pioneering scholarship on friendship in U.S. history, which has inspired and informed my work from the moment at which I embarked upon this project through to its completion.

Ever since I began reading the letters and diaries in which eighteenth-century men wrote about their friendships, I have been moved over and over again by the intensity of the feelings that these men expressed and their clear sense of emotional commitment to one another. Even though much of this book is devoted to showing how different the eighteenth-century world of friendship was from our own, the quality of those premodern relationships strikes a very personal chord for me. They do so, I suspect, because I have been so blessed in my own friendships, which have sustained me through good times and bad, filling my life with love, laughter, and a sense of profound fellowship. This book is dedicated to two friends in particular.

I first met Piotr Gorecki when we were hired in the same year as assistant professors at the University of California at Riverside: we soon became close comrades, and throughout my fifteen years in Southern California we worked, played, laughed, and cried together, celebrating each other's successes and supporting each other through times of adversity. Several years later, at a party in some dark corner of the Inland Empire, I had the good fortune to meet Andrew Cooper: we soon discovered a remarkable convergence of interests, humor, and values that drew us to one another as friends; Andrew's outsider perspective on the idiosyncratic world of academia, often laced with droll and justifiably sardonic humor, has been both entertaining and salutary, but most importantly, I appreciate him as a man of ironclad moral integrity with a heart of gold.

Like many of the friends in this book who found themselves separated from each other, I miss these two remarkable men every day and always look forward eagerly to our reunions, yet I never feel entirely separated from them. They will always shine bright in the constellation of friendships that cast light and warmth upon my life. I dedicate this book to Andrew and Piotr with love and gratitude.

The Overflowing of Friendship

IT WAS SEPTEMBER 4, 1763, and Joseph Hooper, a recent graduate from Harvard College, sat down in Marblehead, Massachusetts, to compose a letter addressed to his former classmate, Benjamin Dolbeare. He wrote:

> The sun never rose and set upon me since I parted from you, but he brought to my longing imagination the idea of my bosom friend; my faithful memory daily represents him in all the endearing forms that in his presence ever rose in my mind. My fancy paints him in the most beautiful colours, and my soul is absorbed in contemplating the past, wishing for a reiteration and longing to pour forth the expressions of friendship, and receiving those that would calm the gloom, soften the horrors, and wholly extirpate the distractions that your absence creates—but I must have done and have scarce time to tell you how much I am your friend.[1]

More than twenty years later, on September 13, 1786, John Mifflin, a Philadelphian lawyer in his late twenties, noted in his journal that this was the birthday of his neighbor James Gibson, currently an undergraduate at Princeton and known to his friends as Lorenzo:

> Serene was the sky and the sun shone bright upon the natal day of Lorenzo—I had scarcely awoke when I recollected it and I congratulated myself on the anniversary of the happy day on which so dear, so affectionate, and so amiable a friend came into existence—I felt a thousand good wishes for him and I thought I could not express them better than in the lines of Pope,
> "Oh be thou blest with all that Heaven can send,
> Long health, long youth, long pleasure, and a friend."[2]

Farther south, two Virginians, William Wirt and Dabney Carr, first became acquainted in the 1790s as eager young lawyers soliciting for clients. Riding together from courthouse to courthouse, they laid the foundation for a friendship that would last throughout their lives. William later reminisced about those early years of their friendship with "a swelling of the heart." When Dabney penned for him a "rhapsody on life, and love, and friendship," William wrote in response, "How grateful are such effusions, how grateful to my mind and to my heart—They make me proud of your friendship—Ah! My dear Dabney, it is at such moments that my soul flies out to meet yours—and as they mix and commingle I feel myself exalted and refined." William rejoiced in the "intimacy and consciousness which seem[ed] to subsist between [their] hearts and understandings." His friend's letters "always spread such a sweet glow through [his] breast" and their relationship, he declared, was "among the purest and sweetest sources of happiness" that he had "upon this earth."[3]

When I first encountered declarations such as these in letters and journal entries written by eighteenth-century American men, I was moved and also intrigued. Indeed, their emotional intensity was so striking and they prompted so many questions that it seemed impossible to pass them by. How common were such expressions of love between men during this period? What did loving friendship mean to these men as a part of their personal and social identities? In what ways, if at all, did male friends express physically or even sexually their feelings for one another? How did relatives and other friends or acquaintances react to such relationships? Did men who developed loving friendships with other men enter into marriages with women and, if so, how comfortably did these two kinds of relationship coexist? How did loving friendships between men fit within contemporary models of manhood? What did ministers and other religious spokesmen have to say on the subject of friendship and love? Why did celebrations of male friendship appear so frequently and prominently in post-revolutionary writings? And what roles did these authors envisage for friendship in the creation of an independent and republican nation? Before I knew it, I was hooked, and this book is the result.

Figuring out what these romantic friendships meant to people living in the eighteenth century involves setting aside modern assumptions about love between members of the same sex. Perhaps it would be helpful to begin by acknowledging those assumptions and discussing the challenges that they pose if we want to understand a world very different from our own. When I read declarations of love such as those quoted above to my students or friends, they usually either squirm in discomfort or wriggle in astonished delight. Once they have recovered sufficiently to start asking questions, they almost always want to know if the authors were "gay," "homosexual," or "queer." In common with many people today, they assume that expressions of loving devotion must imply a desire for sexual intimacy, or, to put it another way, that people who are in love with one another must want to have sex. That modern readers would make this assumption is hardly surprising: the paradigm of sexual orientation—which first emerged in the late nineteenth century, took hold in the early twentieth century, and still dominates Western society's understanding of how people are drawn to one another—teaches us that romantic feelings generally go hand in hand with sexual attraction. Yet however compelling our own models and categories may seem to us, they will not necessarily enable us to see the world as people living in the past saw it.[4]

The modern assumption that most people are attracted—sexually and romantically—to either men or women would have surprised early Americans. Their attitudes toward love, sexual desire, and the relationship between the two differed from ours in significant ways. First, in common with their contemporaries in early modern England and Europe, North American colonists did not think about their sexual impulses in terms of a distinct sexuality that oriented men and women toward members of the same or opposite sex. Instead they understood erotic desires and acts as an expression of social or moral standing. Let me explain what I mean by giving a few concrete examples. Consider the Southern planter who asserted his cherished identity as a gentleman by characterizing sex as a genteel activity, referring to intercourse with his wife as a "flourish," or courtly gesture, to extramarital sex as "promiscuous gallantry," and to venereal infection as a "polite disorder," or the Puritan New Englander who condemned any form of nonmarital sex as a "pollution" of the body that should be kept pure as a temple for the soul and who worried constantly about succumbing to "unclean" impulses. The first individual categorized sexual acts in terms of social identity, the second as part of a larger moral and spiritual endeavor. Both gave meaning and value to sex using categories that were not themselves intrinsically sexual.[5] Early Americans in general were taught to believe that all sex outside marriage—whether masturbation, casual fornication, premarital sex, adultery, or sodomy—was driven by innate moral corruption inherited from Adam and Eve; it expressed moral, not sexual, orientation. We know that there were men in British America who found themselves attracted to other men, yet the modern category of "homosexual" would have made little sense to them or their neighbors; they had their own conceptual frameworks through which to understand their urges and behavior. Strictly speaking, men who practiced sodomy during this period did not engage in homosexual acts, any more than the planter giving his wife "a flourish" was engaging in a heterosexual act.[6]

Early Americans tended, moreover, to think about gender in ways very different from those that characterize modern Anglo-American culture. They clearly associated certain attributes and roles with masculinity and others with femininity, but they did not assume that these roles were or should be attached only to one sex or the other: men and women could embody both masculine and feminine attributes in appropriate contexts. Early Americans thought about behavior and feelings in terms of varied gender roles, not as a unitary gender identity. Again, let me give a concrete example. Puritan men were expected to cultivate a loving and even passionate devotion to Christ, envisaging him as a prospective bridegroom who would eventually marry the souls of the redeemed, male as well as female, consummating that union in ecstatic love raptures. Those same men would meanwhile marry women on earth, developing ardent relationships with their wives that prefigured eventual union with their male savior. In relation to their wives on earth, they were functionally male; in relation to Christ in the spiritual realm, they were functionally female. As we will see, this understanding of the relationship between the faithful and their savior was by no means unique to Puritan New Englanders. For a man to love a male figure such as Christ and to express that love in language that was intensely passionate and romantic would not have struck colonists as problematic. Indeed, early Americans welcomed and respected love between men on earth as well as in the spiritual realm, just so long as that love was nonsexual.[7]

Declarations of love by one man to another would not automatically have suggested to relatives or neighbors that sexual relations might be taking place. Indeed, most Anglo-Americans living in the colonial and revolutionary periods treated emotional ties between male friends as quite distinct from sexual desire. Sodomy was illegal and denounced by religious leaders as an abominable sin, but nonerotic love between men was seen as decent, honorable, and praiseworthy. Acceptable expressions of love between men included not only words, either written or spoken, but also physical affection. Some readers may be surprised that I avoid describing these friendships as "platonic." I do so because this word is often taken to mean a nonphysical as well as nonsexual relationship, which would be misleading since many of the friendships examined in this book were physically very demonstrative. Male friends often referred to the pleasure that they took in touching and holding one another; they delighted in the proximity of each other's bodies. The Anglo-American men about whom I am writing clearly perceived the body as an appropriate medium for the expression of love. Then as now, physical intimacy could and sometimes did become explicitly erotic; but early Americans did not assume that physical affection necessarily expressed a desire for sexual intimacy; indeed they had no difficulty envisaging a passionate yet nonsexual love between two men. Instead of imposing our own assumptions onto the evidence and then concluding that such men must have been in denial about the true nature of their feelings for one another—in other words, assuming that they were closeted gay men—this study acknowledges that premodern American men embraced a range of possibilities for relating to other men that included intensely physical yet nonsexual relationships.

None of this is to deny that loving friendships between men did sometimes include an erotic component. Recent scholars of early modern England and Europe have uncovered examples of male friendship in which love and sexual attraction intermingled.[8] Very occasionally journals and letters that survive from the colonial and revolutionary periods in North America also hint at the possibility of erotic desire. Such evidence has often been downplayed or suppressed by scholars who do not wish to acknowledge such possibilities.[9] Historians interested in male-male sexual desire during the colonial and early national periods face a range of obstacles. These include the understandable reluctance of men to acknowledge openly their attraction to other men in a society that criminalized sodomy and also the lengths to which some embarrassed or perplexed contemporaries went in their efforts to avoid acknowledging same-sex desire. The vocabulary that Americans used during this period to describe sexual attraction or activity was sometimes ambiguous and unspecific, making it difficult to determine exactly what was being described. And last but not least, past scholars have sometimes ignored or suppressed evidence that they found distasteful. I have no intention of aiding and abetting that kind of censorship and welcome recent attempts to recover a long suppressed history of male-male and female-female intimacy; that scholarship can stand proud alongside efforts to reconstruct the lives and experiences of other groups that have been ignored or silenced.[10]

And yet, in avoiding undue reticence or actual suppression of historical evidence, we should take care not to fall into the trap of seeing what we expect or want to see. Sexualized love was just one in a rich repertoire of possibilities open to premodern men as they explored their feelings for male friends. Early Americans created an expansive and eloquent rhetorical space for the expression of same-sex love that was physically affectionate and yet nonerotic. There may well have been cases in which that conception of male love provided a cover for erotic intimacy that would otherwise have endangered the individuals concerned (not only in terms of the legal penalties for sodomy but also in terms of the social and self-inflicted stigma that attached to a man who apparently wanted to have sex with other men). Some of the men we will be meeting tip-toed along the boundary between physical affection and erotic encounters quite self-consciously and even playfully; others were dismayed to identify feelings within themselves and others that they found abhorrent and frightening. Yet we cannot simply assume that men who loved one another must have wanted to have sex, let alone that they actually did so.[11] In common with recent studies of premodern male friendship across the Atlantic, this book refuses to ignore the passionate nature of many such friendships and yet insists that we not impose our own assumptions and sexual categories onto such relationships.[12]

Scholars of early modern England have noted that the specter of sodomy did occasionally cast a shadow over loving male friendships.[13] By the early eighteenth century, there had emerged in London a distinct subculture catering to men who sought sexual intimacy with members of the same sex; such men could meet in specific parks or taverns, the latter known as "molly" houses because of the self-consciously effeminate and often cross-dressing men who frequented such establishments. Lurid descriptions of these gathering places appeared in printed accounts of police raids on such establishments and transformed sodomy from an indistinct threat, often associated with foreigners, to a much more immediate and concrete phenomenon. At the same time, the notion of sodomy as an immoral act that anyone might be tempted to engage in was giving way to the image of the sodomite, a distinct social category referring to a specific cadre of men who were consistently attracted to other men. Some scholars have argued that these developments made men much more reluctant to express affection that might be confused with sexual interest, and it is perhaps no coincidence that by the middle of the eighteenth century Englishmen were shaking each other's hands rather than embracing and kissing one another.[14]

But no such subculture emerged in British America. A wide spectrum of city dwellers on the eastern seaboard were exposed to imported images of the homoerotic through accounts of police raids and prosecutions in London as well as through literary representations such as Lord Strutwell and Captain Whiffle, characters in Tobias Smollett's popular novel *Roderick Random*. Yet American newspapers still depicted sodomy as an alien vice and, more specifically, as a prime example of British decadence; they generally kept silent about its occurrence in their own midst. Descriptions of physical affection between men did occasionally suggest that untoward intimacies were taking place, especially in attacks on groups that were otherwise suspicious, such as the Freemasons; but in general neither expressions of love nor physical affection between men were taken to signify sexual attraction, and so they continued to play an important role in early American male friendships throughout the eighteenth century.[15] Such relationships occupied an almost entirely positive and respected place within colonial society and among citizens of the new republic. As we will see, heroic and biblical precedents for love between men proved far more important than dark associations with sodomy as reference points for male friendship.

Men in early modern England and North America used biblical and classical models to provide a worthy lineage for their feelings. Ministers invoked the relationship between David and Jonathan as an inspiring example of men's capacity for loving and virtuous friendship; they accorded such friendships a central place in their vision for the creation and sustenance of godly community. Male friends responded enthusiastically. One young man hoped that he and his beloved friend would enjoy "the same Christian bond of union that Jonathan and David had." Another likened his love for a male friend to that of "Prince Jonathan" for his "little ruddy Captain David." Given the important role played by classical literature in early American education and polite society, it is hardly surprising that educated men also drew inspiration from the love that bound Greek heroes to one another, using friendships such as those between Damon and Pythias or Achilles and Petroclus as models for their own relationships.[16]

Loving friendships between men also acquired legitimacy through their characterization as a form of kinship. People on both sides of the early modern Atlantic routinely used familial language to depict a broad range of social, political, and religious relationships. Monarchs, for example, figured as parents of their subjects, just as God governed his creation as a loving, though often stern, father. As we have seen, believers envisaged Christ as a spiritual bridegroom who would one day unite with them through marriage in heaven, creating a conjugal family of the saved. Meanwhile, in this world, the faithful represented their spiritual and emotional ties to one another in familial terms: referring to each other as brothers and sisters in Christ, they rejoiced in their kinship as children of God.[17] This expansive conception of kinship extended well beyond the spiritual realm. Just as husbands and wives became members of their spousal families, though not related by blood, so friends also became elective kin. Family incorporated not only biological kin and conjugal relatives but also friends with whom one felt a sense of kinship. Friendship and family membership overlapped as categories of association: people often referred to blood relatives as friends and addressed friends to whom they had no biological relationship as if they were kinfolk.[18] The characterization of friends as family members was neither perfunctory nor merely honorary; it indicated a very real and meaningful connection between individuals. Friends sometimes figured as elective parents: we will, for example, meet young eighteenth-century evangelicals who addressed older ministers with whom they developed close friendships as fathers. But it was much more common to describe the emotional bond between male friends in terms of "loving brotherhood" or "fraternal love." Different forms of voluntary kinship could coexist within the same relationship: male friends sometimes combined the language of fraternity with that of marriage. This overlapping terminology, though perhaps both confusing and jarring to us, captured for these premodern friends the multilayered and multivalent nature of their commitment to one another.[19]

The conflation of kinship and friendship enabled a much broader network of personal association than that encompassed by blood or marital kinship. Loyalties associated with friendship seem for the most part to have complemented rather than clashed with those of blood and marriage. (One striking exception to this was a group of evangelical clergymen who, as we will see, eschewed conventional marriage in favor of their relationships with each other as well as with their savior.) Some scholars of early modern England argue that by the seventeenth century the emotional intimacy associated with friendship did become competitive with the love and affection that ideally blossomed within marriage.[20] If so, this does not appear to have happened in British America or the early republic, where most male friends neither envisaged nor apparently experienced tension between their marital relationships and long-term attachment to male friends. William Wirt, whose effusive and sentimental correspondence with Dabney Carr we encountered in the opening paragraph of this introduction, wrote in a similar style to his wife Elizabeth. Both of these relationships—one with his wife, the other with his male friend—were deeply loving and indispensable to his emotional well-being. There was nothing unusual about this twofold commitment of the heart: early Americans took it for granted that loving relationships between men—and also between women—could coexist with heartfelt love for a person of the opposite sex.[21]

As men developed loving friendships with one another, they did so with the active approval and encouragement of their biological families and of society as a whole. Early Americans believed that male friendship not only conferred personal happiness but also nurtured qualities that would radiate outward and transform society as a whole. They envisaged society not as an abstract entity but as the sum of individual and intensely personalized relationships, including loving friendships between men. Historians have paid close attention to the ways in which the premodern family household functioned as a microcosm of society, training children in the roles that they would perform as adults and serving as the principal metaphor through which people in the colonies articulated all social, political, and religious relationships. The role played by friendship in enabling sociability has attracted much less attention. As a recent scholar points out, we tend to think of friendship as "essentially private" and become uncomfortable when personal allegiances seem to be shaping public decisions or behavior. Yet in the early modern period people believed that personal friendships should inform and enrich social and public interactions, creating affective bonds between individuals that would then serve as the emotional sinews of a larger identity. Private relationships played, then, a crucial role in shaping the structure and tone of public life; contemporaries routinely asserted that ties between friends had both a deeply personal and also a broad public significance.[22] Friendship was itself a multivalent term, signifying both practical collaboration and emotional connection. As we will see, the latter meaning assumed greater salience during the early modern period, but the overlap and interplay of affective and practical impulses remained intrinsic to eighteenth-century conceptions of friendship: the friend figured both as a personal good in his own right and as a means to a larger social good.[23]

Male friends often characterized the feelings that bound them to one another in terms of *sensibility* and *sympathy*, associating themselves with a culture of emotional awareness and expression that was highly influential in eighteenth-century transatlantic polite society. According to those who wrote about sentimental friendship, whether in general terms or as a personal experience, developing an intense capacity for emotion and a loving empathy with the feelings of others constituted an important part of becoming a worthy and refined man. Writers on this subject depicted the cultivation of sensibility and sympathy as a self-conscious process that involved four distinct stages. First, one must learn about the experience, expression, and significance of feeling from newspapers, magazines, novels, letter-writing manuals, sermons, and (for those with the time and education) more demanding philosophical works on the subject. Second, one had to pay close attention to one's own feelings and those of friends. Third, one had to open oneself to experiencing those feelings as intensely as possible. Finally, one must be able and willing to express such sensations, both physically and through the spoken or written word. Emotional feeling was, then, much more than a state of being: it was a form of work—a labor of love.[24]

This book reconstructs that world of feeling as it was experienced by early American men. In doing so, it calls our attention to overlap and interchange between male and female realms of experience. Printed discussions of friendship saw feeling and its fruits as a form of endeavor that men and women shared in common. Historians have established that loving same-sex friendships played a central role in women's lives. Literate women wrote of their feelings for one another in letters that bore a remarkable resemblance to those passing back and forth between male friends. Indeed, men were eager to learn about the experience and expression of sympathetic friendship from women. Male friends developed relationships that quite self-consciously paralleled female friendships and used a similar language to express their devotion to each other, which tells us something very interesting about the way that gender functioned in this period. Sentimental friendship was clearly gendered in that contemporaries identified the emotional processes at work as feminine, but not in the sense that only one sex was involved. Male experience of sensibility and sympathy reflected premodern notions of gender, which accommodated both masculine and feminine attributes within the same person; men could thus embrace roles and qualities identified as feminine without endangering their sense of themselves as men. A close examination of sentimental friendship as experienced by men not only broadens and deepens our understanding of eighteenth-century manhood, both in its personal and in its public incarnations, but also challenges us to reconsider the ways in which we think about gender in this period.[25]

In arguing that the culture of sentiment and sympathy played a significant role in the lives of these male friends, I do not mean to suggest that this was true of all eighteenth-century American men. Opening one's heart to such feelings was a deliberate act of will, and not all men chose to embrace that possibility. Alongside a discourse of sentimental friendship and affective association, a very different literary tradition celebrated satirical and bawdy humor as well as a lusty and competitive male bravado. Even those Americans who embraced ideals of loving friendship recognized that putting those ideals into practice involved an uphill struggle in the face of vicious rivalries and deep-seated enmities that poisoned colonial and post-revolutionary society. But what follows is an explicit challenge to the notion that male interaction during this period was predominantly contentious and competitive. A significant body of literature in the eighteenth-century encouraged Americans to envisage a very different version of male sociability, and at least some men made it a priority in their lives to cultivate a camaraderie of mutual sympathy, support, and love. They hoped that in time those ideals would infuse individual relationships and in turn transform the tone of social engagement as a whole. Meanwhile, fraternal orders such as the Freemasons depicted their organizations as the spearheads for a new social order based on the cultivation of sympathetic love between men.[26]

That culture of sentimental friendship was a transatlantic phenomenon, by no means unique to early American society.[27] But it would acquire a particular and explicitly political significance for North Americans during the revolutionary period, when the encouragement of intense and loving male friendships came to be seen as crucial to the nation-building project and its creation of worthy republican citizens. As Americans grappled with the challenge of translating republican principles into practice, friendship became doubly significant: first, as a way of encouraging empathy between citizens in a society that no longer cohered through shared loyalty to a monarch; and second, as part of a larger project to reimagine the family in ways appropriate to a new and somewhat democratized era. Drawing on the ideas of moral philosophers who stressed the importance of sympathetic friendship in nurturing social benevolence, republican thinkers crafted a blueprint for nationhood that shifted attention away from patriarchal authority toward fraternal collaboration and called for the active encouragement of brotherly love between friends. Such friendships, along with marital and parental love, would nurture social and moral instincts crucial to the well-being of a post-revolutionary society. Post-revolutionary thinkers envisaged a new national family bound together by parental affection, marital friendship, and loving brotherhood. The latter featured as an essential component of that enlightened trinity.

Recent historians have examined the moral and emotional responsibilities that women were expected to assume as republican wives and mothers in the new nation, but less attention has been paid to the importance attached by contemporaries to male emotional labor in the early decades of Independence, including the cultivation of sympathy between male friends. We are accustomed to thinking of men building the new republic through their activities as soldiers and strategists; as voters and political representatives; as thinkers, inventors, and writers; as producers of crops and goods. But men also saw themselves as contributing through their cultivation of feeling. Indeed, affective association would make all else possible as fraternal love and sympathy became the basis for collective action, replacing the corrupt instincts and alliances that had tainted public life under British rule. Given the reassurance and support that individuals drew from friends in times of challenge and uncertainty, it should not surprise us that Americans turned to friendship as an emotional anchor for the new nation itself as it struggled to establish social and political stability. Ideals of republican manhood celebrated sentiment and sympathy in part because these attributes enabled personal happiness, which the founding fathers had, after all, enshrined in their Declaration of Independence as a fundamental goal of any civilized society; but they also had a crucial public dimension, laying the foundation for effective collaboration between citizens, thereby ensuring the very survival of the new nation.[28]

ॐ

This book examines male friendship in British America and the early republic from three perspectives: as a private relationship between two men; as a social fact that encompassed relatives, other friends, and acquaintances; and as a topic of intense public interest. It uses an array of personal and public writings—letters, diaries and journals, newspaper and magazine articles, sermons, and political tracts—to reconstruct the ways in which men gave voice to their love for each other, paying close attention to the spectrum of feelings involved, and also the place that these friendships occupied in early American society. By no means all male friends wrote about their feelings; those who lived in the same neighborhood, for example, could express themselves in person and so may not have felt any need to put their feelings down on paper. Yet a striking number of men who went away on travels or found themselves more permanently separated from close friends did articulate their love in letters to one another, some of which have survived. Letter writing was an indispensable means of communication in this period and a routine part of daily activity for literate Americans, not only as a way to pass on information and consult on practical matters but also as a medium for the expression of feelings. If we add up the time that most of us spend in an average week speaking on the phone, emailing each other, and sending text messages via our cell phones, we will perhaps get some sense of the place that writing and receiving letters occupied in the lives of literate eighteenth-century men. These letters allow us to reconstruct not only the professional, public, and intellectual lives of their authors but also the feelings that men chose to articulate, including their love for one another.

Less privileged men rarely left behind them any trace of their personal lives or feelings. Many of these men would have been exposed to sermons on friendship and also the hundreds of articles on male friendship and love that were printed in eighteenth-century newspapers, either because they read these publications themselves or because they heard them being read aloud in taverns or at home. Yet while we can be confident that a broad range of Americans were exposed to a public conversation about male friendship, we cannot be sure how they responded. Those who could and did write on this subject often depicted sympathetic friendship as the expression of a refined sensibility that was at least implicitly exclusive in tone; as we will see, social commentators writing in the aftermath of Independence clearly hoped that the spirit of sentimental friendship would bring propertied and educated Americans together in constructive collaboration, but that version of civil society would by no means include all men. How those excluded from this fairly restrictive vision of loving brotherhood felt about such celebrations of friendship in post-revolutionary newspapers and speeches is open to question. Given how little we know about the views of less privileged Americans on this subject, the pages that follow limit themselves to addressing the significance of male friendship as it played out in the personal lives of literate, educated men and as it figured in post-revolutionary political discourse. The men about whom I am writing are, of course, interesting in their own right and played important roles in shaping eighteenth-century colonial and republican society, but I do not claim to be writing about all American men.

Those Americans about whom I am writing drew on a wide range of literary and rhetorical genres to articulate their feelings. It might be tempting to dismiss their effusive declarations as merely rhetorical gestures that tell us little about what they actually felt and did. But this book argues that treating their words as nothing more than genteel performance would be ill-advised, blinding us to a world of emotional experience that was real and meaningful to eighteenth-century Americans, even though that world may strike some modern readers as both alien and improbable. One friend writing in 1749 acknowledged that the stylistic devices he used in his letters had been lifted from "all kinds of polite literature," but then avowed "the sincerity of [his] heart in all these affirmations." Just because his prose style was hackneyed did not mean that it was insincere.[29] When friends described in their journals or recalled in their correspondence moments of emotional and physical intimacy, they may sometimes have embellished or even invented them, but they and their contemporaries seem to have assumed that such moments did occur. It seems prudent to treat these accounts as a blend of actual experience, wish fulfillment, and romantic idealization. Words create worlds: in speaking or writing about a world of male love, eighteenth-century American men ensured that they and those who listened to them or read their words experienced that emotional world, even if vicariously. It is also clear that the sentiments expressed by male friends in their letters and journal entries were accorded value in early American society (just as ideals of patriarchal authority carried tremendous significance in premodern society, even though not all men who wrote about or advocated that authority necessarily experienced it consistently in their own lives). Whether or not specific friendships always matched in practice the sensational language used to describe them, ideals of friendship did matter to early Americans, both in a personal context and also as they pondered ways of achieving greater social cohesion, especially in the aftermath of Independence.

In seeking to show the broader significance of friendships during the colonial and revolutionary periods, I do not want to lose sight of their importance as personal relationships. Early Americans perceived their world from a trajectory that proceeded outward from the personal and familial to the local, regional, national, international, and universal. The organization of this book respects that fundamental trajectory. I begin with a chapter that focuses on one young man and his close friendships with two male neighbors. I reconstruct the history of these friendships, their emotional tone, and the place that they occupied in the lives of all three men. The second chapter examines a range of other eighteenth-century male friendships which, when put together, enable us to see how those involved understood their feelings for other men, the ends that they saw their friendships as serving, and the roles that friendship played throughout their adult lives alongside their marital commitments. The remaining chapters consider social, religious, and political contexts in which early Americans perceived loving friendships as serving exalted and also radical ends that transcended and yet relied upon personal ties. Chapter 3 focuses on the role played by fraternal love within three religious movements: seventeenth-century Puritanism, pre-revolutionary revivalism, and post-revolutionary evangelicalism. All three movements were, by contemporary standards, remarkably democratic and egalitarian. This was no coincidence, since for each of these faith communities loving brotherhood figured as part of a larger shift from vertical to more horizontal conceptions of social identity. Chapter 4 examines the emotional ties that developed between young officers in the revolutionary army and places that loving brotherhood in the context of political transformations that enabled and accompanied the Declaration of Independence. The final chapter considers the place that sentimental friendship occupied within late eighteenth-century republican ideology as Americans envisaged the creation of a post-revolutionary society in which fraternal love would play a central and honored role.

CHAPTER ONE

"The Friend of My Bosom"

A Philadelphian Love Story

IT WAS EARLY EVENING on September 4, 1786, on a genteel street of Philadelphia, and twenty-seven-year-old John Mifflin was waiting impatiently to hear of his friend's arrival. Isaac Norris, Mifflin's junior by just a few months, had been away for three years on a tour of Europe, but a few days ago he had disembarked in New York and was now completing his homeward journey by coach. John had wanted to accompany his friend's mother as she traveled to meet Isaac on the road, but a bout of fever and dysentery had kept him at home. He noted in his journal that he was taking laudanum and also "a dose of rhubarb" to help clear his system. Mrs. Norris had promised that she would send the carriage around for him as soon as she and her son reached home. Meanwhile, John did his best to think his way into feeling better: "I will not be sick," he told himself, "I will conceit myself a well man." The young man was in a restless and fretful state of mind, "listening to the noise of every wheel to mind whether or not it stopped at the door" and "looking frequently at my watch to mark the progress of the hours which must pass before I meet that dear friend from whom I have been separated longer than thrice the annual course of the sun."[1]

At dusk it began to rain, and John feared that mother and son would not reach Philadelphia until the next day, but at last a messenger knocked at the door to announce his friend's arrival and to tell him that the carriage was on its way. "The welcome wheels soon confirmed the report," he wrote in his journal. John wrapped himself up and hurried outside for the short drive to the Norris residence. A combination of lingering fever and overexcitement sent John "into a perspiration" and he was "obliged to throw off some of [his] clothing." Once they arrived, John was "in such haste to get out that [he] missed the step and had [he] not caught hold on the carriage should have fallen." He hurried into the house "with all [his] invalid drapery flowing after [him]."

Isaac was in the back parlor with his mother: "As soon as he saw me enter the door, he sprang to me, caught me in his arms, and we clasped each other in the most affectionate embrace." John wrote that "what with the agitation of leaving home, the whirl along [the] street, and the transport of meeting," he "felt such a glow of health that [he] found it difficult to believe [he] was sick." He "talked and laughed and felt a new principle of life within": "In short I seemed to feel as I used to—feelings I have been a long while unaccustomed to." Isaac was evidently just as thrilled to be reunited with John. Later that evening, he told his friend that "he was determined we should never part again. 'I will give myself up to you,' said he, 'I will go whereever you go—and one shall not go without the other.'"[2]

This sentimental and dramatic account of John Mifflin's reunion with Isaac Norris was entirely in keeping with the reputation that both men enjoyed among their relatives and friends. Like most of the young men and women in their social circle, Mifflin and Norris had literary nicknames. The use of these nicknames—some of which were classical, others drawn from well-known plays or novels—expressed playful intimacy as well as self-conscious sophistication. Mifflin, Norris, and their friends were clearly engaging in a literary performance through which they asserted membership in an educated and genteel transatlantic society. Yet as they did so, they were not necessarily shedding their own personalities: indeed, the characters to which their nicknames referred were not so much alternative identities as literary personae that matched their temperaments. John Mifflin was known as Leander, Isaac Norris as Castalio. In Greek mythology Leander was the devoted admirer of Hero; he swam across the Hellespont every night to visit her, until he drowned one night when the light Hero had lit for him blew out in a storm. Castalio was one of the main characters in a well-known English Restoration play, *The Orphan, or, The Unhappy Marriage*, written by Thomas Otway and first performed in 1680; Castalio was a lovelorn young man who married his sweetheart Monimia in secret; she mistakenly admitted Castalio's perfidious brother to her bedroom on their wedding night, with unfortunate consequences for all concerned. Both of these particular figures had romantic, melodramatic, and ultimately tragic connotations. As we will see, this was entirely fitting, given the sentimental and self-dramatizing tendencies of our two Philadelphians, including and especially in their relationship with each other.[3]

On a more mundane level, John Mifflin was a lawyer and the son of a successful merchant. His family had a number of rental properties in Philadelphia, and in addition to conducting legal business, the young man regularly made the rounds collecting rent from the family's tenants. Isaac Norris was the eldest son of another affluent Philadelphian patriarch; his father was deceased, and his family had high expectations of Isaac. As one of his cousins put it, they had "fixed their hearts" on him and awaited the "fruits" of God's "great blessings" upon this "eldest son of a worthy father and family."[4] Travel was supposed to complete a young gentleman's education prior to the assumption of adult responsibilities, and so it was arranged that Isaac would leave for Europe on an extended tour in June 1783. At first John had planned to join him. Deborah Norris, Isaac's sister, predicted that traveling together through Europe would "cement" their friendship: "You would lay in a kind of joint stock of ideas," she enthused, "to serve you in future life."[5]

Unfortunately a rather nasty bout of illness left John weakened and unable to travel. Isaac's mother broke the news that John was "far from being in a good state of health" and that Isaac must "give up the hopes of seeing him" until his return to America. The separation was painful for both young men. Given that John and Isaac grew up in the same neighborhood and social circle, it seems likely that their friendship had developed over many years; Isaac's relatives described John as his "old" and indeed "first" friend.[6] Isaac now wrote that their separation left a "void" in his life "that nothing can replace." "One of the greatest pleasures in life," he confided to his sister Deborah, "is to have a friend whom you may treat with unreserve, but in traveling, when new objects are continually striking you, the pleasure must double and in this situation I have often had to lament my being alone." In another letter Isaac lamented the absence of a friend "to whom one may think aloud . . . It is so seldom, so seldom that one meets a congenial mind!" The young man placed a high premium on the "sympathies" that bound friends together: "The few friends I have in America are dearer to me than I can express, and I will not allow myself to think that anything can detach them from me."[7]

Back in Philadelphia, members of the Norris family vouched for John's steadfastness in their correspondence with Isaac. "He loves thee," declared Isaac's cousin, Mary Dickinson, and "possesses that inestimable jewel sincerity where he professes friendship." Mrs. Norris told her son that John visited "very often." "He is the same lively and sincere friend," she wrote: "He longs for thy return." Mrs. Norris cannot have been in any doubt as to the intensity of the bond between the two young men. John added a postscript to one of her letters for Isaac before she sealed it: "My dear Castalio," he wrote, "I know not how I should bear a disappointment of seeing you in the spring—come, I beseech—I crave you."[8] Isaac's mother welcomed such feelings, hoped that her son's friendship with John would "always continue," and treated John as if he were a member of the family. All of her own children had now left home to travel or marry. Finding herself alone in the Norris residence, she invited John to move in as "guard of the house."[9] The young man sometimes accompanied his friend's mother on social visits and, as she wrote in a letter to Isaac, "by his kind attention endeavoured to make up for the absence of my children." Indeed, she referred to John as "my adopted son."[10] Other members of the Norris clan were also clearly fond of John and acknowledged his position as Isaac's particular friend. When a cousin, Hannah Thomson, wrote in May 1786 to tell John that she expected Isaac to arrive in New York that July, she added that she and her husband would "be pleased when he arrives to see J.M. here." Following Isaac's return, she issued an invitation to them as if they were a couple of sorts. "I wish," she wrote in a letter to John, that "cousin Isaac and you would come and eat your Christmas dinner here."[11]

Isaac's absence had been a torment for John, who felt "friendless and forlorn" without him. "How I want a confidant," he confided to his journal.[12] John waited impatiently for "letters from my dear Castalio," not least because they might contain news of his imminent arrival. He planned to take a stagecoach to New York as soon as Isaac's ship laid anchor and then accompany him on his journey back to Philadelphia. But when his friend would actually arrive was anyone's guess. At the beginning of June, a letter arrived "with an assurance of his speedy return," and John's response in his journal was little short of ecstatic: "with what alacrity shall I fly to meet him." As the weeks passed by, he struggled to maintain "high spirits, anticipating the happiness of meeting my dear Castalio, from whom I have been so long separated."[13] In July 1786 news reached Philadelphia that a French ship had sailed into port at New

York. John dashed frantically through the streets, knocking on the doors of friends and acquaintances who might have news as to whether Isaac was one of the passengers, but all to no avail: "[I] got back to Mrs. Norris's as uncertain as I went, in a great heat and almost out of breath—had a very restless night, with broken dreams." The next morning he "went out to make further enquiries . . . but could get no certainty." Later in the day a letter arrived from relatives in New York to inform Isaac's mother that he was definitely not on board, "a wretched disappointment and Mrs. N[orris] very much distressed at it." John also had been depending upon his friend's return: "The hope of his arrival had inspired me with a kind of new life and for our mutual enjoyment I had laid a succession of plans for the remainder of the season." The young man's distress now bled onto the pages of his journal: "The return of a friend—the joys of meeting—the sentimental happiness of long accustomed friendship and happiness—all—all have vanished for the present—'like the baseless fabric of a vision.'"[14]

A few days later Mrs. Norris received another letter informing her that Isaac would not reach home until the following month. "Alas!" declared John. "Year after year, month after month steals on and Castalio is still absent—life seems to stagnate unemployed in friendship." Yet he did draw solace from the degree of certainty that this latest missive seemed to convey: "But one month more and I trust my friend will return to cheer the heavy moments." The young man waxed poetic as he yearned for his friend's arrival:

> Fly swift ye hours, you measure time in vain
> Till ye bring back Castalio again.
> Be swifter now and to redeem that wrong
> When he and I are met, be twice as long.[15]

A little more than a month later, on August 30, John read in the newspaper that another French ship had sailed into port in New York City. He rushed over to the Norris residence with the announcement. Soon afterward, a letter arrived with "the joyful tidings of my dear friend Castalio's arrival at New York—it was such a burst of pleasure to me that I scarce knew how to deport myself and I believe I behaved myself for a while as if I were a little frantic." Prevented by his sickness from traveling to greet his friend, John had to reconcile himself to a few more days of waiting, "all impatience," until Isaac's final arrival in the city transformed his torment into a "delirium of joy."[16]

The morning after Isaac's arrival, John wrote in his journal, "Visitors soon began to come to pay their congratulations"—as much to John, it would seem, as to the Norris family. That same day John's physician told him that Isaac's arrival had evidently done him a power of good. Doctor and patient "had a long agreeable conversation made up of philosophy and sentiment," after which John wrote that he was "happy to hear him speak in such terms of approbation of my friend."[17] Over the weeks and months that followed, Isaac and John enjoyed many hours of intimate company, often in the Norrises' beautifully maintained garden. Deborah Norris, Isaac's sister, later described the garden as "a spot of elegance and floral beauty . . . laid out in square parterres and beds, regularly intersected by graveled and grass walks and alleys, yet some of the latter were so completely hid by the trees by which they were bordered as to be secluded and rural." The Norrises often made their grounds available to fellow Philadelphians as a venue for recreation and display: "A walk in the garden," wrote Deborah, "was considered by the more respectable citizens as a treat to their friends from a distance, and as one of the means to impress them with a favourable opinion of the beauties of their city." But it also provided the setting for more private gatherings of family members and friends. On one particularly idyllic afternoon, Isaac and John "sat some time in [the] pear grove, then strolled round the gravel walks of the garden." Mifflin wrote that "the conversation was very interesting to us both—what a comfort, what a happiness to have a friend to adjust one's private sentiments by." That night John "amused [himself] reading over [Isaac's] old letters, a delightful banquet," and a few days later Isaac produced "a bundle of [John's] old letters" for them to read over together.[18] But their conversations did not dwell only on past pleasures. One evening the two friends had "a long and very interesting conversation" in Isaac's chamber, devising "a plan of future life and happiness." When Mifflin got home, he lay "awake very late, reflecting on it." The next day they "walked up and down the grand walk of the garden for near an hour, conversing on last evening's subject." Mifflin relished such tête-à-têtes: "How delightful! how happy to have a friend who gives such unequivocal proofs of his friendship."[19]

Yet all was not well. During his stay in Europe Isaac revealed to his family back home that before leaving Philadelphia he had converted in secret from Quakerism to Catholicism, a dramatic shift in religious allegiance. Isaac's relatives were appalled, as was his friend. Soon after Isaac's return to Philadelphia, John "c[a]me to a determination to talk seriously to him" about his conversion, though he worried that he was "unequal to the task": "I have not studied controversial points sufficiently to combat all the arguments he may bring to defend himself in his errors."[20] Equally disturbing was that Isaac was sinking into a deep depression. His brother Joseph, who visited him in Europe, wrote that he found Isaac in low spirits and increasingly withdrawn: indeed, he spent much of his time "cubbed up in a little pitiful dark chamber."[21] Back in Philadelphia, Isaac's spirits did not improve. The precise cause of his melancholy was (and remains) obscure, but its increasing severity became a source of grave concern to those who loved him. On one occasion John arrived at the Norris home to be informed that "Castalio had not made his appearance below stairs although it was past twelve." John was "really concerned lest he injure his health by his present inactive mode of life." Later that afternoon he called in again and went upstairs "to rally him for his indolence." Within weeks of his return home, Isaac began to think about leaving again. "From some conversation I have had with him today," wrote John, "I am a little apprehensive that he intends, or at least wishes, to return to Europe." Isaac began to concoct "wild schemes" that alarmed his friend, though John took some comfort from knowing that he was "woven into all his schemes and I know his attachment to me is such that he can resolve on none without me."[22]

As the weeks passed by, Isaac became more and more a recluse. "He seems never easy but when I am with him," wrote John, "and frequently when we are together he will not talk." Isaac sometimes behaved "almost as if he had been stricken." In November 1787, Mrs. Norris wrote to a relative that Isaac was looking "better, but far from well." She thought that he would improve further if he "exert[ed] himself more and mix[ed] a little more in the world," but he "exclude[d] himself too much, he converse[d] with nobody hardly, but his friend John Mifflin."[23] As Isaac's condition worsened, John made every effort to draw him into social activities with relatives and friends or, at the very least, into spending time together as a twosome. Yet even he found Isaac increasingly mercurial and unresponsive. He wrote in his journal entry for February

16, 1787, that the day had been "quite vernal . . . the sort of charming weather which makes me wish for a confidential, sentimental ramble with one's friend—a day which enlivens the affections and makes friendship seem to be the business of life." Yet Isaac "could not be prevailed upon to venture out," though the next day his friend did persuade him to take a "stroll" in the garden. One evening, wrote John, "I was in wretched spirits and wanted [Castalio] to come home with me—but he would not—and I do not remember when I wanted more the exhilarating society of a friend." Isaac's bouts of illness and depression took their toll on John: "The spirits of my friends are always of consequence to me," he declared, "I am ever influenced by them—Castalio's spirits always affect me."[24]

&

Fortunately for John Mifflin, Isaac Norris was no longer his only intimate friend. Mrs. Norris had written to Isaac during his absence in Europe about "a young neighbor of ours (a son of the late John Gibson)," "a fine amiable youth" who had recently accompanied Mifflin on a trip out of town. Fifteen-year-old James Gibson, known to his friends as Lorenzo, was an undergraduate at Princeton University. His widowed mother lived on the same block of Chestnut Street as the Norris family. John Mifflin and James Gibson had met at a lecture in Philadelphia on March 14, 1785. The subject, appropriately enough, was electricity. Each had found his way to the front row of the crowded gallery in the lecture hall and John was, as he later wrote in his journal, "indebted to my new friend for a seat." James's "gentle manners and modest politeness" kindled in John "an immediate attachment to him." When the lecture came to an end, they walked home together, and on parting they agreed to meet again at the next lecture.[25]

Two years later, John recalled that meeting in his journal. "Today," he wrote, "is one of my happy anniversaries—one of those days which I remember with heartfelt sentimental pleasure—about six o'clock this evening it is two years since the commencement of my acquaintance and friendship with Lorenzo—I may say they commenced together, for I felt the dawnings of a friendship for him as soon as I saw him—a presentiment of that native worth which a close intimacy hath since confirmed, and taught me to esteem and love." Had it not been for that fortuitous meeting, he wrote, "We might have lived in and passed through the world without ever knowing or caring for each other." John adorned this particular journal entry with a couplet:

O! may that eve all happiness portend
Which gave Lorenzo for Leander's friend.

He acknowledged in retrospect that he was at the time feeling "rather friendless and forlorn without a confidant," Isaac having left for Europe, so that he was the "more open and disposed to be impressed with [James's] merit." John considered it "among the fortunate moments of my life to have made such an acquisition, for it hath been a source of happiness to me since by dispelling that gloom which in my then solitary state was beginning to encroach upon me."[26] The friendship that blossomed between John and James was affectionate and sentimental. The young Princetonian may have been nicknamed Lorenzo after a character in Edward Young's *The Complaint and the Consolation, or, Night Thoughts,* a poetic work first published in England in 1742 but popular on both sides of the Atlantic. Young's Lorenzo was a frivolous and irresponsible youth, which is certainly how John sometimes depicted his friend.[27] But each clearly loved the other. James referred to John as "my dear Leander," while John wrote of James as "my Lorenzo" and "my dear little Nassauvian" (Nassau Hall being where Gibson lived at Princeton).[28]

Unfortunately James was away much of the time at college, leaving John to pine for two friends instead of one. As he finished his breakfast one morning, he "suddenly felt a very strange kind of sensation—whether it proceeded from faintness or sickness of stomach I could not tell for the sensation was new to me, but it was very aweful and I could not help reflecting on the frailty and imbecility of human nature and the slender thread of life by which mortality hangs—oh my Lorenzo, at that moment did I think on thee and how did I wish for thee that I might unbosom my thoughts and my fears to my dear and affectionate friend." In the summer of 1786, as John waited impatiently for Isaac's return from Europe, James was also very much in his thoughts as he strolled in the Norris garden and "sat in [the] pear grove." John enjoyed promenading in gardens with his friends and family, as befitted an eighteenth-century gentleman. But for him the Norrises' pear grove was also a sentimental locale, a "dear delightful spot" that "ever sheds a charming influence over my spirits" and "always brings Lorenzo very affectionately to my mind."[29] Talking about James and spending time with people whom he associated with him also helped to console John in the absence of his "dear little Nassauvian," just as discussing Isaac with his nearest and dearest soothed John's spirits. When John introduced Mrs. Norris to some of James's Princeton friends who were visiting Philadelphia, she pleased him by asking them about James and telling them that he was "her particular young friend." John took the visitors into the pear grove and "charged" one of them "to tell Lorenzo he had sat there (our scene of friendship)." They then went over to visit Mrs. Gibson "and partook of a very delicious melon."[30]

John's sentimental yearning for James, "the friend of my bosom," accompanied him wherever he went. On a trip to Maryland in June 1786, he "saw a number of things" that brought to mind a recent journey he had made to the same neighborhood "with my now absent Lorenzo." One afternoon, he "rambled down" to an orchard on the property where he was staying "and sat upon the same fallen tree on which Lorenzo and I sat—thought on my dear absent friend and wished he were with me." How easily, he mused, did memories resurface of those upon whom "the mind loves to dwell." John calculated that he was "at this time about ninety-five miles from him and three thousand from my dear Castalio—what a distressing distance, yet hope I shall see the one almost as soon as the other."[31] Toward the end of his trip John noted that it was now "a month since Lorenzo and I parted." He had received "many enquires" from friends in Maryland about James and was delighted to hear "his praise highly trumpeted—that he was good natured—agreeable and good company—not proud like most citizens but easy in his manners—and moreover (which Lorenzo must not know) that he is a handsome lad." (As we will see, John appreciated his friend's humility and did not want him to lose it.) On his return to Philadelphia, he found that "a long and very affectionate letter from my young friend" had arrived during his absence: "How sensibly I feel myself attached to the dear amiable fellow and satisfied I am that he loves me with equal sincerity."[32]

John acknowledged his "dependence on Lorenzo's good nature" and his loneliness when his young friend was away at college. In November 1786, as James prepared to return from Philadelphia to Princeton, John "was a good deal sad at the thought of parting with my friend—our fortunes and adventures for these six weeks past have been so intimately connected that it seems natural and necessary for me to see him every day and I know not how I shall do to part with him—but it must be so." Once James left, John found it difficult to face the prospect of month after month without him: "I already want to see him so much that I know not how I shall bear the long separation of four dreary months—for till the commencement of the spring vacation will be four months from today." But there were palliatives to alleviate his affliction. A few weeks later, he had "a sick, sick headache all day." That evening "a strong dish of tea" gave him some relief, but it was the arrival of a letter from James that "almost completed the cure."[33] Letters were not the only salve for headaches and a friend's absence: the young men also exchanged sentimental gifts. On one occasion, John gave James a ribbon for his hair; on another, James gave John an unspecified but clearly treasured "token of friendship." John became quite distraught when he thought he had lost this "little pledge," and when he found it, he "could not help putting it to [his] lips." At breakfast one morning with Hannah Thomson, a cousin of Isaac Norris, the conversation turned to "trinkets and watch-keys." Hannah "so much admired" James's "little present" to John that "had it not been a token of friendship, politeness would have inclined" John to give it to her. But he could not part with it.[34]

About a year after they first met, the two young men began to keep journals in which they recorded their day-to-day activities and their feelings for one another; John also wrote about his feelings for Isaac. James began his journal first and then suggested to his friend that he also start one. John later wrote that his journal was "began by the desire of Lorenzo," a remark that captured neatly both his friend having taken the initiative and also the heartsick loneliness that drove John to write.[35] His first entry, for May 12, 1786, recorded their parting as James left home to resume his studies: "took leave of my dear Lorenzo—God bless him." The next day John was "not in very high spirits" and "in the morning rambled in the garden—missed my friend." A few days later he confessed to his journal that he was "a little uneasy" because he had as yet not heard from James. To his relief, "a packet from my dear Lorenzo" arrived soon thereafter. A few days later he again "rambled in the garden—sat in [the] pear grove—the scene of friendship," and "thought on Lorenzo."[36] When it rained heavily later that month, Mifflin wrote in his journal that he hoped James had a fire in his room at Princeton and was taking "bark" (a medicine believed to prevent colds). Confined inside by the weather,

John wished that either James or Isaac were with him: "Such days lag heavily without a friend."[37]

John and James read each other's journals when they met and also sent each other portions to read through the mail. During one of their reunions, James helped his friend to organize the segments of his journal, "placing the names of the months at the top of each page" and sewing the pages together.[38] When traveling away from home on business, John sometimes had difficulty finding paper of the same size as the pages on which he had already written. He complained in one letter that "cutting journal paper" was "very troublesome," and asked if James could send him some "right sized paper." His friend wrote in his own journal that he was happy to comply, "provided he pays me well and my price is that he will not grow tired but always continue to write long journals."[39] A year after beginning the journal, John declared that he was "much indebted to it for the satisfaction it hath yielded me—it hath frequently diverted me when I have been in good spirits and often beguiled a solitary hour when I have not—it hath served as a barometrical diary of my hopes and fears, my distresses and happiness." But journal-writing was not just a "solitary pleasure," he wrote, "for I have a hope at the same time of amusing Lorenzo." James had told him that he was "exceedingly entertained by it." Yet not all of John's journal was available for his friend's perusal. He declared in one entry, "I love and esteem him because he is innocent and artless, because he is unassuming in his manners, because he is affectionate and amiable in his temper, because he is sincere in his professions, because he has an understanding and a prudence beyond his years, and moreover because he has such a noble honor about him that he never yet deceived me." John wrote that James "must not see" this "eulogy," though he hoped that if he did so he would realize it was not "flattery" but sincere and well deserved.[40]

When James was in residence at Princeton, the two friends had to rely for their means of communication on the vagaries of the postal service and the unpredictable movements of friends who agreed to carry letters or journal installments from one to the other. In June 1786, John waited impatiently for a letter from Princeton. When a packet finally arrived, it was clear from its contents that James had sent another a few days earlier, though that previous letter had not reached him. John, assuming the earlier one to be lost, "blamed [himself] for not having wrote" to James while he was waiting. It turned out that the person bringing the earlier letter had been delayed, and so it was not until the day after Leander wrote to his "dear friend, called on his mama in the evening, and forwarded his books and buckles," that the first missive finally arrived.[41] James also waited impatiently for letters from his friend. In his entry for June 14, 1786, he wrote that he "expected a letter from Leander—thought of him—wondered that I did not receive one—shall expect the next to be a very long one." In mid-August of that same year, James was again "anxiously expecting" a letter from his friend, who was currently on a trip to New York. He "desired the servant to call at the post office as soon as the mail came in . . . after waiting some time, I went over myself—the postmaster informed me that there was no letter for me—I stood aghast and firmly believed he mistook and asked him twice if there was no letter for me—he answered in the negative." But the young man then noticed a packet from John's host in New York, addressed to Dr. Smith. He rushed it over to the addressee "and desired him to open it as I believed there was a letter enclosed for me." Sure enough the packet contained a letter from John, which James read eagerly as he returned to college.[42]

The unreliability of delivery was not the only obstacle to communication. James was not always the most diligent of correspondents, much to his friend's and also his mother's frustration. One evening John "called on Mrs. G[ibson] about nine and helped to reprobate Lorenzo, a sad negligent fellow." The next day's entry was more emotional: "Very uneasy about Lorenzo—and I very angry at him—but it is in vain to complain of his negligence—he will only do as he chooses at last—almost conclude to send him no more journals or letters." After another lapse in communication, John wrote James a scolding letter to accompany his latest journal entries. Once he finished, he "had half a mind not to send it" because the letter was "so harsh," but he then decided that James "fully deserved it." Letters, declared John, were "a great banquet to one who has such an epistolary appetite," and he did not appreciate being put on a diet.[43] Several days later he finally received an "affectionate" letter from James, which had been gathering dust at the tavern for almost a week: "My heart smote me for the severity of my last to him, which I now find he so little deserved." In another letter that arrived two days later, James responded to his friend's latest castigations with waggish humor, suggesting that John's resentful tone must have been the result of "an anodyne pill." "The saucy rogue thinks," wrote John, with what reads like a blend of amusement and pique, "that a silence of more than two weeks was not enough to put me out of humour with him."[44]

John quite literally counted the days until he would next see James and became very upset whenever his friend delayed his plans to come home, just as Isaac's postponed return from Europe left him despondent and distraught. When James wrote to tell him that he would be staying at Princeton for several days after commencement, John "grew very angry and almost low-spirited." John did, however, acknowledge that Gibson's absence at college was in some ways beneficial to them both. In December 1786, he wrote that he could tolerate the brevity of his friend's letters while he was at Princeton because John presumed that he was busy "laying up volumes of knowledge in his mind, which is to be a mutual resource for us both hereafter." There was, moreover, no reason for the two friends to let the academic calendar control completely when they saw each other. Not content with waiting for Gibson's periodic visits home on vacation, Mifflin made several trips to Princeton.[45]

Both John and James wrote at length in their journals about one such visit, which turned out to be a dramatic—one might say melodramatic—test of their feelings for each other. In July 1786, when John heard that a ship from France had arrived in New York and thought at first that Isaac might be on board, he wrote to James that he would visit him on his way to meet Isaac and then stop again at Princeton on their way back to Philadelphia so that his two friends could meet. When it turned out that Isaac had not traveled on that particular ship, John postponed his departure. But James had no way of knowing this, and John lamented in his journal that "Lorenzo (poor fellow) I suppose has, as I directed him, been on the watch for me at the stage house." What with one thing and another, John was "not in good spirits." The day after that, he decided that there was no reason to "derange" his plans completely on Isaac's account: he would leave town as soon as possible in order to visit James at Princeton and from there he would proceed as originally planned to New York, where he would spend several days with friends and relatives.[46]

Meanwhile, James had arranged for his friend to stay with Mrs. Knox, at whose boardinghouse he ate his meals ("at two dollars per week"). He slept in college, sharing a room in Nassau Hall with another student named John Rhea Smith, but perhaps did not relish the food that was served in the residence hall. James anticipated eagerly John's arrival: "Very happy on thinking I shall so soon see him—have a great deal to say to him—but I am sure I shall not mention half what I have to say to him while he is here—and shall be sorry when he is gone that I did not." There followed several days of disappointment, with James visiting the stage-coach office repeatedly only to find that John had still not arrived. He wondered and worried: "I hope that sickness prevents him not—I attribute it to business that detains him."[47]

John eventually arrived in Princeton on July 29. He had been awoken by the Philadelphia watchman at two in the morning to catch the stage-coach that left the city at three. He then suffered a "miserably cold" journey during which the passengers were severely "rattled" by the speed maintained by their driver and "like to be suffocated" by what they thought at first was a deluge of dust "beat up" by the speed with which the coach was moving but turned out instead to be a broken keg of hair powder. On arriving in Princeton—shaken, dusty, and exhausted—John went immediately to Mrs. Knox's establishment, where "they were all in the suds," this being the day of the week devoted to housecleaning. He was "shown upstairs to evade the deluge below and a young Ethiopian was dispatched to college for Lorenzo." An hour or so later, he awoke from a nap to find that James had not arrived: "My impatience was great—I arose to dispatch another courier and then lay down again— Soon Lorenzo came and in so soft a step did he ascend that I heard him not till he was at my chamber door, which he gently opened and discovered to me 'the face of my friend'—the joy of our meeting was mutual and our hearts were equally dilated with gladness." After the midday meal James had to return to college and John tried to sleep again, "but it was all in vain . . . and after tossing till near five Lorenzo came and relieved me with his papers, journals, and cheerful concourse." His friend's account of that day noted that at around eleven in the morning someone had come from Mrs. Knox's house to fetch him: "I went," he wrote, "and lo! It was Leander himself—I firmly expected him today and my expectations are verified—very happy on seeing him—found him lying on the bed upstairs—spent the morning till dinner in rummaging his trunk, talking to him, and in reading his journal—how time flies away when a person is engaged in such a manner!" The young fellow was clearly elated to have John with him: "How happy is he who is possessed of a true friend!"[48]

Over the next few days James divided his time between his duties in college and John's company: "A quarter before five went to Leander, found him abed in a doze—stayed with him till prayers—after prayers returned to him again." But John was disappointed that he did not have more of his friend's attention and began to worry that James's affections were fading. James in turn misinterpreted John's "very melancholy mood" as a sign that he had "not quite as much regard for me as he had some time ago." John became "drooping and uneasy in [his] mind." He complained in his journal of a persistent headache, which he thought "arose from low spirits." Two days after his arrival, he "retired in the afternoon to [his] chamber in a very disconsolate mood, reflecting on various distressing subjects." He decided to write "a long letter to Lorenzo, with a plan which my heart did not dictate—a trial of his affection—and almost wept at the conclusion of it." So much of their communication had taken place through correspondence and reading each other's journals that it is perhaps not surprising that he now wrote rather than spoke to James about his doubts.[49]

Once he had finished writing, John sent word to James via another student that a letter was waiting for him at Mrs. Knox's house, "placed it on the table upstairs with a candle by it, and then shut [him]self in the back room to await his arrival." James failed to appear. When the bell rang for nine o'clock, John sent a second message, resumed his position behind the door of the back room, and this time did not have long to wait: "He soon made his appearance—there was something wild and uncertain when he looked at the letter—he seemed to open it hesitatingly and his eyes flew precipitately over every page and then to the cover before he began to read—he had perused but a few lines when his countenance fell and he deliberately drew a chair and sat down—as he read I believe he heard me breathe and looked for a few seconds earnestly at the door—all was hushed and he again returned to his letter—when he had finished, he folded all up slowly and as he went down I thought I heard a sigh—my heart felt a melancholy sadness and I almost repented of my scheme."[50]

John followed and caught up with James "just as he had entered the college gate—the sound of my voice so unexpected made him still more at a loss to account for what he had read." John "asked him to return and told him [he] would explain the whole affair." Once they were back at the boardinghouse and alone upstairs, he revealed the underlying source of his anxiety: he was afraid that his friendship with Isaac, following the latter's return from Europe, would not be as close as it had been prior to his departure; if this fear turned out to be justified, "all [his] hope should rest" on James, and so John had written the letter as "a trial [of] what dependence I might have in his friendship and affection." Not surprisingly, James was upset: "The dear fellow seemed hurt at the experiment, but gave me the fullest assurances of his attachment—and I felt mine doubly renewed to him by the consciousness he testified of his own sincerity." James wrote in his own journal that he had received a message that a letter was waiting for him at the boardinghouse, but he "could not go at that time, being very busy." Then another message arrived to remind him that the letter was still awaiting his attention, so he walked over and read it. He was "very much surprised" at the letter's contents and "could not understand it." On his way back to college, he "heard a voice call me back and found it to be Leander's." Following their return together to the boardinghouse, James recorded laconically, John "explained the reason of his writing the letter."[51]

Earlier that day, James had agreed to "sleep" with John in the room at Mrs. Knox's and had got permission from the college authorities to do so. (What their "sleep[ing]" together actually entailed is a topic to which we will turn below.) James had spent the first three nights of his friend's visit at Nassau Hall, but he now stayed with John as he had promised prior to the evening's drama. The following morning he awoke "at the tolling of the second bell" and "got into hall when prayers were almost over." That day, John ate in college and attended prayers, so that he saw much more of his friend. He also "got liberty" for James "to stay" with him again. Relations between the two young men now seemed much less troubled: "I got into such an excellent flow of spirits that I talked more and enjoyed myself more than I had for weeks preceding," wrote John, "and I believe it was past eleven o'clock before we went to sleep." James wrote that the next morning he "dozed" and "conversed with Leander till past seven." John had planned to leave that day, but the weather was so inclement that he determined to delay his departure. James breakfasted with his friend before going into college and returned soon afterward, having secured permission to spend the morning with him. When the weather cleared up, they and another student decided to procure horses for the afternoon and went for a ride to Rocky Hill (an hour away at a brisk trot). On their return James had to go into college "to make up in the night for the loss of study in the day," and John repacked his trunk in readiness for his departure. The next morning James came over after breakfast, and John "bid him affectionately adieu till I should return again from New York."[52]

Over the next few days James consoled himself for John's absence by reading a portion of his friend's journal that he currently had in his possession and by writing to him. The arrival of a letter and another installment of journal entries "so much engaged" the young man that he "did not regard the dinner bell." That evening, he "wrote a long letter to my dear Leander." Another packet arrived four days later on August 12: "How happy was I at receiving it!" This time "the reading of his journal had nearly driven [that day's assigned reading from] Sheridan out of [his] head" so that "at recitation" he could "scarcely recollect" the passage he should have committed to memory. John, meanwhile, was still in a rather sensitive mood. A few days after arriving in New York, he received a brief letter from James and wrote in his journal: "Think it very evident that writing to me is a task." The student's next missive was much more satisfying: "A letter from my amiable Lorenzo has given a fillip to my spirits." He was less pleased by "a line and a half" that arrived some days later, sent with "respectful compliments." John wrote, "There is something so cold in 'respectful'—had he said 'affectionate' I would have been satisfied."[53]

John returned to Princeton on August 19. James was expecting him, but as usual could not be sure exactly when he would arrive. When the dinner bell rang, he walked over to Mrs. Knox's house for his meal, "saw Leander's coat hanging," and "thence concluded that he was upstairs." The young man "flew up and found him lying down." James wrote that they spent "the whole afternoon" together. John had arrived several hours earlier and had retired upstairs to rest after the journey: "I was now in the village which contained my dear Lorenzo, but as I expected him to call on me as soon as recitation was over I did not send for him— I had one or two short naps and still when I awoke wondered that Lorenzo was not come—When the dinner bell rang he came home to Mrs. Knox's, without knowing of my arrival—as soon as he entered the house he saw the great coat of his friend, and without further enquiry rushed up into my chamber to meet me." John was evidently still feeling insecure about his friend's feelings: "He was rejoiced to see me, but I know not whether he felt the joy that I did."[54]

This visit was much less fraught than the previous one. John stayed for three nights, the second and third of which the friends spent together at the boardinghouse. On the second evening, they "had a good deal of conversation," and the next morning on awakening they "renewed [their] discourse, which fell upon religion." John wrote that he was "perfectly astonished" by his friend's "sentiments on the subject, which were just, decided, and liberal—I have long thought I loved him as well as I possibly could, yet he seems still to be only in a gradation toward my friendship, for every time I am with him I find some fresh reason to attach me more closely to him." Later that morning John went over to Nassau Hall. James was not in his room, so John "took possession and sat for near twenty minutes waiting till [his] friend should arrive." When James did not appear, his visitor sought out another student whom he knew, and they went up to the belfry to enjoy the view. Once James eventually joined them, they came back down to have a look at the library belonging to one of the professors, and then the two friends returned to James's room, where John "took the liberty of rummaging all over his papers and books." In the afternoon John was invited to join a party setting off for Rocky Hill, but James, he wrote, "persuaded me to stay." That evening they went over to Mrs. Knox's together "and he stayed with me all night." In the morning John awoke "at the second bell and roused Lorenzo, but he said it was too late to get to prayers." This was the day of John's departure for Philadelphia and so he "took leave of [his] dear Lorenzo, who went directly up to college." James wrote that he "bid [his] dear Leander affectionately adieu."[55]

*

John and James clearly enjoyed spending the night together and looked for opportunities to do so. We should bear in mind that it was not unusual for eighteenth-century Americans to share a bed for practical reasons, so that sleeping with someone did not necessarily imply an intimacy of some sort in the way that it does today. Lack of space in most homes and inns meant that men and women were quite accustomed to bedding with relatives, friends, and even complete strangers. Visitors staying at private homes would often sleep with members of their host family. In taverns that accommodated guests overnight, it would have been unusual for one person to have a room to himself; a much more likely scenario was that several people traveling separately would share a room and squeeze together onto one or two beds.[56] In the case of our two young friends, however, sleeping together was not just a matter of convenience. At Princeton James had a room in college and John had his room at Mrs. Knox's house, yet they often chose to spend the night together: during one of John's visits, readers will recall, James wrote in his journal that he had "promised to sleep with him." Sometimes they had lengthy conversations before or after sleeping together and they were clearly comfortable spending time together in bed. One morning, wrote John, "we woke early yet we were so much engaged in conversation that it was late before we arose." Another night when he and James "lay conversing till the clock struck twelve," John "had fresh reason to be satisfied" with his friend: "both with his heart and his head."[57]

Back in Philadelphia, Mrs. Gibson welcomed John into her son's bed. (By contrast, John had his own room at the Norris house and there is no suggestion in his journal that he and Isaac slept together.) When James came home from college in September 1786, he was reunited with his friend on the evening of his arrival: he wrote that John "was very happy to see him" as well as "very sleepy," and they "retired to rest" together. The following evening, John, James, and Isaac "held a tripartite tête-à-tête at Mrs. N[orris]'s." Isaac was "in high spirits," reported John in his journal, but James "grew sleepy and would go home." John had promised to spend the night with James and so followed him home: "Leander soon came," wrote James, "and we soon forgot ourselves in balmy sleep."[58] Some of their time alone together at the end of the day was spent in "affectionate attentions," but they also enjoyed youthful horseplay. One evening, wrote John, "as I was wrestling with Lorenzo I fell on the side of my head and hurt myself a little—when I got to bed I felt as if I was somewhat stunned." He ended up with a black eye.[59]

When either John or James was feeling unwell, the nights became an important occasion for them to give one another physical and emotional support. On October 6, 1786, John was afflicted by "a sickness at my stomach and headache." He stayed that night with James, who "did all he could to assist his friend and made me fully sensible of his friendship by his affectionate attentions to me." One evening that November when John went home with James to spend the night, he wrote that they "retired pretty early but [James's] jaw was so painful we did not converse long." James did not get much sleep that night and John "was frequently awake with him." So severe was the pain that James had to delay his return to Princeton. Over the next few days John spent much of his time with the young patient; it was he who wrote to James's roommate at Nassau Hall to explain why his "drooping friend" had not arrived as expected. When John heard one morning that James had been afflicted with "a bad fever all night and was no better," he wrote that the news "seemed to strike a damp through me." He went over to see Mrs. Gibson, who "was not in good spirits—I conversed with her a while about him, but my heart was so full I was obliged to go into the other room to give it vent." What exactly John meant by "giving vent" is not clear; perhaps he needed to have a good cry, but was loath to do so in front of his friend's mother: at this time of crisis in the Gibson household, he probably wanted to be a source of support to both mother and son, not the recipient. Once he had pulled himself together, he went upstairs to sit with James and found, to his relief, that his friend "seemed rather better."[60] Over the coming two weeks John spent many of his nights with the invalid, who grew stronger each day but was still housebound. It was not until the end of the month that James was well enough to leave for Princeton. On the eve of his journey, they again stayed together overnight: "We were so long adjusting the preliminaries of our separation that it was past eleven before we got to sleep."[61]

Even when James was away at college, John sometimes went over to Mrs. Gibson's house and spent the night in his friend's room. The evening before the second anniversary of their first meeting, he visited his friend's mother, "sat up till near eleven" with her, "talking over matters," and then "lodged in Lorenzo's room, all the furniture of which recalled my dear friend very forcibly to my mind—I had such agreeable subjects to occupy my mind that it was after twelve before the drowsy Morpheus took me under his wing."[62] Sometimes he went specifically at Mrs. Gibson's request. Recall that when Mrs. Norris had been left alone in her home, she had asked John to move in temporarily as "guard of the house."[63] One night he "promised Mrs. G. that [he] would take possession of Lorenzo's room" but was detained elsewhere until it was too late to go and wake the household. Yet his promise had clearly not been entirely for her sake: he noted at the end of his entry for that day that it was "a month today since I parted with Lorenzo."[64]

For a modern reader, the love that John and James declared for one another, along with the evident pleasure that they took in sleeping together, might give rise to speculation that their relationship included a sexual component. But just how intimate their relationship became is unclear. If two men wanted to have sexual relations, the very fact that people often slept together as a matter of convenience would have made it relatively easy to camouflage their trysts. Given that eighteenth-century Americans had no difficulty imagining a physically affectionate and yet nonsexual love between friends, it is perhaps hardly surprising that John and James made little effort to conceal their devotion to one another, whether expressed through verbal declarations or physical affection. On one exceptional occasion, they did try to prevent other students at Princeton from seeing them alone together. James wrote that they "locked" themselves up in his study on campus: "I fixing my gown across the window (to prevent the students seeing us) we looked over papers and talked till the dinner bell rang." But given what they proceeded to do together, at least according to the journal, it would seem that this was simply a matter of finding a few moments of privacy in the residence hall; the entry does not necessarily suggest that they were doing anything in particular that other students would have seen as problematic. In general, there is little indication in either of their journals that the two young men had anything to hide.[65]

James's roommate at Nassau Hall, John Smith, also kept a journal for 1786 which, like those kept by John and James, has survived (the sort of happy coincidence that quickens the hearts of historians). Smith wrote little about his roommate's friendship with the Philadelphian lawyer, but what he did say gives scant indication that he or his classmates saw their relationship as peculiar or suspicious. There is one entry that might suggest otherwise, written on the evening of January 19, 1786. John had arrived that day for a visit. Smith noted that several friends were in the room when John came in and that he had felt "a little embarrassed and sorry for James's sake." Smith's embarrassment on behalf of his roommate might have been caused by the fervor with which one or both of the two friends greeted each other, but it could equally have been due to John Mifflin being a stranger who was over a decade their senior and apparently rather stilted in appearance and manner. Smith might also have been embarrassed that he and his fellow students were idling their time away in his room instead of studying.[66] But he went on to write that "we soon got settled and into conversation and then I felt very easy." He finished this entry by noting in a matter-of-fact tone that James had gone "to the tavern to sleep with Mr. Mifflin." Smith himself was no stranger to physical intimacy with male friends. One evening he went back to his room with a fellow student named Johnson: "Throwing [them]selves on the bed," they slept together "through the whole night." When Johnson visited his room a few weeks later, Smith lay "down on the bed with him for quarter of an hour" and then "g[o]t up to study, leaving him asleep." On another occasion, he "played with little George Clarkson for an hour on the bed."[67]

One striking passage in John Mifflin's journal might suggest that he craved a kind of intimacy with his "dear little Nassauvian" that he himself saw as illicit. Consider his account of "a very odd dream" that he had in December 1786:

> I thought Lorenzo and I (and I know not whether there was another person or not) were in a very small boat inside of a long kind of pier-wharf which ran a great way into the river—I thought we had neither oar, paddle, or anything else to guide our course and we were driving fast into the current which was very strong—but just as we got almost to the outside of the pier I caught hold on something to stop us and then pushed our boat from one thing to another till we reached the wharf—the people on shore all the time hollering to us and very anxious for our safety—I climbed up the pier (which was very high) and then drew Lorenzo up after me—he seemed to be stark naked and as we were running along hand in hand to the place where his clothes were—I awaked—greatly agitated by the danger from which we seemed to have escaped.[68]

The interpretation of dreams is, of course, a slippery business. John himself wrote in another journal entry that "dreams seem to be made of the shreds and fragments of reason, worked together into incoherencies."[69] But the image of John and James drifting away from safety, John's realization that his friend was "stark naked," and their running together hand-in-hand to recover his clothes are at least suggestive. That there may have been someone else in the boat (perhaps Isaac?) is also striking. John's dream may have expressed desires and fears that he could not address directly when awake: "If I had any faith in dreams," he wrote, "I should think this ominous of some future event of our lives—wished very much to hear from Lorenzo today." Perhaps most revealing is that those gathered on the shore were not hostile but worried. Whether in his dreams or in his waking life, John did not have to hide his emotional attachment to James, whether expressed in words or physical affection. What would have aroused anxiety among his relatives and friends was the possibility of their loving friendship becoming sexual. John's dream suggests an awareness, at some level of consciousness, that his feelings for James might end up drawing him into a kind of intimacy that contemporary moralists and, it would seem, John himself would have condemned. Yet love itself was not an issue. John and James made no more effort than did John and Isaac to conceal their devotion to each other. The three young men articulated their feelings quite openly through physical as well as verbal expressions of love.

⁊

When John Mifflin befriended James Gibson, it was not his intention that their blossoming relationship should supplant his older friendship with Isaac Norris. As we will see, loving male friendships were rarely exclusive, and this was certainly true of John's relationships with Isaac and James. Though John did fear that his relationship with Isaac might suffer as a result of the latter's prolonged absence in Europe, what he hoped for was that his older friendship with Isaac would survive their separation and thrive alongside his newer friendship with James. He hoped, furthermore, that the two relationships would not merely coexist but become entwined. John wanted his two friends to become acquainted immediately on Isaac's return from Europe and was clearly anxious that they should make a good impression on each other. He worried that James was "not a prominent or striking character, but of that amiable kind for which your esteem increases with your acquaintance," and also that Isaac might have changed during his absence. Indeed, while John was waiting for news of his long absent friend's arrival, he dreamed that the three of them met at Princeton, that Isaac "was so altered both in person and manners that he appeared quite a new being to me" ("his face was flat and sallow, his figure long and gangling"), and that his two friends "took not the least notice of each other."[70]

John had planned that his two friends would meet for the first time at Princeton as he accompanied Isaac on the last leg of his journey back to

Philadelphia. But when John's precarious health prevented him from leaving home to meet his friend en route, he sent instead a letter of introduction that James was supposed to leave at the stagecoach office so that it could be delivered into Isaac's hands as he passed through the college town. It turned out that Isaac did not receive the letter, so his first meeting with James had to wait until the student's next visit to Philadelphia. John, ever insecure, wondered if the letter had arrived in time, or if James had failed to leave it at the coach office for some reason. "I was not satisfied with it," he wrote in his journal, "but I would not give myself leave to draw those reflections from it which might discompose my present happiness." Whatever the letter's fate, James wrote in his journal that he had been "very happy on hearing the news" that he could expect a visit from Isaac and was "a good deal disappointed" when he went to the stagecoach office on the morning that he expected him and "saw the stages come in, but no Castalio in them."[71] Isaac in turn was eager to meet James. The day after his arrival in Philadelphia, John "gave him some account of Lorenzo." Isaac "was pleased and seemed desirous to meet him." A week or so later, John described James's "temper and disposition" at greater length as he and Isaac sat in the pear grove and then "strolled round the gravel walks of the garden." Isaac "quite longed to see him and said he thought he had a perfect idea of him from what he had heard me say of him at different times."[72]

Yet John worried that Isaac's future plans might "run counter" to the "attachments and affections" that John had formed during Isaac's absence. He was presumably referring to Isaac's thoughts about returning to Europe with John, which would involve the latter abandoning James. As it was, John felt guilty during the days following Isaac's arrival that he gave so little thought to James and neglected their correspondence. "My dear little Nassauvian," he wrote, "will think I have forgotten him amid all my joy." It was at this point that he thought he had lost the "token of friendship" that James had given him and, when he found it, "could not help putting it to [his] lips."[73] When Isaac asked to see the journal that John had been keeping, the latter refused on the grounds that it was intended only for James's eyes (though James apparently had no objection to Isaac's reading it). Now that John found himself preoccupied by Isaac's arrival and fretted that he was paying insufficient attention to his relationship with James, he may have wanted to protect this private venue that he and James had created for the expression of their feelings. Given the effusive tone of his comments about James in the journal, John may also have been trying to avoid making Isaac jealous, though denying him access to the entries was just as likely to make Isaac resentful; John made no mention of how Isaac responded to this refusal.[74]

Once James returned home from college, the three men spent much of their time together, sometimes in "tripartite tête-à-tête," sometimes in the company of their families, and sometimes out and about with "chums" in the city. John wrote that his two friends were "very much alike," especially in their shyness "before company." He "could not help smiling to think how two such silent people would be put to it to make out a conversation" when left alone. On one occasion he found the two of them in the Norris dining room, "sitting at the west window in as profound silence as if the God of it were holding his fingers to their lips." Yet this behavior does not appear to have resulted from a specific discomfort or dislike between Isaac and James. Though Isaac did become increasingly reclusive that fall, his reluctance to spend time with others was not targeted at James in particular. Nor did his depression seem to have any significant connection to James's presence in his friend's life. As long as Isaac remained capable of sustaining social relationships, John's hopes were for the most part fulfilled as his two friendships converged.[75]

John's sentimental attachments were no more confined to one sex than they were to one person. Indeed, one of the principal topics that engaged the three friends was their courtship of various young ladies in the city. They confided in each other about these attachments, did not hesitate to pass judgment on each other's infatuations, and took care to nurture those of which they approved. In December 1786, John informed James via his journal that he was currently fascinated by two sisters, Eliza and Leanora: "I was almost ready to sing, 'How happy could I be with either!'—what a whimsical friend will Lorenzo think he hath gotten—yet it will assure him he hath my full confidence as I keep nothing from him—and will it not also convince him of the reliance I have on his prudence and friendship." John did not see the twelve-year difference in age between him and James as conferring upon himself an automatic seniority in knowledge and confidence about matters of the heart. Indeed, he wished that James could "inspire" him "with a little portion of his courage and resolution" in such matters: "Nothing is in the way but my indecision and a spice of diffidence." Fifteen-year-old James does seem to have been quite precocious. John noted that during one of his regular visits to drink tea with Mrs. Gibson he "met a belle there, a *quondam Dulcinia* [former sweetheart] of Lorenzo's." He added that "Lorenzo had some taste even in his youthful day."[76]

For all his self-proclaimed diffidence, John was evidently popular with the ladies in his social circle, both as a friend and as a potential suitor. Deborah Norris described him as "a great favourite with us" and "an agreeable friend of mine, in spite of Patty Jones's poor opinion of platonic sentiments." In eighteenth-century English the word "platonic" was generally used to denote a close but nonromantic and nonsexual relationship with a person of the opposite sex.[77] Some young ladies in Philadelphia seem to have doubted whether "platonic" friendships with men were either possible or desirable. John could evidently play either role: he enjoyed his "platonic friendships" but also relished the game of courtship. Indeed, Eliza and Leonora were the latest in a train of young ladies whose charms had beguiled the susceptible young man. Following Isaac's return from Europe, John had "a very confidential conversation" with him to impart "some things which I had kept in reserve for him—a story which (if my life were written) would make a conspicuous part in my history—my adventures with a certain lady who had been laid out for me— the progress of our acquaintance to the breaking off of our intimacy." This courtship had been one of several impediments that delayed John's departure for Europe before his illness prevented him from going at all. Yet however disappointed Isaac may have been by John's inability to accompany him on his travels, he does not appear to have seen his friend's amorous pursuits as a threat in their own right. When John told him about his "history" with this particular young lady, Isaac responded with "joy and congratulations at the conclusion of it," but not because he wanted his friend to avoid marriage. Isaac declared that "there was but one person in the world he would consent I should marry and left me to guess—it was no difficult thing for we had just left her—the amiable Maria."[78]

"The amiable Maria" lived with her widowed mother, Mrs. Rhoads, across the street from Mrs. Norris. She was now the main focus of John's romantic interest in women. He escorted Maria to and from houses in their neighborhood as well as to public events. One evening there was an oration at the University, where he played "le galant" for "l'aimable petite demoiselle de mon coeur [the delightful little lady of my heart]." Isaac was delighted. Indeed, by early 1787 one of the few activities that could arouse him from depressed lethargy was encouraging John's pursuit of Maria. That February, the two young men had a "long and very interesting conversation" on "the charming subject of Maria," and the next day they "walked up and down the grand walk of the garden for near an hour, conversing on last evening's subject." "How delightful!" declared John, "How happy to have a friend who gives such unequivocal proofs of his friendship—I am convinced of Castalio's sincere attachment by his solicitude for my happiness."[79] A few weeks later, Isaac "elated" John by what he told him regarding a recent visit to the home of their neighbor Mrs. Pemberton. John recounted that "[Isaac] was there before me and he said he took notice of Maria who sat rather silent and inanimate before I came, but as soon as I was announced her whole countenance and manner brightened up immediately." Isaac was actively involved in finding opportunities for John to spend time with Maria and her companions. One morning, after eating breakfast at Mrs. Norris's house, John "went up to Castalio and had a long conversation in his chamber—we agreed that he should go over and bring the girls to walk in the garden—that I would go to Mrs. G[ibson]'s and wait till I saw them arrive and then come over to them." A few days later Isaac busied himself with "laying a charming European scheme" that involved "a tripartite party" of himself, John, and Maria. On another occasion when John "was rather out of spirits" about his pursuit of Maria, Isaac reassured him that all was going well. "I am so diffident a being," wrote John, "that I require to be often reminded by my friends of the most flattering circumstances in my favor."[80]

Just as the Norris garden played an important role in John's relationships with Isaac and James, so it figured prominently in his courtship of Maria. The young people in John's social circle spent a good deal of their time collecting, cultivating, and admiring plants. For genteel Philadelphians such as these, gardening combined the practical (most gardens, for example, featured a variety of fruit trees and were well stocked with herbs), the scientific (becoming acquainted with the recent findings of botanists and perhaps dabbling in horticultural experiments), the ornamental (creating a decorative space in which to promenade and engage in polite conversation), and also the romantic. John took great delight in giving Maria choice specimens, most of which came from the Norris grounds, where John had been growing them in partnership with Isaac. As he walked Maria home one evening from a visit to Mrs. Pemberton's, "she reminded me of my promise of a myrtle tree and I renewed it with the addition of an orange—what would I not give to one to whom I would willingly give myself." A few days later he asked her "to send over her pots for the orange tree and hyacinth which I was to give her." The plants were in the Norris garden and "she seemed to fear Castalio would think it strange of her to send, but I told her the tree and flower were mine which I thought satisfied her scruples." A few days after that, John was going into Mrs. Norris's house when he "saw Maria at the door over the way— she looked so charming that I crossed over—she was quite alone and invited me into the front parlour." He offered to give her "two elegant hyacinths" if she sent pots over to the Norris greenhouse. When the pots arrived, Isaac "put the flowers in them" and John delivered them, arranging them "in the little parlour window" before sending the servant to summon Maria.[81]

Many of John's visits with Maria took place with Isaac in attendance, watching as carefully as John himself for signs of how things were going. One evening in March 1787, they went over to see Mrs. Rhoads and her "jeune demoiselles": "The sofa was drawn before the fire—Castalio seated himself at the further end and I took my seat at the nearest." To John's delight, "the dear amiable Maria brought her chair from the table and placed it between us—never before did I find more frankness and sprightliness in her manner and conversation—and to me, happy Leander, were her attentions directed." Before long he "went to look at the dear little nursery—she followed me—how delighted was I to see my fragrant little presents flourish so under her care and tutelage—the sweet girl's joy seemed equal to mine while we were viewing the precious tokens—tokens of Leander's love—we returned to our seats." Throughout the evening he kept a close watch on "such little airs and graces as flattered my heart and made it tingle with joy," such as "observing her shadow on the wall and by it adjusting her head-dress—'setting her cap at Leander,' thought I, 'happy swain'—for by little things we may often discover matters of importance—oh my full heart, 'tis flushed with fond beliefs and happy hopes." Once they returned to Mrs. Norris's house, "Castalio gave his opinion of my prospect of success decidedly and told me some circumstances which added to my present happy expectations." The next day John "read Dr. Ladd's *Love Poetry*."[82]

Just as John was left in no doubt that Isaac would do all he could to foster his friend's relationship with Maria, so he had every confidence that the progress of his courtship would please his other close friend, James Gibson. That same evening, after his debriefing with Isaac, John visited Mrs. Gibson, "ate half a cranberry tart with her," and "gave her a minute history of [his] evening's adventures." Mrs. Gibson's verdict was highly favorable, which would in turn reassure James that all was going well: "How will this account delight my dear Lorenzo," John declared in his journal that night.[83] This was one of many occasions on which John discussed the "pleasing and flattering subject" of Maria with Mrs. Gibson, who always "inspired [him] with hope and assurance." Just as Mrs. Gibson nurtured the loving intimacy between John and her son, so she encouraged his courtship of Maria: as far as she was concerned, there was ample room for more than one kind of love in John's life. After one such parley with Mrs. Gibson, he then visited the Norris home and "had the second part of the same conversation" with Isaac. Propping up John's romantic enterprise was clearly a communal effort.[84]

In March 1787 John celebrated the second anniversary of his meeting James ("one of those days which I remember with heartfelt sentimental pleasure") in the same entry that described him mooning over potted plants with "the charming Maria." Another entry that he wrote a month later expressed with self-conscious pathos John's sense of his various attachments (male and female) as closely intertwined, not just socially but also in terms of their impact on his emotional state. John noted in his entry for April 13 that he had not been invited to Maria's birthday party, presumably because he had told her that he was leaving town for a few days. Maria could not be expected to know that John had changed his plans, and he had no reason to see the absence of an invitation as having any significance, other than her assuming him to be unavailable, but as John wrote in his journal, insecure as always, "There is ever something to make us uncertain whether circumstances are discouraging or not." He "spent a dull evening at home" with "nothing to amuse me but my journal, to counterbalance many things I have to displease and trouble me." These included Isaac's "indisposition," James's "indolence," and Maria's party, "together with other things—yet I think under them all I am a hero."[85]

Not everyone in John's social circle shared his estimation of his own character. Our self-styled hero became increasingly aware that he was being watched. When Mrs. Rhoads "came in from visiting" one day and found John in the house arranging flowers that he had given Maria, "she looked suspicious," and "there was something in her manner different from her usual behavior to me." A few days later John's brother told him that his "attentions to Maria were beginning to be talked of." On a visit to Mrs. Pemberton's home, when Maria "glanced her eyes several times" in his direction, John "thought Mrs. P seemed to watch her."[86] Relatives, friends, and neighbors tended to keep a close eye on courting couples during this period, not least because of concern for the sexual safety of young women at a time when premarital pregnancy rates were rising precipitately.[87] That John was still very attentive to Leonora ("gentle as the softest zephyrs" and "sweetly attentive to me") may have given rise to suspicion that he was playing fast and loose with the affections of young ladies in his circle. He wrote in one entry that he had "dreamed of Leonora" the previous night and had done so "several times lately as well as of Maria—they have been tender and interesting dreams." John acknowledged that he found himself "in a quandary" with regard to the young women for whom he had romantic feelings—"I am such an irresolute being that I know not whether I deserve the anxious good wishes of my friends."[88] His behavior had clearly been raising eyebrows. On January 31, 1787, he paid a visit to Mrs. Gibson and was drinking tea with her when Dr. Benjamin Rush made an entrance. The good doctor's demeanor was "rather queer" and "not in the usual soft complimentary strain." He told the young man "very bluntly that he thought it was time for [him] to be married." John responded that "I thought so too—for I did not want to be an old bachelor."[89]

John did marry the following year, in June 1788, though his bride was neither Maria nor Leonora but instead eighteen-year-old Clementina Ross. James did not marry until four years after John's death in 1813, when he became husband to John's half sister, Elizabeth Bordley. Isaac, the other member of our "tripartite tête-à-tête," had died unmarried in 1802. A year after his own marriage, John wrote of "the shoals" that he had "escaped" and rejoiced that through marriage he had "now happily reached the harbor of his hopes and wishes." The "shoals" to which John referred were apparently those of courting more than one woman at a time. What seems to have disturbed some of John Mifflin's neighbors was his apparent lack of steadfastness in his romantic dealings with young women, not his intense and demonstrative friendships with other men. In pursuing the latter, John, Isaac, and James enjoyed the enthusiastic support of their families and of the social circle in which they moved. Two of these men were unusual in that James married quite late in life and Isaac not at all. As we will see, most men who formed close friendships with other men did marry and at a conventional age; like John Mifflin, they saw their relationships with men and women as complementary. But there was nothing anomalous about the nature or tone of John's friendships with his two fellow Philadelphians. Indeed, eighteenth-century Americans actively encouraged such ties, holding that male love and its overt expression made men into model members of society. Having focused in this chapter on one triad of male friends, it is now time to spread our wings and examine a broader range of men who formed loving relationships with one another. The next chapter reconstructs that world of male love and ponders its implications for our understanding of eighteenth-century American manhood.[90]

CHAPTER TWO

"A Settled Portion of My Happiness"

*Friendship, Sentiment, and
Eighteenth-Century Manhood*

A s Daniel Webster prepared to leave Dartmouth College on vacation in December 1798, the young student may perhaps have welcomed a reprieve from scholarly labors. But what seems to have preoccupied Daniel on the eve of his departure was the unwelcome prospect of
having to spend several weeks apart from his friend George Herbert.
Daniel committed his feelings to paper in the form of a poem:

> Yes, George, I go, I leave the friend I love,
> Long since 'twas written in the books above;
> But what, Good God! I leave thee, do I say?
> The thought distracts my soul and fills me with dismay.
> But Heaven decreed it, let me not repine;
> I go; but, George, my heart is knit with thine.

Neither time nor distance, he averred, could "tear my heart from the dear
friend I love":

> Should you be distant far as Afric's sand,
> By fancy pictured you'd be near at hand.
> This shall console my thoughts, till time shall end,
> Though George be absent, George is still my friend.

Despite the consolation of such imaginings, Webster was convinced that
he would "sink in dark despair" were it not for knowing that he and his
friend would soon be reunited on his return to Dartmouth. "Roll on the
hour," the young man exclaimed in fervent anticipation.[1]

George Herbert was not the only classmate to whom Daniel's "heart
[was] knit": "Other friends I leave," he declared, and "it wounds my heart."

Daniel's closest friend and confidant was James Bingham. He described James as "the friend of my heart, the partner of my joys, griefs, and affections, the only participator of my most secret thoughts." Daniel and James were bound to each other, he declared, "in the indissoluble bonds of fraternal love." Following their final departure from Dartmouth, the two young men both became lawyers and practiced in different towns. But they established a regular correspondence through which they expressed "eternal attachment" across the New England countryside, providing each other with emotional sustenance that they had previously given in person. "You and I should certainly be always friends if we never wrote another syllable to each other," wrote Daniel, "but we should be friends to little purpose, if we never mutually contributed anything to soften care and cheer the heart . . . There is not half room enough left to enumerate all the good wishes my heart feels for you." Daniel addressed James in these letters as "Jemmy," "lovely boy," and "dearly beloved." As the years passed by, Daniel wrote to James "with undiminished love and tenderness." "I need not tell you," he wrote, "what pleasure I receive from your letters, nor with what exultation my heart glows under the impression that our early congenial attachments will never be sundered." He assured his friend that their correspondence had become "a settled portion of my happiness." "The force of habit is added to the force of esteem," he declared, "and if you should intermit writing for a long time, there would be a kind of vacuum in my pleasures."[2]

Daniel had not anticipated just how emotionally challenging his separation from James would prove: "I knew not how closely our feelings were interwoven; had no idea how hard it would be to live apart." He mourned the loss of "my true and honorable friend, as dear to me as are the ruddy drops that visit my sad heart," and compared his feelings to those of "the dove that has lost its mate." It is not surprising, then, that Daniel treasured his friend's letters, which "always carrie[d] joy to the bosom of Daniel" and through which he could experience, transmuted into words, the tender potency of their feelings for one another. "O Bingham and Bingham forever!" he declared, "There is a kind of magic in your pen." Daniel wanted his friend to be able to envisage him as he read and replied to the words that flowed from James's magical pen: "A letter from you always gives me two happy half hours, one when it is received, and another when it is answered. Figure to yourself, then, a large room lationships, just as young women who attended boarding schools in the early nineteenth century often formed intense and enduring friendships.[6] Most of the evidence through which we can glimpse these male relationships was left behind by friends who lived at a distance from one another. John Mifflin and James Gibson began their journals as a way to survive their separation while James studied at Princeton; sadly we have no way of knowing how this particular friendship developed in later years, in large part because John and James spent the rest of their lives as residents of the same city and so had no need to maintain a written correspondence; if either of them kept a journal after 1787, it has not surfaced. But when friends ended up living far apart from one another, their geographical separation prompted them to write each other letters, some of which have survived; that correspondence enables us to reconstruct their relationships as they evolved over many years. This chapter examines the efforts of eighteenth-century men to sustain youthful friendships and turn them into long-term relationships. It considers the tone of such friendships, the ends they served, and the ways in which men perceived these relationships as fitting into their lives as husbands and fathers. It also establishes the importance of shared feeling in the version of manhood that these men embraced. That conception of sympathetic affection between friends would inform a new civic ethos that emerged during the revolutionary period as Americans sought to envisage a republican masculinity through which citizens could find new ways of relating to and working with one another.

Men who became close companions in college and then continued as friends long after graduation saw such ties as a precious gift that sustained them through various trials in adult life and provided a link back to a phase of their lives that seemed, at least in retrospect, both happy and carefree. William Livingston—a native of Albany, New York, who graduated from Yale College in 1741—compared his correspondence with former classmate Noah Welles to "the balmy dew on withering flowers, delightful as the fragrant odours of Arabia, and more reviving than the spicy gales of Sabea." On leaving Yale, Livingston had moved to New York City, where he became a student of law and soon thereafter a highly successful attorney. Welles, who hailed from Colchester, Connecticut, went into the ministry: after working for several years in short-

in the third story of a brick building, in the center of Boston, a sea
fire, and a most enormous writing-table with half a cord of books
Then figure further to yourself your most obedient, with his back t
fire, and his face to the table, writing by candlelight, and you will
cisely see 'a happy fellow.' " It was almost as if Daniel were conjurir
for his friend a setting in which they could meet, at least phantasr
"to soften care and cheer the heart"—a cozy setting, complete with
ing fire, in which he could once again consider himself "a happy fe
Yet despite the "magic" of the pen, Daniel became increasingly disc
late about their separation: "I don't see how I can live any longer wit
having a friend near me, I mean a male friend, just such a frien
one J.H.B."[3]

Daniel's letters to another college friend, Thomas Merrill, als
pressed his craving for lost intimacies: "O Thomas, Thomas! I w
could see you," he declared. "My heart is now so full of matters and tl
impatient to be whispered into the ear of a trusty friend that I th
could pour them into yours till it ran over . . . I desire most earnes
hear from you, to hear directly from your heart and your heart's
cerns." Just as Daniel wanted his friends to visualize him as he wro
he needed to imagine them in their various settings. "My heart fe
sort of vacuum," he wrote in one of his letters, "when it cannot fanc
situation of my friends. While you resided at Dartmouth College, I
trace you in your morning vocations and in your evening walks. At
set I could see you enter the chapel, could hear the bell, and follov
through every scene of business and amusement. How is it at Mi
bury? You have there too, I suppose, vocations, and walks, and cha
and bells. But I know nothing of them; tell me, therefore."[4]

It might be tempting to see the bonds that developed between y
men such as these as one phase in their emotional histories that w
have ended once they left early manhood and entered marital rela
ships. Some of these youthful friendships did indeed fade over time
others proved long lasting and became for those involved, to parapl
Daniel Webster, a settled portion of their happiness.[5] Many life
friendships began in college, which is hardly surprising: the intima
these all-male environments, the need to form new emotional bond
first leaving home, and the shared memories that classmates accu
lated during their college years would have fostered close and lastin

term positions, he answered a call to the pulpit in Stamford, Connecticut. Both men lamented their separation, but they did at least have the consolation of writing to one another. It was, declared William, "a great alleviation of the cares of the world to throw out one's soul on a sheet of paper to a bosom friend, without restraint or disguise." Letters from "a bosom friend" provided "exquisite relaxation amidst the labour of study and the fatigues of business." They would enable, William hoped, "the perpetuation of that friendship the foundation whereof was laid at college" until one of them "quitted this wretched and distempered world." Once he became confined to a sedentary life by old age, he planned to devote an hour each day to "reading the bundles of your letters (the unquestionable testimonials of our long and inviolate friendship)," while continuing to exchange new letters as long as they both survived.[7]

Yet Noah's letters were a mixed blessing. On the one hand, they kept alive a primary source of emotional fulfillment in William's life and prompted "a most delightful retrospection" of their "academical pleasures" at college, "the most agreeable scene, integrally considered, that ever I acted in." On the other, their need to communicate via letters instead of spending time together in person reminded him how unfortunate it was that the two friends had not "settled in the same place." If William did not hear from his friend for a while, the eventual arrival of a letter produced nothing less than "raptures" and "transports." Like "the dew from heaven that fructifies the barren mountains," Noah's words "again quite invigorated and refreshed" his parched heart. When Noah found the time to write only a brief note, William would berate him, gently yet eloquently: "giv[ing] birth" to the "sublime pleasures" that William "ever enjoy[ed] in reading [Noah's] letters" without fully "gratifying them" was, William declared, "so cruel that, had you not made an apology for it, I should have thought you barbarously designed to string me up for a second Tantalus." According to the Greek myth, Tantalus was doomed to stand for ever up to his neck in water, trees heavy with fruit dangling over his head: whenever he tried to drink, the water would disappear; whenever he tried to pick fruit from the branches above him, the wind would blow them away. This was, to put it mildly, a vivid image of deprivation.[8]

Harvard graduate Israel Cheever responded to letters from his college "chum" Robert Treat Paine with a similar blend of joy and melancholic craving. When Israel received a packet from Robert and saw his friend's "sweet name affixed at the bottom of the lines," his heart "skipped like lambs upon little hills." But he read the letter "with tears in [his] eyes for desire of seeing the author of it." Indeed he told his friend that he wept whenever he recalled their "parting." The pain of separation comes across very clearly in letters such as this. Bostonian Ellis Gray, who traveled abroad in the 1760s, wrote wistfully of his yearning for "the conversation of a friend who could make even a desert delightful." Ellis was thinking in particular of his friend Benjamin Dolbeare, whom he assured that "no distance of time, no change of place or of circumstances can ever erase the memory of my dear friend from my breast." Ellis wrote "with all the ardor of friendship" and consoled himself by "anticipating the pleasing moment that shall bring me to my native land, to the enjoyment of my friends, and in that enjoyment the sublimest pleasure this world can give."[9]

When another Bostonian, Arthur Walter, left on a two-year European tour, his friend William Shaw showered him with affection through the mail and left him in no doubt as to how much he was missed. "I have frequently thought of you by day and dreamt about you by night," William told his absent friend. The two men had met at Harvard in the early 1790s, and following graduation, both worked with law firms in Boston. William wrote of the "fond affection," "the ardor of attachment," and "the beautiful love" that they had shared since their student days at Harvard. He described Arthur as "the man who loves me, with whom I can converse without guile, without dissimulation, and without reserve." No wonder, then, that he awaited so eagerly the arrival of letters from his absent friend. He wrote on one occasion that he had read Arthur's latest missive "with raptures which I shall not attempt to describe—so full was it of affection, love, benevolence, friendship, and zeal." William responded with effusive declarations of his own loving devotion: "You know not how necessary your presence is to [my] happiness," he avowed. "Goodnight, my dear Walter—Love me always and believe me to be affectionately and unalterably your friend."[10]

Not long after his return to Boston and his beloved friend, Arthur Walter died of tuberculosis. Joseph Buckminster, a mutual friend of theirs who was visiting London at the time, wrote to William on hearing the news of Arthur's death. Parting from his friends in Boston had been "painful in the extreme, but continually relieved by the belief that [he] should see [them] all again after some time of absence." He now had to console himself with the hope that his separation from Arthur—"dear, dear fellow"—was "only a little lengthened." Joseph was also ailing from tuberculosis: "We shall embrace again . . . in a world more worthy of his noble, pure, pious heart than this." Yet "resign[ing] ourselves to the loss, till we meet him again," was no easy matter, and he wished he was with William in person "to give vent to [his] sorrow." William replied that both he and Arthur had been waiting eagerly for Joseph's return, but now that Arthur was gone, he "wished for [Joseph's] company more than ever." William wrote frankly about the profundity of his loss: "I need not tell you, who were so well acquainted with us both, how much I loved him . . . There was no good I ever enjoyed, there was no pleasure I ever anticipated, with which [Arthur] was not most intimately associated."[11]

Just as memories, however precious, could never fully compensate for the loss of a loved one, so letters could never replace the pleasure of immediate companionship. Indeed, separated friends often declared themselves frustrated by the inadequacies of the written word. Thomas Wait, a publisher in Portland, Maine, had to adapt to the absence of his friend George Thatcher when the latter was elected to represent Maine in the U.S. Congress. Thomas lamented in a letter to George that pen and paper were "but vile interpreters of the language of one's heart." Yet Thomas managed to convey his feelings for his friend in language that was vivid and direct: "As to my friendship, you must know, my dear G.T. Esq., and if you don't God Almighty does, that I love you more fervently than did Prince Jonathan the little ruddy Captain David." He finished one letter by noting that there was "barely room" left on the page "to say what I have so often said—I love you very much." Another ended with his signing off as "yours for ever—and ever—and ever." Thomas evidently felt his love for George as a palpable force. In a letter that described the problems he was having with his heart, which was "palpitating" and had "an unsteady and vibrating pulse," Thomas assured George that "this heart of mine, however feeble and how soon soever it may cease to move, its last pulsations shall vibrate for you."[12]

Eighteenth-century men often wrote that they craved physical affection from their male friends and that they felt their mutual love as an overtly sensual experience. Daniel Webster recalled "press[ing]" Thomas Merrill's hand and wrote that he wanted to pour the effusions of his "heart," which was "now so full," into his friend's ear "till it ran over." William Wirt, a Virginian lawyer who established a close friendship with Dabney Carr in the 1790s as the two men traveled together in search of clients, later wrote, "O! That you were here. Am I ne'er to see you more?—I long for your hand—I hunger after your face and voice—can you not come down this winter, if not sooner?" Time and again loving friends wrote of their feelings as suffusing and overwhelming them; those feelings were then conveyed through letters into their friends' hearts, creating a reciprocal response. William described such letters as "voluntary effusion[s] of [the] heart" that sent "a warm glow through [his] breast."[13] Ezekiel Dodge declared his love for former classmate Robert Treat Paine in prose that was rhapsodic and vividly passionate:

> Thanks be to my genial stars that it was my happy lot to contract
> such an acquaintance with you that the silver cord of friendship hath
> wrapped our united souls in such a glorious concord. O! Had I all the
> tuneful art or did the noble fire which inspired the poets' breasts of
> old inspire mine, it would not be sufficient to describe the arduous
> love and noble value I have for you. When I think of representing my
> anxious love and my ardent affection to you, alas! My fainting muse
> folds up her wings, unable to sustain the task. What words shall I
> seek or what numbers shall I choose to paint my ardent passion
> and my warm desires?

Though Dodge claimed that no words could express what he felt for Paine, though he sensed his muse swooning under the weight of the task (and also, perhaps, the heat of his passion), the language that Dodge and other loving male friends did summon to convey their love for one another leaves no room for doubt that they felt their intimacy as a powerful and visceral experience, engulfing the "whole self."[14]

Whether such feelings ever translated into erotic attraction or expressed themselves in the form of sexual relations is for the most part impossible to tell. It seems presumptuous to assume either that they did or that they did not. Virginian John Randolph wrote that he "burned with desire to see" his college friend Henry Rutledge, yet Randolph celebrated their friendship in a 1795 letter as "pure affection between man and man." Perhaps he wanted to distinguish his feelings from those of other men whom he knew or suspected to be less "pure" in the expression of their love. Or perhaps he sought to disown feelings within himself that he feared and condemned. That men rarely acknowledged any sexual attraction toward each other in their correspondence is hardly surprising, given contemporary attitudes toward sex between men. (We should also bear in mind that even married couples rarely mentioned the sexual component of their relationships in diaries or journals, even though sex between husband and wife would have been entirely licit.) Yet male friends were not reluctant to express physical affection for one another that was certainly intense and at least sensual, if not sexual, in tone.[15]

Some of these friends clearly enjoyed sleeping with one another. Readers will recall that John Mifflin and James Gibson relished the "affectionate attentions" that they shared when "lodging" in each other's beds and also the intimate conversations that often preceded or followed their repose. When Israel Cheever wrote to Robert Treat Paine from his teaching post in Wrentham, complaining that he had "not the fashionable people of the world to converse with, nor no sweet chum to confabulate with upon a bed of ease," his turn of phrase was by no means metaphorical: he went on to declare how much he missed his "dear chum, with whom I have lain warm so many nights." Israel informed his friend that he had "no bosom friends in the night upon [his] lodgings." He then declared jokingly that he was referring to "bed bugs," but he also seems to have wanted to reassure Robert that no new "chum" had supplanted him in Israel's bed. William Wirt and Dabney Carr first became friends as young lawyers riding from courthouse to courthouse looking for work; they almost certainly slept together as they traveled, perhaps from choice as well as for practical reasons. Wirt recalled that period of their friendship with "a swelling of the heart." "Gone forever," he lamented, "are those pleasures!"[16]

Though we should beware of leaping to unwarranted conclusions about the kinds of intimacy that "dear chums" enjoyed when lying "warm" together, it is of course not inconceivable that in some instances "those pleasures" might have included erotic stimulation or even sexual activity. Some letters are a good deal more suggestive than others in expressing nostalgia for nights spent with a close friend. Virgil Maxcy, who lived in Smithfield, Rhode Island, assured his "chum" William Blanding in Rehoboth, Massachusetts, that he missed sleeping with him: "I get to hugging the pillow," he declared, "instead of you." One night when "a stranger" slept in the same bed with Maxcy, the other man commented in the morning that Maxcy had "hugged him all night," and indeed Maxcy remembered waking up "several times" to find "both my arms tight around him." We cannot know for certain if the physical intimacy that Maxcy missed had any sexual component to it, but he did make a rather striking remark in that same letter. "Sometimes," he wrote, "I think I have got hold of your doodle when in reality I have hold of the bedpost." A "doodle" that could be confused with a bedpost was hardly in a state of repose, and Maxcy signed this particular letter "your cunt humble." One cannot help but wonder.[17]

Whether or not some loving friendships did include a sexual component, it is clear that many were emotionally intense and lasting. Following George Thatcher's departure from Maine in 1789 to serve in the U.S. Congress, he and Thomas Wait never again lived in close proximity, but they remained devoted friends. The prospect of occasional reunions became a sustaining force in their lives: "I have thought of you almost every hour since the commencement of the New Year," wrote Thomas in January 1810, "and have hoped to see you." By 1813 Thomas was in his early fifties, and he still missed George. "You do not know how often I think of you," he wrote that December, "nor how ardently I wish that we were nearer each other." George had apparently suggested in a recent letter that this might become more feasible as they "arrived at old age." Thomas replied, "I know of no event of the kind which would give me so much pleasure as that to which you refer." A few days later he wrote again and told his friend that once he started a letter to him he "never kn[e]w where to end it; and so ke[pt] gabbling on till [he] reach[ed] the end of the sheet." But what he really wanted was to "*see*" his friend (Thomas's emphasis), to "talk an hour about politics, and an hour about religion, and an hour about new books, and an hour about old friends." Eight years later, in 1821, Thomas was still lamenting that he and George lived "at too great a distance from each other": "What shall be done? We are so old, and have so little time to lose—I ask again—What shall be done? But I have neither room nor power to answer." Their one consolation, he suggested, was that they could live out their separate lives "in a manner that shall ensure, in another life, a nearer and happier residence."[18]

An essay printed in *The New Universal Letter-Writer* at the end of the eighteenth century described friendship as "made for life." Thomas would certainly have agreed. Year after year, decade after decade, he assured George that his letters remained "of great consequence" to him, striking a chord in "heart and soul." Like John Mifflin and James Gibson, Thomas and George sometimes became insecure about each other's feelings during lapses in communication. When George apparently complained that Thomas was neglecting their correspondence, the latter was stung by his friend's accusatory tone: "How could you talk of drawing a letter from one who has long since freely given you his heart?" Yet Thomas himself became disconsolate when he did not hear from George. "I love you," he reminded his friend when several weeks went by without a letter arriving, "and long to hear from you." Many years later, when George was again silent for "a long time," Thomas became pleading: "What is the reason? Is it my fault? Pardon me if it is. I wish to offend no one, particularly one whom I have loved so much and so long." Thomas pointed out that "love without tokens of affection" resembled "faith without works," and that although George had "for twenty or thirty years" proven "the sincerity" of his feelings for him "by kind actions, kind words, kind letters, and kind looks," he still "require[d] a continuation of kind actions, words, etc." As he "wish[ed] to do as [he] would be done by," he now wrote "this kind letter" and hoped to hear back soon.[19]

Despite the challenge of sustaining a relationship via correspondence, some of these men succeeded in doing so for many decades. William Wirt and Dabney Carr maintained their friendship throughout their adult lives, for the most part through letters. William treasured these expressions of the "intimacy and consciousness which seems to subsist between our hearts and understandings." He wrote that Dabney's letters "always spread such a sweet glow through [his] breast as to refuse participation to any other subject." One such letter, containing a "rhapsody on life, and love, and friendship," had a particularly profound effect on William. "Ah! My dear Dabney," he replied, "it is at such moments that my soul flies out to meet yours." Transported across the miles that lay between them by the sheer emotional power of Dabney's words, their souls could "mix and commingle." William described "filing away and reperusing old letters" as "one of the purest, tenderest, holiest banquets that the heart of man can know," especially "when the correspondence has flowed from a friendship like ours." He assured Dabney that he had "preserved every scrip of a pen that [he] ever received from [him]" and that they were "among [his] most valued treasures."[20] He and Dabney also experienced moments of insecurity about the persistence of their love, as when his friend questioned (in a letter that has not survived) whether William still felt as deeply for him as he once had. But the latter's response left no room for uncertainty: "Can you, my beloved friend, who have known the very bottom and core of my heart so long and so intimately, who have had a home in that heart for twenty years, suspect, for one moment, any decay of my affection for you?" William's final letter to his friend was dated December 25, 1833. Dabney noted in the margin that it was the last he received "from this dearest of friends." He wrote that William's death was an "irreparable" loss: he had "loved him with the most unbounded affection" for "nearly forty years."[21]

Dabney was not William's only long-term friend. Indeed, William rejoiced that he had around him a circle of "well tried and dearly beloved friends," few of whom lived nearby but on whom nonetheless he relied to "relax [his] 'brow of care' and checker with soft and genial light the dusky path of life." "Need I tell you," he wrote to his former law partner, Littleton Tazewell, "how balmy and precious to my heart are the expressions of your friendship[?] We have been separated, indeed, by the duties of our profession and the course of fortune; but I can truly say that there has never been a time since our first acquaintance in which you have not been an object of my admiration and my love."[22] William's circle of friends provided him with a sense of consistent, true-hearted, and affectionate support as he faced "on every hand duplicity and sordid[ness] covered under a specious exterior." Each encounter with noxious "villainy" prompted William to "sigh for the simplicity, the sincerity, the fervour, the benevolence" of his "dearly beloved friends," to whom his "affections cl[u]ng" with "renewed determination." He told Benjamin Edwards that his "friendship and affection" were "among the purest and sweetest sources of happiness that I have upon this earth." He had "read, a half o' dozen times, with swimming eyes," Ben's most recent and "precious letter." He wrote to another friend, George Tucker, that he thought of him "always with affection and respect—not coldly and philosophically, but tenderly and warmly and deeply." And then there was William Pope: "From the year 1798 (when I first saw you) which is 26 years this summer," William assured his namesake, "I have been, with constant love, and shall ever be, your friend."[23]

Yet William's love for these other friends paled in comparison to the intense feelings that he had for Dabney. "I have certainly never loved man as I love you," he declared, "and never shall." William confessed quite openly to "jealousy" at the thought of Dabney developing close relationships with other men: "I do not want you to love any new friend quite so well as I hope you do me, and as I certainly do you."[24] As the years passed by, William left his friend in no doubt as to how important their relationship had been and remained to his emotional well-being. "Our delightful intercourse," he wrote, "fortifies me against the chances of the world and newly strings my system for the labors of my profession." Indeed their friendship had provided a "counterpoise" against "all the ills of life." "I should find," he assured Dabney, "ample consolation and refuge in your esteem and affection from the desertion of all the world of men beside." And this was possible because their separation had never been entirely real: "You have lived," declared William, "in my heart's core."[25]

As William approached old age, he began daydreaming of "an old times society" that he and his friends might form together. Given how long their friendships had been sustained by the writing of letters, it is hardly surprising that he imagined them engaged in "a scribbling expedition" to "recall the days of our early manhood": the reunited friends would summon their heartfelt past from the depths of their memories, and then they would commit it to paper. This would be, he wrote, "a sweet sunset." William now felt his "affections cling with more anxious and jealous tenacity." Worried about their prospects for reunion after death, he urged those of his friends who had not embraced his own evangelical faith to convert so that they could become "fellow traveller[s] to the eternal world." As we will see, religious faith played a key role in some of these relationships, not least in the ways that friends envisaged a future together. "I would love and enjoy you forever in heaven," William assured his beloved Dabney. And to another friend he wrote, "I am most anxious to have some foundation of hope that we shall meet again, in a happier world, to part no more."[26]

The feelings that men such as these developed for one another were intense and passionate, but also self-consciously high-minded and purposeful, dedicated to the nurture of knowledge, virtue, and religious faith. According to William Shaw, a friend was to be treasured for "the wisdom of his head and the goodness of his heart." In his own life, he wrote, friendship had been "one of the greatest sources" of "instruction" as well as "pleasure." Daniel Webster saw friendship, love, and virtue as entwined in a glorious symbiosis:

> Let love and friendship reign,
> Let virtue join the train
> And all their sweets retain,
> Till Phoebus' blaze expire.

Jeremy Belknap, founder of the Massachusetts Historical Society, copied into his commonplace book an extract from an essay on friendship that appeared in a 1750 issue of the *Rambler*, an English magazine devoted to moral improvement. According to the essayist, true friendship consisted of mutual love and also "equal virtue," the latter ensuring that friends would respect and learn from each other: "We often are, by superficial accomplishments and accidental endearments, induced to love those whom we cannot esteem; we are sometimes by great abilities and incontestable evidences of virtue compelled to esteem those whom we cannot love. But friendship, compounded of esteem and love, derives from one its tenderness and its permanence from the other; and therefore requires not only that its candidates should gain ye judgment but that they should attract the affections."

William Wirt would surely have agreed with this depiction of friendship: as he looked back on the years he had lived apart from Dabney Carr, William felt the loss not only of companionship but also of his friend's improving influence. "If I could have lived alongside of you all the days of my life," he declared, "I should have been happier and I am persuaded should have made a better figure both in law and literature." Yet his friend's letters had exercised a profound influence upon his "mind" and "soul": he felt "exalted and refined" by their correspondence. William declared himself "proud" to have such a man as his intimate friend, asserting in another letter that there was "nothing valuable in life but virtue and friendship."[27]

The selections from Greek and Roman literature that eighteenth-century American boys encountered in their schoolbooks often included effusive celebrations of ancient heroes and their devotion to one another. Yet these classical antecedents differed from eighteenth-century friendships in significant ways. Whereas the former often brought together an older and younger man, the latter mostly involved men of a similar age (often classmates in college, as we have seen). And classical friends were in certain respects less than ideal as exemplars, that is, from the perspective of many early Americans. In praising Greek and Roman friendships, eighteenth-century writers had to shift attention away from the pagan beliefs of those whose characters they were praising and also the sexual intimacy that many of these friends apparently enjoyed with one another. Some authors acknowledged quite explicitly and then repudiated the undesirable characteristics of those involved in heroic friendships; others simply ignored them. A 1752 translation of Cicero's letters to Atticus chose the former strategy, praising classical friendships for the "passion" that animated them, "strong as their love and sacred as their religion," but disavowed "the impurities that sometimes debased the one, and the superstition that always polluted the other."[28] William Livingston noted approvingly in a letter to his own beloved friend, Noah Welles, that "the ancients" made friendship "a principal ingredient in the character of their heroes":

> The friendship of Achilles for Patroclus is one of the finest as
> well as most interesting parts of the whole Iliad. Here that
> thunderbolt of war, who generally delighted in blood and slaughter,
> is humane, affectionate, and dissolves with tenderness. Aeneas sel-
> dom does anything of importance without his beloved Achatos . . .
> And next to glory, friendship was the predominant passion even of
> the ruthless Alexander, of which there needs no other proof than
> his own declaration when he cried out near the statue of Achilles,
> "O Achilles, how happy do I esteem thee for having a faithful com-
> panion in thy life."

William was careful to emphasize that he valued these classical friendships for their "affectionate . . . tenderness" and not for the "delight" that these heroes took in "blood and slaughter" (let alone their sexual passion, which he declined to mention). In another letter to Noah, William declared that to him the term "great man" signified not "a person of prime quality, of an affluent fortune, or those who butcher a million or two of men through pride, ambition, or false glory," but instead a man "whose heart is strongly disposed to acts of humanity and benevolence." He went on to note that "this description" was "a faithful representation" of Noah himself.[29]

William told Noah that his "ardent desire" to sustain their relationship was fueled in large part by appreciation of his friend's "great learning" and "great goodness." This was "so rare a thing that it is impossible to set too high a value on the friendship and correspondence of the person to whom that amiable character belongs." William had written "repeatedly" to other classmates with whom he hoped to establish an improving correspondence, but they had proven "generally a pack of lazy fellows" with "an aversion to writing." And there was little hope of finding virtuous, high-minded friends in New York, where he had the misfortune to reside. William regularly bemoaned "the depravity of taste this town is fallen into with relation to all intellectual pursuits and everything worthy [of] a reasonable soul." The "levity of mind" that characterized "modish company" in New York was such that few people had "any relish for learning" or "attend[ed] to anything but such impertinences as raise their silly mirth." Living as he did in a place where "the cultivation of the mind" was "neglected for the decoration of the body," he was "the more desirous to converse with a man who can find a noble entertainment in the works of the learned and the free communication of his knowledge." Fortunately for William, Noah's letters provided "an amiable picture of a sincere and upright heart." They reaffirmed those qualities truly "ornamental to our nature": "moral rectitude and a life of true purity and religion."[30]

In declaring that his correspondence with Noah "abundantly compensate[d]" for the "sterility" of New York City and in committing to use his friend's character as a model for his own life, William recognized that his motives for nurturing their relationship were at least partly self-interested. Indeed, "the character of a friend," he averred, "if it be searched to the bottom," would "be found to spring from self-love and private interest": "The pleasures of a judicious well-grounded friendship are so sublime and refined that I can scarce help thinking the person who enters into it does it more for his own sake than the happiness of his friend." And yet one could "distinguish" virtuous friends "from the bulk of mankind," since the latter did not understand "that there is anything in friendship capable of inspiring such exalted a satisfaction." He who made "reason his guide and piety the rule of his actions" was "the glorious

symbol of the eternal power that created him." Because "friendship between men of virtue" nurtured qualities that were "the glory of human
nature," he and Noah could enjoy each other without fretting about the
self-serving nature of their motives. Indeed, they should "cherish so
noble a passion."[31]

Just as early American women of faith sought to follow in the footsteps of biblical role models such as Bathsheba, so early American men
had their own religious exemplars, including and especially the friendship between David and Jonathan.[32] When Robert Treat Paine's friend
Nathaniel Smibert died in the fall of 1756, Robert mourned him as "the
delight of our eyes, the pride of our society, the pattern of our conduct,
the rival of our virtues." Robert had been with Nathaniel in his final
hours, "performed for him the last office, and prepared his body for the
grave." "I need not hint to you," he wrote to a mutual friend, "what are my
reflections on this melancholy occasion; you can better conceive than I
express. I shall only add that while I stood over him in his dying moments,
my busy thoughts, impatient of confinement, flowed in the strains of
David's elegy for his friend Jonathan." Robert inserted into his letter a
paraphrase of the biblical lament:

> The beauty of virtue is slain in the height of life! How is the mighty
> fallen! Tell it not in the land of vice, publish it not in the concourse
> of the prophane, lest the prostitutes of wickedness rejoice, lest the
> devotees of sin triumph. From the spoils of vice, from the profits of
> vanquished temptations, the valour of Nathaniel turned not back, his
> soul returned not empty. O Nathaniel! Thou wast lovely and pleasant
> in thy life and in thy death we trust thou wert not divided from hap-
> piness. Thy vigilance was swifter than of eagles, thy fortitude was
> stronger than of lions! Ye fair daughters of virtue, weep over Na-
> thaniel, he clothed you as in scarlet, he displayed your illustrious
> merits, he gave you rational delights, he prided in your lasting joy.
> 'Twas his glory to array you in the golden ornaments of virtue, 'twas
> his pleasure to conceal every foible.

Robert remembered his friendship with Nathaniel, "the patron of virtue,"
as "inexpressibly delightsome" and (again echoing scripture) as "far more
profitable than the love of women." He was determined that his friend's
"name and virtues" should live on and declared that the best way of en-

suring that was to invoke him as a role model. "An image might convey his person," Robert wrote, "but his virtues, his godlike virtues—let us imitate where he followed truth." Robert shared this elegy "as the effort of an inflamed friendship rather than of poetical judgment." He hoped that his friend would "therefore excuse the forcedness of the paraphrase and sympathize with [him] as a partner in a common loss." That mutual loss would, he hoped, root them "more firmly . . . in the growing bonds of friendship" as well as in "closer attachment to reason and virtue."[33]

Robert Treat Paine was not the only member of his social circle to quote the biblical David. Though colleges in eighteenth-century North America were no longer devoted exclusively to the training of clergymen, religious education still played a significant role in the lives of students. For these young men, celebrating God's love, loving to learn, and learning to love one another were closely related experiences. Ezekiel Dodge, one of Robert's classmates at Harvard, addressed him as "quo non charior ullus [thou than whom no other is dearer]" and declared, "Friendship is that delectable bond by which friends are united, than which nothing can be more pleasant. To this David of old seems to allude when he saith, 'how good and how pleasant is it to see brethren thus dwell together in unity.' May it not with the same justice be said of classmates as he said of brethren?" Ezekiel framed his expressions of love in explicitly religious terms: "A constant remembrance of each other in our prayers," he wrote, was "the best pledge of love and friendship." He seconded Robert's "desire that our souls might have the same Christian bond of union that Jonathan and David had," writing, "I can truly say my desires answer yours as face answers face in a glass. O my fellow disciple, always to be loved, would that our souls should always be joined in Christian love and friendship, and may be united in ardent prayers for grace and knowledge, each supplicating for the other."[34]

By no means all eighteenth-century friends modeled their relationships as explicitly as did Robert Treat Paine and Ezekiel Dodge on that between David and Jonathan, but the blend of friendship, love, and virtue to which Robert and Ezekiel aspired would not have surprised their contemporaries. Indeed, it is striking how many male friends emphasized the nurturing of moral character in their expressions of love to one another: loving friendship and a love of virtue were closely entwined in their minds and hearts. Joseph Hooper reminisced in a 1763 letter to his Harvard classmate Benjamin Dolbeare about the "pleasant and precious minutes" they had spent in conversation as students, which "not only gave an agreeable relaxation to our wearied faculties" but also "refreshed the mind and gave us better notions, and greater knowledge of mankind and a method of conducting ourselves when we entered on this vast theater of the world, than the same time spent in the most laborious studies would." Other members of the circle surrounding Benjamin Dolbeare also saw the mutual encouragement of virtue as an essential component of friendship. Ellis Gray was drawn to Dolbeare in part because of his character: "If you have any foibles, from which I won't exempt you, dear as you are to me, I have not yet had the penetration to find them out, so that I suppose them known only to yourself." Ellis hoped that his friend would remain "preserved from the pollutions of an evil world and from every folly and vanity [that] youth, our unguarded hearts, our corrupt passions, and unheeding innocence are ever exposed to." Thus Benjamin's happiness would be ensured not only in this world but also well beyond "this fluctuating state" so that he would "at last shine forth as the brightest of the stars forever—these are the wishes, the ardent desires of your sincere, your affectionate friend." Ellis sent Benjamin this telling benediction: "Be virtuous, my friend, and be happy."[35]

Just as William Livingston sought to shield himself from the banal and corrupting influence of New York society, so John Mifflin and James Gibson were also well aware of the dangers that young men faced in their hometown if they associated with unworthy companions. By the late eighteenth century, Philadelphia had become notorious for the sexual libertinism that some of its residents embraced.[36] John wrote in a journal entry for October 1786 that he had just attended a dinner party with James at which they heard "the melancholy history and catastrophe of a youth with whom I was once very intimate, but who by the impropriety of his conduct had for a few years past interrupted our intercourse." John "shed a silent tear to his memory," recalling "when he was amiable and deserving—he was of a sprightly genius which with proper culture would have made him shine—and had a heart capable of exalted and benevolent virtues." Unfortunately, "a warm heart and a lively genius at his own direction left him open to the designing and worthless who drew him from the paths of virtue and happiness and involved him in inextricable ruin." This "history" made John "sad and pensive." James "saw my distress," he wrote, "and endeavoured [to] comfort me . . . his friendship was like a balm to me."[37]

Late eighteenth-century literature that would have been familiar to educated Philadelphians such as John and James expressed serious concern about the potentially corrupting influence of male rakes upon innocent young women and also other young men whom they might lead into a life of debauchery.[38] Yet contemporaries also believed that men could influence each other in more positive ways through mutual support and reciprocal tutelage: together they could quell their corrupt tendencies and inspire each other to become better men. Both John and James transcribed into their journals the following poetic tribute to "virtuous friendship":

> Is ought so fair
> In all the dewy landscapes of the East,
> In the bright eye of Hesper, in the morn,
> In nature's fairest forms, is ought so fair
> As virtuous friendship?

John saw the preservation of his own virtue as a high priority. On reading about the period of Charles II's reign, he "rejoice[d] that [he] was not born in that reign, when to establish the character of a wit and a genius it was necessary to be a drunkard and a debauchee—refinement and sober sense were of little consequence—and of course neglected." He also cared deeply about the moral welfare of his friends, in part for their own sakes but also because he acknowledged that he could not sustain his own commitment to virtue without their assistance. In this regard as in many, James Gibson was a fine catch. John wrote that he treasured his young friend's "thousand virtues" and at the same time appreciated his "laying up volumes of knowledge" at Princeton that would be "a mutual resource for us both hereafter."[39]

John was clearly relieved that James did not need to be redeemed from youthful vices, and he enjoyed hearing praise of his young friend's many fine qualities. James was apparently "a handsome fellow" and received many a compliment on that account, but beauty was for John at least in part a reflection of virtue and intelligence. He recounted in his journal a conversation that he had with an acquaintance about "different ideas of beauty." According to John, the two men "concluded [that] there was no standard for it, but that each one's opinion of it was governed by the idea of some virtue which he annexed to it—or rather that beauty ever presented itself as the semblance of some virtue." During a visit to a neighbor's home, John sat next to Mrs. Wharton, "a sensible woman." She was "a prodigious admirer of beauty either in gentlemen or ladies, but she agreed with [John] that a handsome ignorant man was one of the most insipid and insufferable of beings." John was especially pleased if the praise that his young friend attracted dwelt primarily on his virtue. In one journal entry, he wrote that he had just heard "a most flattering account of Lorenzo, that 'he was so prone to morality and sobriety that he could not do wrong if he would'—I hope Lorenzo may deserve all this, nay I believe [he] does."[40]

John believed that it was his responsibility to encourage and protect his friend's "thousand virtues," so he was not happy that James wanted to follow in his own footsteps and become a lawyer. John had come to the conclusion that lawyers were "a rapacious set of cormorants feasting and fattening upon the miseries and misfortunes of their fellow citizens . . . Just Heaven, and is it possible my Lorenzo can think of devoting himself to such a profession? Could his good heart and gentle spirit brook such an ungracious, ungenerous, inurbane line of life, the prosperity of which depends perhaps on the wretchedness of thousands?" John was convinced that his friend's "nature" was "so kindly tempered with philanthropy it would recoil at it."[41] James, however, was adamant, and so John determined to play a central role in his friend's professional development, including his initial placement. In January 1787 he "paid a morning visit to Mrs. G[ibson]" and "had a great deal of conversation about Lorenzo, particularly his destination and the uncertainty of procuring him a good place." Over the next few days he made a number of enquiries around town about possible placements for his friend.[42] His "hopes and expectations" for James were "the highest that an affectionate friendship can form—Alas! Should he not come up to them it will be sapping the foundation upon which I have built much promised happiness—but should he continue himself under the guidance of my mentorship I trust I shall pilot him safely through those shoals and rocks among which he shall shortly be launched—and then, ten years hence, I may look back with delight on this day's journal and find all my hopes and expectations accomplished." If James's moral integrity could survive and flourish despite his choice of profession, John wrote, his virtue as much as his knowledge would be "a mutual resource for us both hereafter."[43]

Even as eighteenth-century friends such as these committed themselves to the mutual cultivation of minds and souls, they also acknowledged that this exalted enterprise became possible only through the workings of the heart. It was a man's capacity for emotion, nurtured in the context of loving friendships with other men, that would open the channels of communication and support through which he would grow both rationally and spiritually. Such friendships placed a premium on what Jeremy Belknap and Ebenezer Hazard called "mutual feelings" and "the sympathy of friendship." Indeed, most of the men we have met thus far declared quite explicitly that their relationships with one another depended on two fundamental attributes: *sensibility*, a capacity for refined and yet profound emotional feeling, including and especially in response to the feelings of others; and *sympathy*, a compatibility in temperament combined with a commitment to empathetic feeling that enabled supportive companionship. The eighteenth-century culture of sensibility, which flourished on both sides of the Atlantic, sought to cultivate an intense emotional susceptibility that should be felt as a visceral force throughout the body. Belknap could conceive of no greater blessing than "a sympathetic and congenial soul, with whom I can *mix essences*." Hazard treasured "the sympathy of friends" as "a cordial which even *mens conscia recti* [a soul with a clear conscience] does not render unnecessary." That emotional bond between men of feeling was profound and all-encompassing: "My whole self loves yours," he declared.[44] Advocates of sensibility stressed that to embrace one's potential for feeling was in no way to forsake the exercise of reason or virtue: indeed, the feeling heart would align with moral instincts and rational faculties to create an integrated and enriching sensibility. London's *Universal Magazine* for December 1785 defined sensibility as "a refinement of moral feeling, which animates us in performing the dictates of reason, and introduces many graces and decorums to the great duties of morality, which are plainly felt by the sentimental mind, though not easily defined." William Shaw defined friendship as "congeniality of feeling" and "assimilation of minds, which shall mutually interest and delight," so that "the happiness of the one in some measure be interwoven in that of the other."[45]

Men such as these were doubtless influenced by celebrations of friendship that appeared in eighteenth-century newspapers and magazines. These essays and poems emphasized the role played by sentiment and sympathy in bringing two men together. According to this genre, every man craved "the sympathetic affection of the soul." He wanted a friend who "from benevolence of disposition and sensibility of soul" could "sympathize with him," "a friend whose clay is replete with softness and refinement, whose understanding is strong and enlarged, and whose heart is faithful," with whom he could enjoy "sympathetic affectionate interviews," nestled "in the retired bower of friendship."[46] As the *Providence Gazette and Country Journal* put it, a friendship "without sentiment" was nothing but "a name" and "a shadow." It was its "sympathizing power," declared another piece, that made friendship so potent: its initiates were "bound by mutual sympathy."[47]

It was a happy coincidence for separated friends that letter writing had now become the preferred medium for expression of shared feeling. Eighteenth-century novelists, the self-appointed apostles of sensibility, encouraged their readers to embrace what Samuel Richardson called "the converse of the pen," through which individuals could communicate their emotions and sustain relationships based on sentiment and sympathy. Richardson claimed that "correspondence by letters" constituted "the cement of friendship" and indeed improved on companionship in person: it was "more pure, yet more ardent, and less broken in upon, than personal conversation can be even amongst the most pure, because of the deliberation it allows, from the very preparation to, and action of writing." As the power of the pen transformed "distance" into "presence," that conjured presence would transcend literal proximity: "[It] makes even presence but body," declared Richardson, "while absence becomes the soul."[48]

Letter manuals taught that friends should express their feelings openly; self-restraint was appropriate only when writing to those with whom one had no personal relationship. "When you write to a friend," *The Complete Letter Writer* explained, "your letter should be a true picture of your heart." Such effusions of the heart should be spontaneous and appear on the page "naked," neither buried beneath layers of diffidence nor "dressed in the borrowed robes of rhetoric." The author of this particular manual insisted that a friend would be "more pleased with that part of a letter which flows from the heart, than with that which is the product of the mind." He conceded that "the passions themselves" could "be dressed in wit," but only if "it sits easy and natural, and seems rather expressive of the thoughts, than placed there for any beauty of its own." As we have seen, male friends embraced this mode of expression with great enthusiasm, conveying through their correspondence the intensity of their emotional connection with each other and recording the tangible symptoms of their love: hearts pulsated as they yearned for the comfort of absent bosoms; faces glistened with tears of affection.[49]

As eighteenth-century friends wrote to each other, they drew inspiration from letter-writing manuals, epistolary novels, shorter stories and essays in magazines, and new editions of classical works. The declarations of feeling that male friends penned for one another, based on these models, might at times strike modern readers as rather affected and formulaic. "It was when the tuneful larks had sung their vespers," Ezekiel Dodge averred in a letter to Robert Treat Paine, "and the sun had dipped itself in the western ocean, when the wakeful stars to make their splendid appearance while a crimson red hung over the blushing horizon, 'twas then my pensive soul, sorrowing at your absence, would repair to the groves to tell the rocks its grief and make the grove a witness of its sighs." As "the Queen of silent shades began to roll her pale chariot over the soft bosom of the silent night," as "herds lay prostrate on the ground and eased their hearts of toil," and as "all nature seemed to nod and take its ease," Ezekiel lay awake: "I unhappy, I all night, perplexed with anxious thoughts until Aurora's harbingers of day proclaimed the rising morn." Yet when a letter from his friend arrived that morning, he "revived," and "sympathy throbbed in every vein" as he read that his friend had been equally afflicted since their recent parting. Yet however mannered and derivative passages such as these may seem, it would be rash to dismiss the feelings they described as therefore unreal or spurious. Another of Paine's friends, Israel Cheever, anticipated that Robert might wonder if Israel's feelings were as hackneyed as his prose style. He acknowledged that Robert's partiality for "all kinds of polite literature" had influenced the way in which he chose to write, but he assured his friend that his declarations were sincere and heartfelt: "If there were a crystal casement in my breast, through which you might espy the inward motions and palpitations of my heart, then you would be certified of the sincerity of my heart in all these affirmations."[50]

Though much of the correspondence that passed back and forth between friends addressed practical interests and concerns, their fundamental purpose was often and quite avowedly to express feeling. Virginian John Custis maintained a correspondence with fellow botanists through which they shared information, specimens, and above all their common passion. He thanked one of his friends for a specimen as follows: "If you will please to figure to yourself any passionate joy beyond the reach of expression, you may have a faint idea of my satisfaction." In another he declared, "I have my heart's desire when you tell me what I have sent you is acceptable and if it were in my power would ransack the universe to gratify and oblige my dear friend."[51] As William Livingston put it, "We ought to esteem each other's letters most beautiful when they abound with those soft and melting expressions peculiar to those whose bosoms are warmed by cordial affection." William rejoiced that his "bosom-friend" Noah, whom he nicknamed "Mr Eloquent," could write letters that "abound[ed] with all the embellishments of rhetoric," "majesty of style," "pomp of expressions," and "ravishing strains of eloquence" that could "move the passions, elevate the soul, and charm the imagination." William described his friend's literary "embellishments" as "perspicuous," or transparent and lucid. Far from obscuring or impeding the flow of emotion, they illuminated feeling and enabled the recipient to experience the pulsation of heartfelt friendship along with his beloved. Livingston considered himself "superlatively happy" to have such an "ingenious correspondent."[52]

Contemporaries often characterized the culture of sensibility as feminine, in large part because emotion itself was often associated with femininity. But that did not mean that the ethos of shared feeling was seen as the purview of women alone: indeed, cultivated men were expected to display this particular feminine attribute. Premodern Anglo-American culture made a clear distinction between masculine and feminine qualities, but attributes associated with either gender were not attached inflexibly to male or female bodies. In certain contexts women could assume male-identified roles and qualities, just as men could adopt feminine roles and attributes in specific circumstances without qualm or public reproach. By no means all feminine qualities carried positive connotations, and allegations of "effeminate" behavior, which usually meant the adoption of undesirable feminine attributes, could inflict serious damage on a man's reputation.[53] But for a man to display approved feminine attributes—such as a capacity for sympathetic friendship—was not problematic. The transition to a much less fluid gender culture was just beginning in the period with which we are dealing, so that even late eighteenth-century men could still cultivate without discomfort feelings which they identified as feminine. As one newspaper columnist declared in 1789, "Besides the real and obvious advantage, and the more manly pleasure, derived from friendship, many pleasing, refined sensations are mutually created by its tender offices; there are a thousand little delicate nameless emotions excited at *her* shrine [my emphasis], which polish and ennoble the heart."[54]

It was not unusual for male friends to acknowledge the ways in which they combined masculine and feminine attributes. In one of his journal entries, John Mifflin described James Gibson and Isaac Norris as "a brace of male Epicenes." His use of the word "Epicene" (meaning one who shares the characteristics of both sexes) may perhaps have been mildly satiric, but it also reflected his understanding that becoming a civilized young gentleman in the late eighteenth century involved the cultivation of traits that contemporaries defined—and praised—as feminine. William Wirt equated sentimental friendship with femininity and was forthright in avowing those "feminine" attributes within himself that he felt were necessary in a good friend. "My heart is so friendly or so feminine," he told Dabney Carr, "that I can't hold out [from writing to you]." William was not always wholeheartedly enthusiastic about this aspect of his emotional makeup: as conceptions of gender became more fixed, so male assumption of even approved feminine traits could seem problematic. William, writing in the early nineteenth century, sometimes worried that his "feminine" capacity for feeling threatened to "overcome" his "manhood." Yet on other occasions he celebrated "that happy mixture of almost feminine tenderness and manly energy which has never failed to attach me deeply and permanently." William suspected that his friend Dabney Carr was unwilling to identify as feminine his evident capacity for sensibility and sentimental friendship. In 1814 he wrote to Dabney that on reading one of his letters he had experienced "some of the most delicious suffocations that ever touched me." He then added: "I don't know if you have enough of the woman in you to understand this expression." He did not "doubt" his friend's "sensibility" ("I know that well," he declared). But, he continued, "I don't know that it ever takes you by the throat. Your manhood might rebel at such a liberty, and yet I have seen it make pretty free with your eyes." However inconsistent William himself may have been in his attitude toward the incorporation of "feminine" qualities, reflecting perhaps the period of transition in which he lived, his version of manhood did unequivocally place a premium on emotional susceptibility: "I would not exchange the sensibility which has made me so happy in my friends," he declared in a letter to William Pope, "for all the honors on earth."[55]

The characteristics and vocabulary of sympathetic friendship could be acquired not only from articles, poems, and novels but also from women in one's own social circle. This was for John Mifflin an important source of inspiration. Mifflin saw his relationships with James Gibson and Isaac Norris as closely analogous to the loving attachments enjoyed by his female friends and relatives. John showed a keen interest in reading the letters that these women wrote to each other. Some of that correspondence survives, and it is effusive in tone. Isaac's sister, Deborah Norris, wrote to Sally Wister that her "heart" was "dilated with the purest sentiments of friendship, tenderness, and affection" whenever she thought of her. "Thee has indeed no reason," wrote Deborah in another letter, "to fear a rival in my heart. Love me as I love thee and then thee will love me with the sincerest, the warmest affection that it is possible for one to love a dear, dear friend with." One of Isaac's cousins, Mary Dickinson, wrote to Deborah that it was her "sentiment, and I know it is also thine, that to enjoy the company of those who truly share our esteem and love is one of the greatest pleasures this life affords." Mary's feelings on this subject bore a remarkable resemblance to those expressed by John, Isaac, and James. "The company of a friend," she declared, "to whom we can disclose our sentiments without restraint or fear of any other construction but what proceeds from the friendship of the heart, where you may *think aloud*, how delightful it is to enjoy the privilege—very, very few indeed are the number deserving of confidence or formed for what I call friendship."[56]

On one occasion John persuaded Deborah to read him part of a letter she was writing to Sally Wister and also "an extract" of a letter written by Sally to her. Deborah assured Sally in a letter describing this incident that John had not actually seen the letter, but "sat at a respectful distance" while she "cull[e]d out the prettiest part" to read to him. John apparently said that he "liked the style." Deborah wrote to another close friend, Sally Fisher, that John had "expressed a wish to see some of [her] letters." On this occasion Deborah "did not satisfy his curiosity," though after telling Sally of this, she wrote, "Shall I do it, my dear?"[57] But it was not only from women that one could learn the art of sentimental penmanship. John also shared with James the letters that he had received from a former male friend who was now deceased. One afternoon he showed him "all the secret depositories of my escritoire—opened my sanctum sanctorum and showed him some of the letters of my dear departed Eugenius, to whom he has succeeded—they made me pensive, as indeed they always do." John evidently used his desk not only to store his letter-writing equipment but also as an archive of love. This private tour of its contents was in part a sentimental and nostalgic exercise that acknowledged James as an intimate friend, but John's sharing of the letters written by Eugenius may well have been intended as instructional, especially given that he was not always satisfied by the length or tone of James's letters.[58]

Just as male friends saw the cultivation of sensibility as a collaborative endeavor that included both men and women, so most of the men who appear in this book saw loving male friendship and marriage to a woman as complementary. As we have seen, James Gibson and Isaac Norris encouraged their friend John Mifflin in his courtship of various Philadelphian ladies; likewise William Wirt and Dabney Carr kept each other abreast of their amorous adventures and celebrated their successes in wooing young women. When both men became engaged in the same year, their mutual response—as "first and dearest friends"—was "to rejoice and be happy." William declared that he could feel, quite literally, his friend's excitement about his impending marriage. "How your transport kindles me," he wrote. "Yes—at this moment I have the very swelling of the heart which you describe. O! It is a delicious pain. I wish I had hold of your hand—you should be electrified with a vengeance."[59] The word "pain" might suggest that William felt some anguish as he and his friend prepared to leave behind their bachelor days, and as we will see, some men did look back with nostalgia on the period of their lives when their male friendships had precedence over all else. But neither William nor Dabney seems to have feared that their friendship would suffer as a result of their marriages. Indeed, William saw it as gaining a new significance in the light of the marital happiness that they both found: "To be sure, we are both married—but is that any reason why we should cease to love each other? Answer, 'no.' Somebody asks what pleasure is there in traveling through a beautiful country, unless we have someone with us to say to, 'What a beautiful country is here.'—So, blest as we are in the bosom of our families, there is no small satisfaction in having a friend to say to, 'O! How happy, how superlatively blest am I!'" William could write to Dabney about his happiness as a married man confident in the knowledge that Carr's "own heart" would "respond," presumably in part because he was also a newly married man, but also because they understood so intimately one another's feelings.[60]

William considered his "domestic joys" and those "valuable friends by whom I am known and beloved" to be the foremost blessings of his life. These blessings were, for the most part, symbiotic. As he imagined meeting with old friends in the "sweet sunset" of life to reminisce together, William assumed that their wives and children would also participate in these gatherings.[61] Far from seeking to conceal from his wife the intensity of his relationship with Dabney, William shared his friend's letters with her and also hoped that they would inspire his children. "I look forward," he declared in one of his letters to Dabney, "with a kind of plaintive pleasure to the period when, after my bones are in the grave, my children, in turning over my old letters, will meet with your and my dear Peachy's, and, with eyes swimming with tears, hand over [that is, turn over or examine] your warm and affecting expressions of love and friendship."[62] William hoped that their children would "learn to know and love each other as their fathers have done before them." Dabney named one of his sons after his closest friend, who then reciprocated three years later.[63] There was nothing unique about this intertwining of friendship and family. William Livingston hoped that he and Noah Welles "might strike up a match between a couple of our children," thus perpetuating their friendship and in a sense producing their own joint progeny via their offspring.[64]

Just as virtuous men could use their influence as loving friends to protect each other from the corrupting influence of male libertines, so they could warn their chums against the pursuit of unworthy women, especially those who deployed "external ornaments" to conceal their lack of "intrinsic worth." Just as the authors of didactic stories and essays urged young ladies to beware "the glittering appearance" of "a flattering beau" who might rob them of their virtue and then abandon them, so morally fastidious young men such as William Livingston reminded male friends that in dealing with women they should put "a just estimate upon the internal beauty of the mind and incomparable charms of virtue," guarding against those "artifices" through which fashionable beauties won "daily and innumerable conquests over the undiscerning males" of their acquaintance. Yet Livingston was confident that his friend Noah would select a wife of impeccable character. In writing to congratulate Noah on his impending marriage, William declared, "I would stake my life on the wisdom of your choice because it is yours." When William himself embarked upon a serious courtship, he assured Noah that the young lady in question was "amiable" and "religious." He avowed that he had "so impolite a turn of mind" and was "so widely different from the gay part of the world" that "in an affair of that infinite moment" he would "consult virtue before fortune." Indeed, he associated "a happy marriage" with "all the pleasures of friendship, all the enjoyments of sense and reason, and indeed all the sweets of life." He believed Noah to be "of the same complexion."[65]

Most of these men professed themselves happy in their choice of wife, yet some of the letters that they sent to each other as married men did hint at nostalgia for the intimacies of male friendship that marriage had, at least in part, superseded. Jeremy Belknap was delighted when his particular friend Ebenezer Hazard "fixed upon a partner." He sent him felicitations "warm from the heart" and hoped that his friend had been "prudent" enough to select a bride according to the same criteria "as the Vicar of Wakefield, who chose his wife as she chose her wedding gown, for such qualities as would wear well." Jeremy and his wife wished Ebenezer and his future wife "all the comforts arising from the nuptial connection" and "rejoice[d] in the prospect of [their] domestic happiness."[66] Yet he subsequently confided to his friend that his own wife's company, however congenial, was no match for that of "a sympathetic and congenial soul with whom I can *mix essences,* and talk upon *every subject* with equal ease and pleasure [Belknap's emphases]. I have not one of the right sort," he lamented, "within a dozen miles of me." By "right sort" Belknap presumably meant a close male friend. Prior to his marriage, Ebenezer himself alluded rather wistfully to an alternative version of their personal history that might have taken place had they both remained unmarried.

Jeremy had recently suggested that another friend of his "seem[ed] inclined to undertake" a scholarly work that he was finding "daily more impracticable" and that this friend might well succeed in the endeavor if he could "attain to the virtue of celibacy." Ebenezer responded as follows: "How strangely thoughts pop into one's head! I was just going to wish that you had 'attained to the virtue of celibacy,' and that things were so ordered that we could be fellow travelers in quest of knowledge."[67]

Ebenezer Hazard was not alone in fantasizing about a life that centered on partnership with a male friend instead of marriage to a woman. Daniel Webster reacted to his postcollegiate separation from James Bingham by proposing that he relocate so that they could again live together: "Yes, James, I must come; we will yoke together again; your little bed is just wide enough; we will practice at the same bar, and be as friendly a pair of single fellows as ever cracked a nut. We perhaps shall never be rich; no matter, we can supply our own personal necessities. By the time we are thirty, we will put on the dress of old bachelors, a mourning suit, and having sown all our wild oats, with a round hat and a hickory staff we will march on to the end of life, whistling as merry as robins, and I hope as innocent." Daniel imagined the two men living together as a couple and sleeping together in the same bed, though their life together, he stressed, would be "innocent." He finished his letter, perhaps somewhat defensively, by dismissing as "nonsense" his dream of two "old bachelors" living in domestic bliss, "yoked together" and "whistling as merry as robins." But this was not the first occasion on which he used the language of domesticity to characterize the possible future of their relationship. In a previous letter he assured James that he would "continue to occupy the parlor of [Daniel's] affections until Madam comes." If and when Daniel married, his wife "must have the parlor, but even then," he assured James, "you shall not be cast off into the kitchen. Depend on it, if Madam treats you or anybody else who is an older proprietor than herself with prankish airs, we will soon away with her into Lob's pound." (Most eighteenth-century communities had a pound, an enclosure used to confine stray or trespassing livestock.) William Livingston also envisaged that his preexisting friends would be treated as part of his domestic circle and could not conceive of "a greater pleasure than that of receiving a friend into one's house and making him for a while, as it were, one of his own domestics [i.e. family members]."[68]

The transition from a life that was nominally single but actually structured around close friendships to a married life in which older emotional bonds had to reckon with new loyalties could not always have been straightforward, especially for friends who remained single while their chums became married men. As Daniel Webster watched his friends marry off one by one, he became convinced that matrimony did threaten the intimacy that they had previously enjoyed. In a letter to one of his married friends, he poured scorn on what he saw as a spurious distinction between marriage and friendship, a distinction apparently embraced by some of his erstwhile companions: "A wife, I take it, reverently be it spoken, is like a burning-glass, which concentrates every ray of affection that emanates from a husband's heart. We single dogs have attachments which are dispersed over society, our friendships are scattered all over the world, and we love at a thousand places at the same moment; but you husbands carry all your wares to the same market. You have one bank, in which you deposit all your tender sentiments, wherefore I hold you all pardonable for forgetting your friends." To "philosophize" thus was all "very pretty," Daniel wrote, but his "heart" told him that "every syllable" was "a lie" and that "its attachment to any one object, however ardent, however near approaching to adoration, could never sever the ties that hold it to its friends." There could be "no monopoly" in "the commerce of affection," he declared: "It rebels against the doctrine of concentration aforesaid, and kicks the business of the burning-glass to the devil." But then, he concluded sarcastically, "These things are all mysteries to us, the uninitiated, and it is presumption to reason about them. You husbands, happy race, could, if you would, tell us all about it."[69]

Remarks such as these point to the danger of generalizing about the trajectory of male friendships. Daniel Webster was much more committed to sustaining his friendships with other men than to forming relationships with women and resented what he saw as the competing demands of marriage and friendship. Though he claimed in one letter that his heart "overflow[ed] with affection" for ladies of his acquaintance, he admitted in another that he saw "little female company." This was "an item," he wrote, with which he could "conveniently enough dispense." Daniel wrote a few years later that he doubted he would ever marry. "The example of my friends sometimes excites me," he wrote, "and certain narratives I hear of you induce me to inquire why the deuce female flesh and blood was not made for me as well as others; but reasons, good or bad, suppress hope and stifle incipient resolution."[70] Yet other men saw close male friendships and marriage as equally desirable and quite compatible. While some did let their friendships lapse once they married, others saw friendship as a crucial and sustaining component in their emotional lives, lasting from early adulthood throughout married life and into old age.

Many of these men not only envisaged that their longstanding friendships with other men would become interwoven with their conjugal families but also characterized their feelings for male friends by using familial terms. Ezekiel Dodge, who at twenty-two was one of the oldest students entering his class at Harvard, became known among his classmates as "Father Dodge." He himself referred to one of the youngest in his year, thirteen-year-old Cotton Tufts, as "Son Tufts." William Wirt referred to his professional mentor Benjamin Edwards as "his dear and ever beloved friend and father."[71] But male friends of a similar age generally thought of themselves as brothers. Wirt urged Dabney Carr to think of him as "a brother as well as a friend" and also addressed William Pope as his "dearly beloved brother."[72] Daniel Webster wrote that he and James Bingham were bound to each other "in the indissoluble bonds of fraternal love." And William Livingston told Noah Welles, "I fancy myself talking to a brother." It clearly meant a great deal to him when his friend addressed him by the affectionate diminutive "Billy" and also as a brother: "The epithet of 'Brother Billy' at the beginning of your letter affects me with singular delight, nor is any part in the sequel wanting to keep the pleasure alive kindled by so affectionate an introduction."[73]

The epithet "brother" and the phrase "fraternal love" cropped up frequently not only in letters between male friends but also in contemporary discussions of male friendship and its significance. In describing each other as brothers, male friends affirmed that kinship resulted not only from biological and conjugal relationships but also from emotional affinity and long-term commitment between friends. According to Livingston, the ties that bound "persons of the same family" were "vastly" inferior to "friendship between men of virtue, arising from a kind of equality of temper, and preferring one another for intimates before the rest of mankind." Such friendships were "voluntary" and arose "from our free choice, whereas that of relations is accidental and was not in our power to prevent." In this regard, friendship and marriage were very similar. The kinship that friends asserted through declarations of brotherhood was, like that of most married couples, a voluntary relationship. (Though young people were expected to take their parents' views into consideration when choosing a spouse, most contemporaries considered it inappropriate for parents to insist on a particular marital choice over their child's objection.) Furthermore, in common with a husband and wife, they were not bound to one another by ties of blood. Yet the elective kinship experienced by friends as well as by husbands and wives felt very real and profoundly meaningful to those involved.[74]

Given that premodern Anglo-Americans saw the family as a microcosm of larger communities, routinely using familial terms to articulate social, religious, and political relationships, the appropriation of fraternal language to describe loving male friendships had profound implications, bestowing upon those friendships a broad social and political significance. The chapters that follow explore the public ramifications of these friendships as they were perceived by eighteenth-century Americans. We begin by examining the ways in which loving male relationships figured as a theme in religious culture throughout the colonial period and into the early republic. When contemporaries treated the bond between David and Jonathan as a model for their own friendships, they drew on a potent conception of male love that informed key religious movements in early American history. As we will see, that spiritual version of male fraternity had radical implications: in the second half of the eighteenth century, it would combine with the culture of sensibility and the ideology of the American Revolution to produce a powerful moral vision for post-revolutionary society that placed love between men at its very center.

CHAPTER THREE

"The Best Blessing We Know"

Male Love and Spiritual Communion in Early America

STITH MEAD, a young Methodist itinerant who preached throughout western Virginia in the early 1790s, spent much of his time journeying on his own from one community to the next; only occasionally did he have a traveling companion. Riding the circuit—often along primitive roads or barely passable tracks, sometimes in ghastly weather, with no guarantee of a friendly reception at the next stop—was "difficult" enough "when two are together," Mead wrote, "but much more so when one is left alone." Yet he was never truly alone. Not only could he feel the "sweet" presence of his savior, but he also sensed the love, support, and example of fellow preachers toiling elsewhere, especially his beloved friend John Kobler, who was Mead's senior by a few years. Despite their physical separation, Mead and Kobler remained "united in faith and love," sustaining each other through prayer and correspondence. "How are you, my dear," Mead wrote, "I am daily with you in spirit." The two men wrote long and effusive letters to one another as they each labored to awaken Southern souls. In one of these letters Mead expressed his feelings for Kobler in the form of a poem:

> Although we ride so far apart,
> I love you in my very heart.
> I've often thought, if I could be
> A pattern as in you I see,
> I'd often feel [God's] spirit beam
> And catch hold of the living stream.
> O could I see your solemn face,
> I'd take you in my arms embrace.

Mead dwelt lovingly in his letters on the "ineffable sweetness" of reunions with his beloved Kobler: "Nothing less than rivers of love," he wrote, "could give us such heavenly feelings and glorious consolations as we enjoyed together." The prospect of more "sweet moments" together "revive[d]" his "drooping spirits and add[ed] new strength" to his "wasted body." "I daily think of you," Mead declared, "with sweet delight."[1]

The close and loving relationship that Mead and Kobler enjoyed would not have struck their fellow itinerants as unusual or problematic. Indeed, evangelical preachers who traveled throughout the South in the closing years of the eighteenth century laid great stress upon the need for "sweet" and "sympathizing" love between brothers in Christ that would provide support and a sense of familial belonging as they strove to save souls, often in the face of virulent hostility from those who did not welcome their particular brand of Christianity. Many of these itinerants committed formally as covenant brothers to sustain each other through prayer and loving correspondence as they traveled in service to their God. Mead, who entered "into band" with Kobler, thought of his friend as a "dear brother" and "sympathizing mate."[2] As late eighteenth-century evangelicals embraced an ethos of brotherly love in service to Christ, they followed in the footsteps of pre-revolutionary revivalists and also seventeenth-century Puritans. All three movements venerated love between men as a sanctified expression of membership in a transcendent spiritual family. Not only should the faithful cultivate fraternal affection, modeled on the relationship between Jonathan and David, but they should also envisage their relationship to Christ himself as a passionate union akin to marriage that enveloped male as well as female believers. As we will see, the emphasis that all three movements placed upon brotherly love reflected an egalitarian spirit that had profound social and political implications. Their conception of spiritual community as a family that held together through bonds of affectionate mutuality between brethren in Christ would provide an important context for late eighteenth-century republican ideology as Americans sought in the wake of Independence to create a new and democratic society.[3]

,♡

In early 1630, as John Winthrop prepared to cross the Atlantic and join the Puritan settlement of New England, he found himself saying goodbye to friends and loved ones. Some, including his wife, would remain in

England for a time and then join him in North America. Others he would never see again. Among the latter figured his "most sweet friend" Sir William Spring. Winthrop sent Spring a parting letter in which he declared: "I loved you truly before I could think that you took any notice of me: but now I embrace you and rest in your love and delight to solace my first thoughts in these sweet affections of so dear a friend. The apprehension of your love and worth together hath overcome my heart and removed the veil of modesty, that I must needs tell you, my soul is knit to you as the soul of Jonathan to David: were I now with you, I should bedew that sweet bosom with the tears of affection." Winthrop was "so straightened in time" and his thoughts "so taken up with business" that he feared himself "unfit" to write the kind of letter that Spring deserved, but his friend's "exceeding love" had "drawn" from him these words of devotion. In the past, he wrote, their farewells as one or the other set off on a trip had been "pleasant passages," but now "this addition of for ever" was "a sad close." Winthrop confessed quite openly to Sir William his "envy" of their mutual friend Nathaniel Barnardiston and Spring's wife, neither of whom would suffer the anguish of permanent separation. Of Barnardiston, Winthrop wrote, "He shall enjoy what I desire." And as for Spring's wife, he "must repine at the felicity of that good lady." Winthrop consoled himself with the thought that Providence must have ordained this separation for their ultimate good: "Bitter pills help to produce good health." And if he and Spring never did see each other again in this life, they would, Winthrop trusted, "meet in heaven." Meanwhile, their "prayers and affections" would sustain their friendship "and represent us often with the idea of each other's countenance." Winthrop prayed that Christ would bless and sustain their "bond of brotherly affection: let not distance weaken it, nor time waste it, nor change dissolve it."[4]

Envious though Winthrop was of Barnardiston and Lady Spring, there was another loving companion to whom he could entrust his friend without any twinge of jealousy, that is, their mutual savior. "I know not how to leave you," he wrote, "yet since I must, I will put my beloved into his arms who loves him best and is a faithful keeper of all that is committed to him." In common with other Puritans, Winthrop envisaged Christ as a prospective spouse and relished "the most sweet love of my heavenly husband." Winthrop imagined himself as "the loving wife" in Canticles (the Song of Solomon), rushing to the door when she hears "his voice, whom her soul loves." He addressed his spiritual husband-to-be in a rhapsody of romantic infatuation: "O my Lord, my love, how wholly delectable art thou! Let him kiss me with the kisses of his mouth, for his love is sweeter than wine: how lovely is thy countenance! How pleasant are thy embracings! My heart leaps within me for joy when I hear the voice of thee, my Lord, my love, when thou sayest to my soul, thou art her salvation." Winthrop would have to wait for union with his savior until the afterlife, when he hoped to join other redeemed souls in marriage to the heavenly bridegroom. Meanwhile, in his sleep, he "dreamed that [he] was with Christ upon earth" and was "ravished with his love towards me, far exceeding the affection of the kindest husband." On awakening after one such dream, he found that the experience "had made so deep impression in [his] heart as [he] was forced to unmeasurable weepings for a great while, and had a more lively feeling of the love of Christ than ever before." Now that he was leaving England and would no longer be able to "bedew" William Spring's "sweet bosom with the tears of affection," he would find solace in Christ's love and also imagine his friend in their savior's embrace.[5]

Winthrop's dreams of ravishment by the love of a heavenly bridegroom would not have surprised or disturbed his contemporaries. As we noted in the previous chapter, notions of gender in early modern Anglo-American society were in some respects remarkably fluid. Roles and attributes labeled as masculine or feminine were not attached inflexibly to male or female bodies; Puritan men were expected to adopt both male and female roles, depending on the context. John Cotton, Winthrop's pastor in Boston, declared that the relationship between government officials and the freemen who elected them should be equivalent to that between "husbands and wives in the family": men, in other words, should defer to officials as wives deferred to their husbands. That feminine obedience in no way compromised the male privilege that those same men exercised when electing the official in the first place. Likewise, functioning as a husband in this world was quite compatible with anticipating eternal bliss as a bride of Christ in the world to come. Cotton invited members of his flock, male and female, to imagine Christ as a lover and his gift of redemption as equivalent to sexual impregnation: "Have you a strong and hearty desire to meet him in the bed of loves, whenever you come to the congregation, and desire you to have the seeds of his grace shed abroad in your hearts, and bring forth the fruits of grace to him?"[6]

Winthrop saw his loving relationships in this world—with three successive wives and with close male friends—as analogous to the love raptures of the world to come. Once in heaven, he aspired "to deal with [Christ] as I was wont to do with my earthly well-beloved." In Winthrop's mind, earthly and spiritual loves were mutually sustaining, each informing and inspiring the other. Looking over some of the letters that he and his first wife had written to each other, Winthrop found himself in "such a heavenly meditation of the love between Christ and me as ravished my heart with unspeakable joy; methought my soul had as familiar and sensible society with him as my wife could have with the kindest husband." He hoped that the love he and his third wife, Margaret Tyndal, shared would inspire them "to a like conformity of sincerity and fervency in the love of Christ our lord and heavenly husband; that we could delight in him as we do in each other."[7] Winthrop never referred to Sir William as a spouse (at least not in any of his surviving letters), but he did see their loving friendship as a foretaste of the bliss awaiting the redeemed in the life to come: "If any emblem may express our condition in heaven, it is this communion in love." Spring evidently felt the same way, depicting his love for Winthrop and for Christ as parallel devotions: he wrote longingly of Winthrop's "bosom, whither I desire to convey myself and to live there, as we may to [Christ] also that owns that place." Winthrop saw marital love, loving friendship, love of Christ, and Christ's love for the faithful as mutually reinforcing devotions that conflated the earthly and spiritual as well as love for men and women. He finished his letter of farewell to Spring by praying that Christ would bless their love for one another and unite them in love for their savior: "Make us sick with thy love: let us sleep in thine arms, and awake in thy kingdom: the souls of thy servants, thus united to thee, make as one in the bond of brotherly affection."[8]

A few months later, in a lay sermon that Winthrop delivered aboard the *Arbella* as the Puritan flotilla journeyed across the Atlantic, he revealed just how central that ideal of "brotherly affection" was to his vision for a godly life and godly society. The law of nature, he declared, bound men to one another "as the same flesh and image of God," while the law of grace united them as brothers in Christ, joined "in the communion of the same spirit" as one "household of faith." Just as a body would fall apart without the ligaments that held its bones together, so the members of a godly commonwealth would fall prey to contention and disorder unless "knit together" by the "bond of perfection." That "bond of perfection" was love: throughout "the histories of the church in all ages," it had been "the sweet sympathy of affections" that united the faithful, "serving and suffering together" because of the "fervent love among them." Winthrop explained to his fellow travelers that "the ground of love" was a recognition of self in others: "Each discerns by the work of the spirit his own image and resemblance in another, and therefore cannot but love him as he loves himself." In a society built on this principle, each member would seek to sustain others "out of the same affection which makes him careful of his own good." Winthrop declared that this "sympathy of each other's conditions" would "necessarily infuse into each part a native desire and endeavour to strengthen, defend, preserve, and comfort the other."[9]

Winthrop proposed that his audience take from scripture two models for this "bond of perfection," which would gather "the scattered bones of perfect old man Adam" and bring them together as "one body again in Christ." The first of these was the loving and devoted relationship that Adam and Eve enjoyed in the Garden of Eden, each taking "great delight" in the happiness of the other, eager for "nearness and familiarity," sharing in each other's sadness or distress, and never so happy as when the other was "merry and thriving." Many generations later, the spirit of that first human relationship had been "acted to life" anew in another consummate expression of Christian love: the friendship between David and Jonathan. Winthrop evoked that friendship in a deeply affecting passage of his sermon:

> Jonathan, a valiant man, endued with the spirit of Christ, so soon as he discovers the same spirit in David, had presently his heart knit to him by this lineament of love, so that it is said he loved him as his own soul, he takes so much pleasure in him that he strips himself to adorn his beloved, his father's kingdom was not so precious to him as his beloved David, David shall have it with all his heart, himself desires no more but that he may be near to him to rejoice in his good, he chooses to converse with him in the wilderness, even to the hazard of his own life, rather than with the great courtiers in his father's

palace; when he sees danger towards him, he spares neither care, pains, nor peril to divert it, when injury was offered his beloved David, he could not bear it, though from his own father, and when they must part for a season only, they thought their hearts would have broke for sorrow, had not their affections found vent by abundance of tears.

Inspired by the example of these two loving men, New Englanders should "entertain each other in brotherly affection" and "love one another with a pure heart fervently." Unlike those who professed love but did not enact its dictates, the godly of New England must be truly "knit together by this bond of love, and live in the exercise of it." The cultivation of their God-given capacity for love was an absolute imperative since only by "work-[ing] upon their hearts" could "Christ be formed in them and they in him, all in each other knit together by this bond of love." Mutual love and devotion among the faithful, modeled on the first human marriage and the loving friendship between David and Jonathan, would enable a truly redemptive society, preparing believers for union with Christ, the heavenly bridegroom.[10]

Winthrop would have found inspiration aplenty for his vision of a godly commonwealth united by "brotherly love" in the sermons and other writings of fellow Puritans back in England. Seventeenth-century Puritans on both sides of the Atlantic laid great stress upon the need to nurture loving communion among the faithful. Puritans should be bound to one another by their shared beliefs, their similarity in temperament, and their experience of hostility from those who did not welcome their vision for a reformed Christendom. But it was the process of spiritual regeneration that each of them went through and their consequent sense of Christ's love that lay at the heart of this "sweet communion." Their mutual affection was, as Winthrop put it, "the fruit of the new birth." The "beauty" of that loving communion would, declared Puritan preacher Richard Sibbes, "allure and draw on others to a love and liking of the best things." John Cotton, who served as the vicar of St. Botolph's parish in Boston, Lincolnshire, before traveling across the Atlantic to become the first minister in Boston, Massachusetts, entreated his flock to "covet society with faithful friends." Their loving fellowship with one another would not only sustain them as they faced the challenges of their faith, whether in England or New England, but would also mirror the love that bound them to their savior and provide the informing principle for their establishment of a truly Christian society. According to another Puritan minister, George Gifford, "true friendship" was "in the Lord, knit in true godliness." Loving friendship was, then, the product of a shared experience, a celebration of Christ's devotion to the faithful, and above all, the instrument of divine love, the means for realizing God's will on earth.[11]

New Englanders by no means lived in constant amity with each other, but the godly did at least aspire to "love one another with a pure heart fervently." Not least among their reasons for doing so was the need to unite in the face of hostility from outsiders. God's "plantations" in the New World must band together "in as strong a bond of brotherly affection, by the sameness of their condition, as Joab and Abishai were, whose several armies did mutually strengthen them both against several enemies." Connecticut's colonial assembly urged in 1638 that New Englanders should "walk and live peaceably and lovingly together, that so if there be cause we may join hearts and hands to maintain the common cause ... against all opposers." Assemblymen invoked the example of Jonathan and David, whose "love was great each to other" and who "made a covenant to perpetuate the same." The treaty of friendship between colonies that they now advocated would be inspired by this biblical archetype for male love.[12]

When disagreements did arise, godly settlers lamented the "breach of charity and love," since mutual affection was, they insisted, "the principal badge of saints." Those brethren who became embroiled in disputes should—at least ideally—behave in a "friendly" spirit as they sought an end to the quarrel, so demonstrating "the power of God's holy word awing their hearts." They should remind themselves that even though they "differ[ed] in their opinions from one another in many smaller things," they were—or should be—"united in their faith in Christ, their love to God and one another."[13] Winthrop was horrified to learn in 1642 that critics of his model for a commonwealth built on "brotherly affection" were recommending that "there be no kindred, affinity, or close amity" between those in government because it was "dangerous for the commonwealth to have the magistrates united in love and affection"—far better that they "be divided in factions." Winthrop responded by reaffirming his belief that "love and affection" were essential to the welfare of a godly society: "Christ says that love is the bond of perfection and a kingdom or house divided cannot stand." Winthrop noted that "late divisions and oppositions amongst us" should remind New Englanders of the need to reaffirm, not abandon, this commandment. Otherwise, they may as well "take up the rules of Matchiavell [Machiavelli] and the Jesuits."[14]

The covenants that Puritans signed when establishing congregations in colonial settlements expressed their commitment to loving communion. The founding members of the church in Dedham, Massachusetts, pledged themselves "to all such Christian and spiritual duties of love as flows from that union with Christ and one another." They declared themselves "knit firmly in the band of love" by "a mutual consent or profession of the covenant of grace." In order to achieve a "sweet communion," members must become "well acquainted with the hearts and [spiritual] states of one another." New members must therefore profess their faith in public "for the better union of the hearts of other Christians unto them." In order to sustain the "endeared affections of love" that held a congregation together, members must be "free and frequent in communicating to one another the inward workings and dealings of the Lord with their souls." They should also demonstrate "brotherly love" by "watching over each other, admonishing and exhorting one another, etc., in love, wisdom, and pity." Thus they would "cleave together in spiritual love and communion."[15]

Each of these congregations evolved in practice as a densely interwoven network of personal relationships between church members. These devoted and devotional friendships bound the godly to one another, realizing the basic component of social unity as envisaged by Winthrop in his sermon. New England colonists took very seriously the cultivation and expression of friendship. They addressed each other in their letters as "most loving friend," "loving and no less loved friend," "entirely beloved," "dear and desired," "endeared friend," and "beloved in the Lord."[16] Ezekiel Rogers saw Winthrop's own "godly heart" as a model in this regard and wrote of the love that Winthrop had "showed" him "by so many expressions and so constantly," which had been "a great motive to me to stay in these parts." Winthrop was by no means unique in his "expressions" of yearning for physical closeness and affection. "Sir,"

Nehemiah Bourne wrote in a letter to Winthrop, "suffer me to lie in your bosom." The godly often imagined their friends in Christ's arms as well as in their own: their love for one another and the love that they craved from their heavenly bridegroom became tightly entwined in their minds and hearts. Thomas Jenner "lovingly embrace[d]" John Winthrop's advice and in turn envisaged Winthrop "in the arms of our blessed savior." Thomas Harrison looked forward to a time when Winthrop's "spirit" would "be at last folded up, and laid in [Christ's] spirit and be made one with it, in whose bosom (the center of all happy souls) I leave you." And Samuel Newman ended a letter to John Winthrop Jr. by "leaving [him] in the arms of the Almighty."[17]

Winthrop's son and namesake inspired effusive declarations of love from his brothers in Christ. "I do long for your company as much as the teeming earth for the rising sun," wrote Hugh Peter, "Oh how my heart is with you." Peter addressed the younger Winthrop as "honest heart" and "my dear heart."[18] He assured the governor's son that he loved him "as mine own soul" and declared in one letter, "Oh that I were to die in your bosom."[19] Edward Howes, writing from England, addressed Winthrop Jr. as "charissime" (dearest one), "gaudium meae vitae" (joy of my life), and "optatissime amice optime" (best and most desired friend). He sent him "as much love as a man can yield to his friend" and declared that "all the water between us shall not be able to wash away my former professed love to you." Howes declared that Winthrop's "virtue" had "kindled" in him "such a true fire of love" that "the great Western Ocean" could not "quench" it. "It shall be with you," he assured his friend, "wheresoever you are."[20]

Puritan men often described the love that they felt for one another in terms of spiritual brotherhood: they were united, as Winthrop had put it, by "the bond of brotherly affection." To give just a few examples, John Wilson described himself in a letter to Thomas Weld and John Eliot as their "very loving brother." Thomas Thacher ended a missive to Wilson and others by declaring himself "yours in the Lord" and sending his "brotherly love." John Humfrey signed off at the end of a letter to Isaac Johnson by calling himself "your loving and deeply engaged brother." A striking number of the godly were linked to each other through marital alliances and so were brothers by marriage, but when George Jenney (who had married John Winthrop's second wife's sister) wrote to Winthrop in 1640, he declared himself a "truly loving brother not only [in] law but also in Jesus Christ." This appropriation of a familial relationship was deliberate and purposeful: it asserted a form of kinship among the faithful that prefigured the loving family they would join in heaven and meanwhile provided them with a sense of visceral connection. It also conferred upon their relationships a basic legitimacy, given that the family household was universally recognized as the primary social unit in early modern Anglo-American culture. Furthermore, as we will see, asserting familial identity specifically in terms of brotherhood had profound and far-reaching political implications.[21]

Puritan expressions of fraternal love stressed that along with mutual affection came the obligation to serve each other's welfare, spiritual and otherwise. Brethren were "obliged in a never to be cancelled bond" and frequently committed themselves in their correspondence to "all service of love."[22] George Fenwick, for example, thanked Winthrop for his "continued offices of love" and assured him that "[i]f there be anything wherein you can use me, I am yours." Fenwick made it abundantly clear that his sense of obligation to the Winthrops was anything but perfunctory. "Your son was with me before your letter," he wrote, "and acquainted me with your own and his desire. I did but express my heart when I told him I should be glad any way to pleasure either of you."[23] Reciprocal service expressed love for God as well as for each other. As Stephen Goodyear put it, "with my love to you I rest in God your friend to use." That enactment of love could sometimes take the form of mundane tasks: Thomas Stanton asked Winthrop Jr. "to be helpful to the gentleman who has bought my three oxen that I had of Jacob Waterhouse: I pray let them be delivered to him or his assignees: and I shall remain bound to you in any service of love to my power." Oxen mattered, but the underlying significance of favors such as this was their expression of feelings that bound brethren together. "Nought else at present," wrote William Lord, "but the remembrance of my service to you and of your loving kindness formerly to me for which I count myself engaged in any service of love towards you."[24]

Many of these Puritan brethren recorded their feelings for one another because they were separated, whether temporarily or permanently. As Winthrop himself anticipated in his farewell letter to William Spring, such separations could prove extremely painful. Yet as Winthrop's son wrote in 1650, letters enabled even those who were "separated by an entire hemisphere" to "nourish a mutual friendship." They could, "so to speak, talk . . . though far long and absent from one another." There was nothing formulaic or perfunctory about the declarations of love that friends sent back and forth between New England settlements and across the Atlantic. Thomas Arkisden assured Winthrop Jr. that no distance could "eclipse the sun of true affection among faithful friends: the moon being in a diameter line farthest from the sun shines brighter than when they are both near together and so ought love among them whom affection hath united in a constellation of friendship." In a letter to James Richards, John Hull conveyed with simple eloquence the love that bound brethren together across even thousands of miles: "The Lord help us both to be frequent in our remembrances one of another at his throne; when our bodily eyes cannot behold each other, yet let our hearts be firmly knit and the eyes of our souls looking to that ever flowing fountain of all supply of whatever we may seem to be deprived of." Hull depicted their exchange of letters as a form of reunion: "When distance of place hindereth me from walking with you and speaking mouth to mouth, yet it is no small favour that we may give each other now and then a visit in such a way as this." Brethren took comfort in their friends' "sweet and comfortable" letters as "manifestations of continued affection" that were "full of life and love and encouragement." Ezekiel Culverwell wrote that John Winthrop's letters "well resemble[d] their parent in constancy of true Christian love."[25]

Expressions of brotherly love and of passionate devotion to Christ the spiritual bridegroom would play a central role in the sustenance of early American faith well beyond the first phase of settlement in New England.[26] In the early decades of the eighteenth century, the tone of religious experience seemed to be heading in a quite different direction as a much less affective approach to faith began to shape the ways in which ministers addressed their congregations, especially those preachers influenced by Enlightenment thinkers and their rationalist perspective. This appealed to some colonists but alienated others and indeed appalled those clergymen who did not embrace Enlightenment principles. Beginning in the 1730s, a wave of evangelical revivals often referred to as the Great Awakening aimed to reinvigorate a "cold" and "dead" religion with the spirit that had animated earlier settlers.[27] Careful though we should be not to accept at face value the evangelists' assertions about "cold" religion, which were clearly polemical and self-serving, it is nonetheless true that the version of religiosity promoted by revivalists such as Jonathan Edwards and George Whitefield harkened back to a version of faith that emphasized emotional intensity: repudiating the notion that humankind could win salvation through rational conviction, the revivalists reaffirmed the central importance of affective response. In particular, they envisaged a society of the faithful united by passionate love for brethren in Christ as well as for Christ himself. According to one prominent evangelist, "mutual love" was "the band and cement" of society without which no community could "comfortably or profitably subsist, yea, hardly subsist at all, for any long duration."[28]

Jonathan Edwards, revivalist pastor of the congregation at Northampton, Massachusetts, is best known today for his sermon "Sinners in the Hands of an Angry God," in which Edwards invited his audience to contemplate the punishment that awaited them if they failed to be reborn. Especially famous is the passage in which he declared, "The God that holds you over the pit of hell, much as one holds a spider, or some loathsome insect, over the fire, abhors you and is dreadfully provoked; his wrath towards you burns like fire; he looks upon you as worthy of nothing else but to be cast into the fire . . . and there is no other reason to be given why you have not dropped into hell since you arose in the morning but that God's love has held you up."[29] Yet this was actually one of very few sermons in which Edwards subjected his listeners to lurid warnings of divine wrath. Much more characteristic of his sermonic style were rhapsodic descriptions of Christ's love and of the loving community that reborn men and women would join as spiritual brethren. In two celebrated sermons that he first delivered in 1738, Edwards declared that it was "not only fear" but also "love . . . a holy fire within" that drove the faithful to strive "after holiness," a love that was "pent up" and "struggl[ing] for liberty." According to Edwards, it was love, "both toward God and man," that "distinguishe[d] true Christians from others." "The nature of the Holy Spirit" was love, and "he that ha[d] God dwelling in him by his spirit" would have "love dwelling in him also."[30]

Like other eighteenth-century revivalists, Edwards insisted that love was "the life and soul" of "a truly practical or saving faith." A "merely speculative" faith, based "only in the assent of the understanding," was "light without heat": it was "in vain, and good for nothing." True faith comprised "light and heat together, or rather light and love." It involved "the consent of the heart." Edwards argued that faith without love was "as dead as the body is without its soul." Love was "the root and spring" of "all the virtues." It "alone" was "sufficient to produce all good practice." According to Edwards, "Every right disposition toward God and man [was] summed up in it, and [came] from it, as the fruit from the tree, or the stream from the fountain." And it was not only God whom the Holy Spirit inspired the faithful to love. It also "incline[d] the soul to flow out in love to God's people, and to all mankind." Love of God and of mankind were "wrought in the heart by the same work of the spirit." Indeed, they were inseparable: "In producing one, the spirit produce[d] the other also."[31]

While in this world, the soul could experience only "a little spark of divine love," but in heaven that would ignite "into a bright and ardent flame, like the sun in its full brightness, when it has no spot upon it." There "the spirit of God" would reign triumphant, "manifested in perfect love in every heart to all eternity." God would fill heaven with love just as "the sun, placed in the midst of the visible heavens on a clear day, fills the world with light." Edwards likened the love that suffused heaven to a "glorious fountain" that would "flow forth in streams, yea, in rivers of love and delight . . . swell[ing], as it were, to an ocean of love, in which the souls of the ransomed may bathe with the sweetest enjoyment, and their hearts, as it were, deluged with love!" The redeemed would live "as in a perpetual spring, without autumn or winter, where no frosts shall blight, or leaves decay and fall, but where every plant shall be in perpetual freshness, and bloom, and fragrance, and beauty, always springing forth, and always blossoming, and always bearing fruit." Each of the redeemed would be "as a flower in that garden of God." "Holy love" was "the fragrance and sweet odour that they [would] all send forth, and with which they [would] fill the bowers of that paradise above."[32]

Edwards described Heaven as "the household of God" and its inhabitants as "one family," "united together in very near and dear relations." All would be "nearly related to God" as "his children," while Christ would now become "the husband of the whole church of saints." On arriving in heaven, the redeemed would "be presented to Christ, as a bride, clothed in fine linen, clean and white, without spot, or wrinkle, or any such thing." Divine love would flow from God "out toward Christ the head, and to all the members through him." The saints, "with one heart and one soul," would "unite in love to their common redeemer," their "holy and spiritual husband." Living as one family, the saints would "love each other" with "full complacence and delight." Their "desire of love" would "never fail of being satisfied," since their feelings toward each other would be "inconceivably pure, sweet, and fervent," as well as "mutual, and full, and eternal."[33]

Edwards encouraged members of his audience to imagine themselves in that "paradise of love," where "the beauty of the beloved objects shall never fade, and love shall never grow weary or decay, but the soul shall more and more rejoice in love for ever!" Those who aspired to genuine faith, he declared, should focus their "thoughts and affections" on that "world of love," including "the friends" with whom they would enjoy its endless delights if and when they arrived there. Here on earth they must "cherish the spirit of love" and "live a life of love," so as to become as far as possible "like the inhabitants of heaven, who are now confirmed in love forever." Embracing that "spirit of love" in their relations with spiritual brethren in this world would enable the faithful to enjoy "on earth the foretastes of heavenly pleasures and delights."[34]

A similar conception of faith and of the loving bonds that united brethren in Christ pervade the sermons and correspondence of George Whitefield, the charismatic young evangelist whose tour of the colonies in 1740–41 unleashed a wave of revivals from New England to Georgia. For Whitefield, faith involved "believing not with the head, not in notion only, but with the heart." It was heartfelt love that bound believers to one another: "Oh how closely does true faith in Jesus Christ, our head, knit all his members in love to one another; what a divine harmony and attraction is there between them, when they have drank into and been made partakers of one and the same spirit!" There was, he declared, "a divine sympathy and attraction" between "all those who by one spirit are made members of that mystical body, whereof Jesus Christ is the head."[35]

As far as Whitefield himself was concerned, that "sympathy" between spiritual brethren manifested itself as a profound and tangible experience. Consider these words with which he began a letter to a "friend" and "brother" in 1739: "Was not my heart with your heart, when we rode by the way and talked to each other concerning the scriptures? I thought our souls tallied together, and that we had both drank of the same spirit.

I have often, since that time, admired the grace of God in you, and even now feel my soul, whilst I am writing, intimately united with yours." In letter after letter, the apostle of love expressed his sense of emotional connection with brethren in Christ. "Ever since you opened your heart so freely in the garden," he wrote to one brother, "you have been much upon my heart. Though absent from, yet I have been present with you." "The agony I was in at your departure," he wrote to another, "and the many strong cryings and tears which I offered up to God afterwards, plainly show that I love you." "My heart has been knit to you," he assured yet another, "ever since God first brought us together." Whitefield responded to the words penned by spiritual brethren with a visceral intensity: "I felt your letter," he declared in response to one such missive. Another letter "warmed [his] heart." Painful though it was "to part from a friend which is as one's own soul," brethren in Christ could find consolation not only in loving correspondence but also in the hope of eventual and everlasting reunion. "The good Lord sanctify my friendship to you," he wrote to one kindred soul, "and grant [that] we may go hand in hand to heaven." Whitefield "long[ed] to be in heaven, chiefly to see God," but "next, that I may have my soul satisfied with the blissful communion of saints."[36]

Whitefield believed that the human capacity for spiritual love, itself "the effect and fruit" of God's love, would play a central role in bringing spiritual renewal to those not yet awakened. A "loving, tender disposition," he insisted, was a crucial qualification for "winning souls to Christ." Whitefield felt "a peculiar love" toward those whom he "touch[ed]" with his ministry. When one of these awakened souls wrote to "acknowledge" Whitefield's role in "awakening [him] to the divine life," the evangelist responded by promising that he would "endeavour to quicken and inflame the heavenly spark infused into [his] soul," so that his "dear brother" would "glow with divine love, and lean by faith on the bosom of his dearest redeemer," who would then "manifest himself sweetly to [his] panting soul." God's love for mankind would combine with the love that believers felt for their almighty Father, his Son, and each other to create a spiritual commonwealth of the heart. "May he unite us more and more intimately to his dear self," the evangelist wrote, "and to one another."[37]

All of those who journeyed with Whitefield—whether literally as his traveling companions or metaphorically as spiritual pilgrims—became his "family," united in "brotherly love." He addressed his allies in the evangelical movement as "dear brother," "my brother, my friend," and "my dear friend and brother." According to Whitefield, their savior was "the friend of all," who would "unite us in the best bonds and bring us to himself at last." "On this account," he declared in one letter, "I make bold to call you brother."[38] Gilbert Tennent, Whitefield's ally and fellow preacher, encouraged the faithful to love one another as "children of the same father." The Lord's Supper should be known as a "love feast," he declared, because "one great design of the ordinance" was to "promote brotherly love." But for both men, by far "the most powerful incentive to the love of our brethren" was "the glorious example of the redeemer's love," which would ultimately take the form of another familial relationship, that of marriage. Once God, "our Father," admitted the saints into their "everlasting home," they would all join in "marriage-union" with "their husband," Jesus Christ.[39]

Eighteenth-century evangelists revived with dramatic effect the rhetoric of passionate marital devotion that Puritan ministers had used in previous generations to describe union with Christ. That rhetoric celebrated spiritual love as an expansive constellation of gendered relationships: it depicted union with a male savior as the ultimate marriage, coupling men as well as women to Jesus Christ in eternal rapture; meanwhile, the prospect of that union should inspire believers to join with one another in marriage and loving friendship on earth. Just as Winthrop had juxtaposed the marriage of Adam and Eve with the friendship of David and Jonathan as models for the love that should bind Christians to one another, at the same time envisaging himself as a bride of Christ, so evangelical preachers sanctified brotherly love among the faithful as a preview of the marital love that male and female saints would enjoy in the arms of Jesus Christ. According to Whitefield, the process of redemption reached its climax when the redeemed became "married to the dear Lord Jesus." Christ had "made a marriage feast, and offer[ed] to espouse all sinners to himself, and to make them flesh of his flesh, and bone of his bone." In a sermon published in 1742, Whitefield urged his audience not "to play the harlot any longer." Instead of resisting the advances of their savior and wallowing in sin, they should "come to the marriage" and embrace their "lawful husband." No matter if they felt unworthy: faith was "the only wedding garment that Christ require[d]."[40]

Evangelists anticipated union with their savior in language of rhapsodic infatuation. Tennent envisaged Christ as an "adorable" husband of "unrivalled beauty and perfection": "Behold, my dear brethren! The blessed bridegroom cometh, clothed with majesty, as with a robe; with light, as with a garment; with zeal, as with a cloak: see, he is girt with a golden girdle, his head and hairs are white as snow, and his eyes are as a flame of fire, his feet like unto fine brass, as if they burned in a furnace, and his voice as the sound of many waters! See the unrivaled beauty of his person, and the inexpressible riches of his love!" Tennent reminded his listeners that Christ's devotion to his betrothed "manifest[ed] itself by love-expressions" in the Song of Solomon: "Open unto me, my love, my dove, my fair one, for my head is wet with the dew, and my locks with the drops of the night!" It was, Tennent argued, entirely appropriate to characterize Christ's love in language that evoked the passion of human relationships: "a human love" could "be properly ascribed to [Christ] as man" since he had "a soul and body, will and affections, blood and animal spirits, as we." Yet the quality of his love had "great preeminence" over that of humankind because it was "perfectly pure," that is, "without excess in its tendencies, and without tumult in its effects."[41]

As eighteenth-century evangelists sought to illuminate and exemplify that spirit of divine love, they sometimes came close to embodying for their audiences a Christ-like persona that was in its own right not only redemptive but also profoundly seductive. Puritan ministers had cast themselves as "friends of the bridegroom" whose task it was to woo their congregations on Christ's behalf. But Jonathan Edwards went further, comparing "the union between a faithful minister and a Christian people" to "that between a young man and virgin in their marriage." Church members should unite with their pastor in mutual "affection and regard." They should "love and honor" him, "their admiration raised, and their carnal affections moved, by having their ears tickled, and their curiosity and other fleshly principles gratified by [his] florid eloquence . . . as the messenger of the Lord." According to Edwards, the relationship between a minister and his flock prefigured the marriage between Christ and the faithful, which he characterized in passionate and even erotic language. The redeemed bride would be "offered up to him in the flame of love," their union "most tender and ardent." The savior would "give her his loves; and she shall drink her fill, yea, she shall swim in the ocean of his love." Edwards quoted lavishly from Canticles 4: "Thou hast ravished my heart, my sister, my spouse; thou hast ravished my heart with one of thine eyes, with one chain of thy neck . . . How fair is thy love, my sister, my spouse! How much better is thy love than wine! . . . Thy lips, O my spouse, drop as the honeycomb: honey and milk are under thy tongue." Edwards stressed that the union between a minister and his congregants was a mere "shadow" of that between Christ and the saints, and that it was a pastor's duty "not only to espouse the church to her husband, but to present her a chaste virgin to Christ." Yet his use of sensual, even torrid, imagery to describe spiritual marriage in a sermon ostensibly discussing the union between a minister and his flock must have had a powerful impact on his audience, particularly given his own widely recognized charisma.[42]

Revivalists hoped, of course, that their preaching would inspire within the hearts of those listening a newfound love for Christ and for fellow believers. Such was in fact the experience of Nathan Cole, a Connecticut farmer who left behind an account of his conversion in 1741. When Cole went to hear George Whitefield speak, he was at first overwhelmed as much by the evangelist's appearance as by his actual words: "He looked almost angelical; a young, slim, slender youth before some thousands of people with a bold undaunted countenance, and my hearing how God was with him everywhere as he came along solemnized my mind and put me into a trembling fear before he began to preach; for he looked as if he was clothed with authority from the great God; and a sweet solemn solemnity sat upon his brow. And my hearing him preach gave me a heart wound." But having received this "heart wound" from the "sweet solemn" youth, Cole "was filled with a pining desire to see and feel Christ's own words in the bible": he "got the bible up under [his] chin and hugged it; it was sweet and lovely." Over the coming days and weeks, Cole felt a "new heart" within him. Both "heart and soul" reached out "abundantly in love and thankfulness" unto his savior. Cole had "found the best friend ever man had" and could "lie and sleep securely in his bosom." Christ's commandment "that ye love one another" resonated within him as he "often saw and felt the movings of God's spirit among" awakened brethren, "all in love seemingly with Christ." Cole "had many sweet meetings with them" and his soul became "much knit" to these "dear children of God." Indeed, his heart was "many times ravished, as it were, with love to the dear saints of God . . . the excellent ones of the earth in whom is my delight." Cole described such meetings in terms of the shared emotions that he experienced: "When I was with them I seemed to feel perfectly their feeling; they felt all as one as if they had been made up all into one man, all drinked into one spirit and oneness."[43]

Another of Whitefield's followers described the preacher as "a son of love," and clearly his ability to inflict heart wounds was central to his appeal. The young evangelist was nothing less than a spiritual cupid unleashed upon the colonies.[44] Yet the outpouring of love that Whitefield sought to inspire and that listeners such as Cole embraced so enthusiastically struck some observers as resembling less a "paradise of love" than an orgy of "gross disorders" and perhaps illicit passion. According to Whitefield's critics, the "ungoverned passions" and "tumults" that erupted during revival meetings—often accompanied by "strange unusual bodily motions"—were "indecent" in their own right and conducive to "unclean" behavior. William Douglas, a Bostonian deist, accused Whitefield of promoting "wantonness" by encouraging converts to embrace each other at revival meetings. Anti-revivalists charged that the physical expression of supposedly spiritual affection between brothers and sisters in Christ subjected those involved to insidious temptations that might lead them down a dark path ending in fornication or even sodomy.[45]

Evangelical ministers clearly did not intend to be sexually permissive. They attacked not only the alleged "deadness" of early eighteenth-century spirituality but also what they saw as an increasingly licentious and immoral society. Yet according to their opponents, revivalists fostered, whether wittingly or not, the very culture of immorality that they claimed to abhor. Evangelical preachers themselves worried that their emphasis upon love between spiritual brethren might lead to impropriety. Jonathan Edwards warned against "a counterfeit of love" among some of the "wildest enthusiasts," whereby the expression of "Christian love" through "mutual embraces" and "holy kisses" degenerated into "unclean and brutish lust."[46] Critics claimed that such degeneration did in fact take place and that evangelical ministers themselves engaged in "unclean" practices with their followers. Revivalist ministers were dogged by allegations that they had seduced female devotees and "had bastards in this or that place."[47]

Rumors of sexual impropriety included accusations of illicit intimacy with men as well as women. Jonathan Parsons, minister of the West Parish in Lyme, Connecticut, wrote that some people who witnessed a revival in his church "complained" that "two men embraced each other in their arms before the blessing was given," which the observers condemned as "an indecency." Parsons acknowledged the embrace as a "fact" but argued that it was not "so very indecent as some would represent it." Theodorus Jacobus Frelinghuysen, a leading evangelical within the Dutch Reformed Church, was damaged by his close association with schoolmaster Jacobus Schuurman. Shortly after Schuurman's arrival in the Raritan Valley, several people accused him of "having offered whoredom" to men with whom he spent the night. Schuurman apparently often embraced and kissed Frelinghuysen in public and private settings. Frelinghuysen's enemies referred to Schuurman, who reportedly "slept with Rev. Frelinghuysen in the same bed," as the preacher's "boy." Frelinghuysen was reported to have told church elder Joris Van Nest that "Schuurman had, at least one time, made attempts upon him." Once the rumors about Schuurman began to harm Frelinghuysen, the preacher "ceased friendly communication with him" and "put him away from him."[48]

Whitefield himself was dogged by rumors of secret sodomitical activity. One evening while on tour in Maryland, he and several male associates had retired "upstairs and shut the door in the house that they put up at." Soon thereafter, "a curious servant" proceeded to spy on the evangelicals through the keyhole to their room and saw one of them rubbing another's naked bottom. According to Whitefield's defenders, the bottom in question belonged to a revivalist who, "being galled in the posteriors, got one in the room to apply a plaister or some tallow to the place affected." The maidservant, however, being "one of a prostituted character and impudent to the last degree," passed on what she saw through the keyhole to some of Whitefield's enemies, who then "cooked up" a "base report" that made its way to Philadelphia, where it sent some of Whitefield's supporters into a frenzy of anxiety.[49]

The rumors swirling around Whitefield may perhaps have been encouraged by his evident affection for fellow preachers and other brothers in Christ, combined with his lack of enthusiasm for marriage to a woman. Whitefield spurned any love that was not purely spiritual as a distraction from his evangelical efforts. "There is nothing I dread more than having my heart drawn away by earthly objects," he declared in 1740. "For alas, what room can there be for God, when a rival hath taken possession of the heart? . . . My blood runs cold at the very thought thereof." Whitefield believed that God did want him to marry and recognized that the acquisition of a wife was "absolutely necessary," not least for the "due management" of an orphanage that he had established in Georgia. During the course of his evangelical tour through the American colonies, he became increasingly eager to find "a help meet" who could "take off some of that care" and assist him "in the work whereunto our dear Lord Jesus hath called me." Yet his interest in finding a wife was entirely practical: "I pray God," he wrote to a friend, "that I may not have a wife till I can live as though I had none." Whitefield was determined not to "preach one sermon or travel one day less in a married than in a single state." He wanted "a gracious woman" who was "dead to everything but Jesus," who was "qualified to govern children, and direct persons of her own sex," a woman who "would help, but not retard me in my dear Lord's work." Christ had apparently promised him that he would "not permit me to fall by the hands of a woman."[50]

Whitefield decided that the likeliest candidate was a young convert named Elizabeth Delamotte. In a letter to her parents, he declared himself "free from that foolish passion which the world calls *love*" and assured the Delamottes that he was proposing only because it was "the will of God that [he] should alter [his] state." Whitefield "would not marry but for Him, and in Him, for ten thousand worlds." He was equally frank in proposing the marriage to Elizabeth herself. "Can you," he asked her, "when you have a husband, be as though you had none, and willingly part with him, even for a long season, when his Lord and Master shall call him forth to preach the gospel, and command him to leave you behind?" Whitefield wrote "not from any other principles but the love of God." He was asking her to marry him "not for lust but uprightly" and quite self-consciously spurned those "passionate expressions which carnal courtiers use": he would love her "only for God, and desire[d] to be joined to [her] only by His command and for His sake." Readers may not be surprised to learn that Elizabeth Delamotte declined his invitation.[51]

Following Whitefield's return to England, he renewed his search and in 1741 announced his marriage to Elizabeth James. In a letter to fellow evangelist Gilbert Tennent, he described James as "neither rich in fortune, nor beautiful as to her person, but, I believe, a true child of God" who "would not, I think, attempt to hinder me in His [God's] work for the world." Following their marriage, Whitefield resumed his travels without his wife and did, for the most part, "live as though [he] had none." As an observer of their marriage pointed out, Whitefield "did not intentionally make his wife unhappy," and in his dealings with other women "he was a very pure man, a strict example of the chastity he inculcated upon others."[52] Seventeenth-century Puritans had welcomed an ardent and sexually passionate relationship between husband and wife as a preview of their coming union with Christ. But for Whitefield, as for that other spectacularly successful preacher of the eighteenth century, John Wesley, marriage with a woman could pose a serious threat to spiritual effort unless very clearly disassociated from the experience of passion. Whitefield's capacity for emotional intensity and passion, which was considerable, seems to have been reserved for his preaching, his savior, and his brethren in Christ.[53]

George Whitefield's somewhat mordant attitude toward earthly marriage was not shared by revivalist preachers in general during the decades preceding the American Revolution. However, evangelicals who swept through the South in the aftermath of the Revolution were much more inclined to follow his lead in perceiving human matrimony as potentially incompatible with their calling as preachers. These spiritual crusaders of the new republic were mostly young bachelors, and their leaders wanted to keep them that way: the heavenly bridegroom should have no rival on earth. Bishop Francis Asbury, who presided over Methodist evangelism in the post-revolutionary South, advocated a life of celibacy for itinerant preachers under his jurisdiction. He estimated that the ministry had "lost the traveling labors of two hundred of the best men in America" because the men in question had married and were then prevailed upon to abandon the itinerant life in favor of a settled residence. Asbury urged ministers to beware the company of women: "Stand at all possible distance from the female sex, that you be not betrayed by them that will damage the young mind and sink the aspiring soul and blast the prospect of the future man."[54]

As Asbury's army of young preachers traveled around the countryside, wooing souls on Christ's behalf, many of them followed his advice and did their best to avoid associations with women that might distract them from their heavenly ministry. Stith Mead had to deal with unwanted attentions from an unnamed "young lady" who had evidently been smitten by Mead's preaching in more ways than one. In May 1793, she wrote the following declaration: "Sir, you are the person that I would wish to place my affection upon and I could wish I was worthy to merit your favour and enjoy your person; notwithstanding my unworthiness I make bold to express my love to you." The young lady was "desirous" to see Mead again and asked him "to come into this part once more." According to Mead, his admirer was "personable" and "well-looking," in spite (or perhaps because) of which he kept his distance. She wrote again the following February, expressing her "ardent wish and desire" to see him. Mead noted in his letter book that he soon afterward had "an appointment to preach in her neighbourhood" and took the opportunity to have "an interview personally" with her, "in presence of a male member of the church." Though "respecting her for her friendly regard," Mead explained that her attentions were futile and so they "parted."[55]

Mead's attitude was by no means unique among revivalist preachers. James Meacham was much saddened in November 1789 when "dear bro[ther] P" told him that "he had some thought of changing the life of celibacy." The following April, a "dear sister" in Christ warned Meacham himself "to take care, that Satan could counterfeit love" and "begged [him] to hold fast celibacy, which by the grace of God" he was "fixed to do." Jeremiah Minter, a fellow preacher and "very dear brother," also seemed "doubtful of [Meacham's] continuance" as a single itinerant. In one journal entry Meacham did "confess" that he had "met with a powerful temptation" from "one of the female sick," but the young man went on to declare, "Bless the Lord, I feel as if I'll die before I'd desist from traveling in his blessed vineyard."[56] Preachers who did fall in love with women often became tormented by what they saw as their infidelity to their mission and to Jesus Christ.[57] Minter became so distressed by his feelings for a married convert named Sarah Jones that he had himself castrated: by becoming "an eunuch for the kingdom of heaven's sake," he could "devote [himself] entirely to the Lord in a single life." This was one step too far even for Bishop Asbury, who excommunicated Minter.[58]

Other revivalist preachers chose less drastic ways of handling their desire for loving, passionate relationships: they simply avoided female company, focusing their romantic energies on Christ himself and their brother preachers. As James Meacham rode the circuit—often cold, tired, and lonely—he imagined himself reposing in his savior's arms. "My soul longeth to be at rest in his sweet bosom," he declared. At night, Meacham often got what he wished for, or so he claimed in his journal. When he went to bed, "Jesus was near and precious," so that Meacham "rested sweetly." One night he stayed "in a little cottage" with "no fire, very cold, and all alone, but [excepting] my Jesus." In many entries, he wrote that throughout the night "arms of love compassed [him] round." One morning, he wrote, "when I awoke I felt for my Jesus and found him standing by my bedside—I hailed him and he turned sweetly to my embrace—I was happy." Whenever Meacham had "a day of rest from the labour of preaching," he would try to secure "a little room for sweet retirement" where he could "feast and banquet with [his] loving Jesus." On one such occasion, closeted in a "little upper room," Meacham's soul "was greatly favoured with peace and power divine": "I am blessed and happy, happy—yes! Happy in my adorable Lord." "Thank God," he declared, "I don't go one day without his sweet smiles." Meacham prayed that his "adorable Jesus" would "fill [his] poor soul with divine sensations." Indeed he often "felt" and "tasted" Christ's love. On one occasion, he wrote, it coursed "all over and through my soul and body." The love that Meacham felt for his savior was passionate and all-consuming: "I long, I pant for more of the religion of Jesus Christ—O! How I love him—he is my all and in all—I've none to fly unto but unto Jesus—neither is there any that I desire like unto him."[59]

In common with revivalists of the pre-revolutionary decades, late eighteenth-century Methodist preachers envisaged Christ as a tender and loving bridegroom. They encouraged those who heard them preach to do likewise, frequently citing the Song of Solomon as the inspiration for their sermons. Freeborn Garrettson wrote that he preached at New Rochelle from "O my dove, who art in the cleft of the rocks, etc." His "greatest freedom in the subject" came when he enlarged upon the line, "Let me see thy countenance, let me hear thy voice, for sweet is thy voice, and thy countenance is comely." A few days later, he gave another sermon based on the text, "Friend, how camest thou in hither, not having on a wedding garment?" Garrettson himself experienced Christ as "a divine sweetness" that "ran through [his] whole frame." His soul was "enraptured with the love of [his] dear saviour": "Sweet Jesus," he declared, "thou art lovely to my soul!—O Jesus! thou hast overcome me with thy looks, and the kisses of thy lips!" Thomas Cleland remembered being part of an "immense" gathering in his early twenties when a preacher used as his text Canticles 2:10, "Rise up my love, my fair one, and come away." " 'Rise up my love' was pressed upon me in the tenderest and most affectionate manner," Cleland later reminisced. "I thought, indeed, it was the heavenly bridegroom calling and inviting his poor, feeble, and falling one to rise from my low condition, and come away and follow him more entirely. My heart was melted! My bosom heaved! My eyes, for the first time, were a fountain of tears." Leland leaned against the back of one of the benches for support, sobbing "till my handkerchief was saturated with my tears." A friend, he recalled, "took hold on me, and gently drew me beside him, with my head in his lap."[60]

Post-revolutionary evangelical preachers also embraced wholeheartedly the notion that love for Christ should inspire a parallel devotion to other believers. Asbury and his fellow bishop Thomas Coke wrote in their expository notes on the Methodist Discipline that Christianity should "strengthen," "improve," and "spiritualize" the "social principle," which they deemed "one of the grand springs in the soul of man." They urged their fellow Methodists to "exercise" that "principle" in "spiritual intercourse, as we well know that one part of our heavenly felicity will flow from friendship and union with our brethren, the redeemed of the Lord, to all eternity." (They then quoted from the second chapter of Paul's Epistle to the Philippians: "If there be therefore any consolation in Christ, if any comfort of love, if any fellowship of the Spirit, if any bowels and mercies: fulfil ye my joy, that ye be like-minded, having the same love, being of one accord, of one mind.")[61] Meacham cherished the time that he spent with spiritual kinsfolk, recalling one such gathering as "a time of love that [would] be long remembered." In entry after entry of his journal, he wrote that they "had a sweet time of it" or "had a sweet little feast of love." Another revivalist, John Taylor, depicted Christ as a model friend. In a sermon inspired by the text, "A man that hath friends must show himself friendly, and there is a friend that sticketh closer than a brother" (Proverbs 18:24), Taylor spoke at length about Christ's "friendship" to mankind. Though "the friendship of the saviour was more to be depended upon than any brother whatever, for that he was God and changed not," Christ's followers should draw inspiration from his devoted friendship to them in their relations with one another. Taylor and his "brethren" parted that day in "tears of cordial friendship."[62]

Many itinerants developed affectionate and clearly intense friendships with fellow preachers. Bishop Asbury, who urged itinerants under his charge to avoid earthly marriage, actively encouraged them to forge for themselves alternative versions of kinship by joining with fellow preachers in covenant brotherhood, a spiritual partnership in which two men would pray for each other and commit to a regular correspondence that would sustain them as they traveled on their circuits. Mead entered "into band" with Kobler, consigning his "heart and hands" to his "sympathizing mate." Though eager to see each other in person whenever possible ("I shall use my endeavours to get into your district as soon as possible," wrote Mead), their letters bridged the miles with remarkable intensity of feeling. "In conformity to the covenant made between us when together last," wrote Kobler, "I now sit down to inscribe the warm feelings of my heart; I still feel the sacred fire glowing that was kindled at our last conference." Mead's letters were no less vivid: "I feel the same uniting flame glowing towards you, often I think of you in love and sympathizing prayers." Despite "the miles that slipped between our well known sweet united flesh," he declared, "yet in the spirit we've each other seen and eat[en] of Isaac's savoury mess." Mead read Kobler's letters "over and over again." They filled his soul "with the overwhelmings of divine love": "O the divine stream that pours forth into my soul while I make mention of it. Heaven is now begun in my soul—hail! O hail! Glory to God—my heart is so full I hardly have strength in my fingers to use my pen or a right disposal of my mind to dictate."[63]

Mead made sense of his relationship to Kobler by envisaging his fellow preacher in not one but three familial roles. He mostly addressed him as a "very dear brother": "I am your brother and your friend," he declared. But Mead also wrote that he "esteemed" Kobler "as a father," even though the latter was only a few years older than him. And he imagined his friend as a spouse, just as he did Christ himself. Mead might be reluctant to marry a woman, but he embraced enthusiastically the idea of marriage to his savior and his "sympathizing mate," John Kobler. Mead expressed his feelings for Christ in fervent and sensual language: "I often sit beneath his heavenly smiles," he declared, "and long to be swallowed up in the bosom of eternal love. My feeble tongue cannot express the unfathomable depths of never-failing love that continually flows from God my saviour." Mead used similar language to address Kobler, as his love for the heavenly bridegroom and for his brother in Christ resonated with and inspired one another: "I love all the dear preachers, yet none seems so much like my own flesh as yourself. I love you with a pure love fervently, I think of you with tears; I dream of you; I dream of embracing you in the fond arms of nuptial love, I dream of kissing you with the kisses of my mouth; I am married to you; O that I could see you and spend a few moments in heavenly converse together." In another letter to Kobler, Mead appropriated a biblical passage that evoked the bond between husband and wife: "Entreat me not to leave thee, or to return from following after thee, for whither thou goest I will go; and where thou lodgest I will lodge, thy people is my people, and thy God my God; when thou diest then I desire to die, and then I desire to be buried; the Lord do so to me and more also if ought but death part me and thee."[64]

Kobler was by no means the only brother in Christ with whom Mead enjoyed a close and loving bond. Horatio Burns addressed Mead as "dear loving Stithey": "I cannot fully express the love I bear for you," he declared, "and I want to see you so much." Edward Mitchell declared in one of his letters to Mead that, although "absent in body," they were "often present in spirit, which still keeps alive that spirit of brotherly love which has prevailed ever since our first acquaintance." This was, Mitchell averred, "one of the great privileges the Christian enjoys, that they love one another, and love taken in the general sense is not only fulfilling the law but it is also a foretaste of that bliss to which we are aspiring—yea, it is heaven itself." John Metcalf wrote to Mead as "a friend, a brother, and a fellow sufferer in the Gospel of Jesus Christ." "My dear love," he declared, "you are my brother, whom I love with a pure love fervently in the bowels of Jesus Christ." And Nathaniel Harris signed off as "Yours in love, the best of bonds." No wonder, then, that Mead described friendship as "the best blessing we know."[65]

Mead clearly treasured his loving correspondence with "sympathizing mates" as he traveled alone from settlement to settlement. But he also enjoyed the more immediate companionship of a "gospel mate," the term he used to describe fellow preachers who occasionally rode the circuit with him.[66] Itinerants often became very fond of their traveling companions. "My dear Billy is still riding with me," wrote Kobler. "He cannot rest at home—his whole desire is to be with me in the work of the gospel." An incident that Mead described in a letter to Kobler suggests the physical as well as spiritual and emotional support that fellow preachers gave each other on the road. A "young man" who was also named Billy (perhaps the same fellow) woke up one night in a sweat after having seen "the approaching fiend." He was sleeping in bed with "Tommy," a twelve-year-old who was apparently Billy's nephew; Mead was sharing a bed in the same room with another man. When Billy awoke in terror and Tommy tried in vain to comfort him, Mead intervened, declaring, "Be not afraid, have faith in God." He changed places with Tommy, saying as he climbed into bed with Billy, "The Devil shall not hurt you." "No sooner was I in bed with him," Mead wrote, "but I felt his palpitating heart thumping within and a cold sweat on his affrighted body." He "exhorted" the young man again "to trust in God," and Billy spent "the remainder of the night quietly." That Mead could feel Billy's "palpitating heart" and the "cold sweat on his affrighted body" suggests that he was holding him closely to give comfort. As we noted in a previous chapter, it was not unusual for friends, neighbors, or even complete strangers to sleep together in the eighteenth century, but evangelical preachers seem to have seen their beds as special places devoted to affection and reassurance. One night when Meacham was lucky enough to have a fellow preacher with him, he wrote that "the arms of mercy and love compassed us about and did keep us while we slept." It is unclear from Meacham's account whether the embrace that enfolded him that night was entirely spiritual; he may well have believed that he was held by his savior as manifested in the form of a human bedfellow. If so, the ambiguity of his language encapsulates neatly the symbiotic conflation of spiritual loves in his heart.[67]

Evangelicals evidently found great comfort and affection—physical as well as emotional—in their fellowship with spiritual brethren. William Capers wrote that although Bishop Asbury was reputed to be an "austere" man, his "sympathies were, nevertheless, as soft as a sanctified spirit might possess." When William's father was reunited with Asbury after a seventeen-year separation, "they embraced each other with mutual emotion," and it was "evident" that "no common friendship had subsisted between them." Asbury first met William as an infant. When their paths crossed again almost two decades later, the bishop apparently declared, "Ah, this is the baby, come and let me hug you." Evangelicals often used affectionate diminutives in addressing each other. Stith Mead was "Stithey" to his fellow preachers, and Francis Asbury, himself known as

"Frankey" within his spiritual family, addressed Capers as "Billy sugar." When Capers spent a night with Asbury and tried to get a fire going in their frigid room, Asbury approached him as he crouched at the fireplace and said, "O Billy sugar, never mind it; give it up: we will get warm in bed." Going over to the bed and lifting the bedclothes, he repeated, "Yes, yes, give it up, sugar, blankets a plenty." Clearly, the two men needed to get warm, but the way in which Asbury addressed his fellow preacher—as "sugar" and "Billy sugar"—suggests an intimate affection that would have given additional warmth to their night together.[68]

Revivalists clearly saw their brethren in Christ as relatives in a very real and meaningful sense. A young Methodist preacher named William Spencer declared that "in church fellowship" he had "fathers and mothers, brothers and sisters." Capers wrote that "at most places [he] had brothers and sisters whom [he] loved as if [he] had been born with them." Yet in the evangelical mind, a spiritual family did not necessarily include both sexes. Freeborn Garrettson described his fellow preachers—all men—as "this happy family." Francis Asbury described Methodist "bands"—same-sex support groups for converts—as "little families of love."[69] Spiritual families had their own fathers, on earth as well as in heaven: as converts acquired kinfolk in Christ, they became "spiritual children" of the evangelist who had awakened them. John Taylor wrote of his "great attachment" to a preacher who was his "father in the gospel" and whose "company at that time was more to me than all other men in the world."[70] Evangelical preachers often preferred to be called "Father" or even "Daddy" instead of "Reverend," underscoring their familial relationship with converts. And younger itinerants often treated their older brethren as spiritual parents. Recall Stith Mead's words to John Kobler: "I esteem you as a father."[71]

Yet the predominant relationship that emerges from evangelical letters and spiritual autobiographies was clearly that of brotherhood. Spending time with a "much beloved bro[ther]," "precious little bro[ther]," or "lovely bro[ther]"—whether on the road, at a prearranged gathering, or having met by chance—provided Meacham with "a season of love to [his] soul" as they "took sweet counsel together and sat together in heavenly places in Christ Jesus." The love that spiritual brothers felt for one another was clearly rooted in their mutual devotion and service to Christ. He wrote of one such brother, "I love him fervently, I believe him to be a servant of my master." Of another he wrote, "My heart and spirit feel deeply united to him and his spirit." This sense of a tangible connection to "brethren in Christ Jesus" was crucial for Meacham and his fellow evangelists: "My relation to them I feel," he declared.[72]

.☙

Seventeenth-century Puritans, early eighteenth-century revivalists, and post-revolutionary evangelicals differed from each other in many respects, but they shared two fundamental characteristics: first, a commitment to deeply felt and "sympathetic" love among the faithful that would hold them together as a spiritual community; and second, a conception of that community as a family in which fraternal relationships played a central role. Their cultivation of brotherly love was quite self-conscious and reflected the radicalism—social as well as spiritual—of all three movements. Each included in its blueprint for godly community a conception of family that challenged fundamental assumptions undergirding early modern society on both sides of the Atlantic. We noted earlier in this chapter that Puritans sought to foster love between covenanted brethren in part because they needed to ensure a united front against their many enemies, which was also true of evangelicals both before and after the Revolution. But however urgent the need to find unity in the face of adversity, another motive also inspired the rhetoric of brotherly love that Winthrop placed front and center of the New England mission and that evangelicals later appropriated for themselves.

Puritans saw these fraternal ties as having a double significance. Not only did they bind the faithful to one another on a personal level, but they would also serve as the ligaments of a reconceptualized society in which familiar kinds of relationship would serve new and radical ends. In a speech that Winthrop gave in London a few months prior to leaving for New England, he characterized the colonists as a "family" that was "knit together in a most firm bond of love and friendship."[73] There was nothing surprising in such a remark, given that early modern English society conceived of all relationships, public and private, in familial terms. But the emphasis that Winthrop and his fellow Puritans placed on fraternity was distinctive and entirely appropriate, given the shift that they sought to bring about from a hierarchical conception of society in which paternal authority played a crucial role to a more egalitarian model of brotherly engagement. As English divine Thomas Brooks pointed out, Puritan communities of faith brought together "the lowest as well as the highest."

They all had "the same spirit, the same Jesus, the same faith." They were "fellow members, fellow travelers, fellow soldiers, fellow citizens, fellow heirs, and therefore must they all be loved with a sincere and cordial love."[74] The egalitarian spirit to which Puritans committed themselves was perhaps most evident in matters of church governance. New Englanders convened as local churches not by permission of an overarching ecclesiastical authority but on their own initiative, coming together and signing covenants as cofounders of a congregation. These were autonomous, self-governing communities of faith: authority within each church was exercised not through a vestry of locally prominent gentlemen, as in the Church of England, but instead through a democratic decision-making process involving all male church members. Members voted to hire and fire their ministers as well as to admit, discipline, and expel fellow members. The faithful had a heavenly Father, but on earth they acted as brothers in Christ.

Meanwhile, in the political realm, voting qualifications were much more inclusive in New England than across the Atlantic, giving voice to most adult white males. Colonial assemblies included representatives from each and every town, which is more than could be said of England's parliament until the mid-nineteenth century. All public officials, including governors, were elected annually. At the local level, all white adult males had the right to attend town meetings and to participate in discussion. Prominent townsmen took the lead in establishing the agenda for such meetings and often had a disproportionate voice in debates, but those debates were by no means muted, and decisions had to reflect the will of the community as a whole, not least because local leaders had no way to impose their will on their neighbors. To a considerable degree, New Englanders separated the right to engage in public affairs from considerations of social rank.

Neither spiritual brotherhood nor a commitment to political inclusion eclipsed completely conventional assumptions relating to hierarchy or imperatives of deference within Puritan society. Indeed, Winthrop argued in his famous sermon that God had ordained social distinctions, making "some high and eminent in power and dignity, others mean and in subjection," in part so "that every man might have need of other, and from hence they might be all knit more nearly together in the bond of brotherly affection." John Cotton, the pastor in Boston, declared that the covenant "between friend and friend" was one component in "a three-fold covenant wherein God doth bind himself to his people," the other two being the covenant "between prince and people" and that "between man and wife." These "match[ed] God's relationship to his people as king, husband, and friend." The first two of these relationships were explicitly hierarchical, but the same could also be said of many friendships, including that between Christ and the faithful. Many of the loving services that the godly performed for one another took place in the context of hierarchical patronage networks.[75]

Yet the society that Puritans established in New England was by contemporary standards a radical participatory democracy. Godly colonists were careful not to allow differences in social status to interfere with their cultivation of brotherhood and all that implied. At a meeting of the Boston church in 1640, William Hibbens apologized for a slip of the tongue that he and some of his fellow church members found both significant and troubling: "Some of my godly brethren, watching over me when I spake the last day in that case wherein I opened my mouth, they put me in mind of an expression that I used in calling one of my brethren "sir" instead of "brother." How it fell from me I know not, but it was an expression unsuitable to the covenant I am in, and the more unsuitable for myself because the title of brother is such a phrase that I have found my heart many times enlarged when in the use of it." Neither Hibbens himself nor his "godly brethren" sought to deny the existence or legitimacy of social hierarchy or deference, but they did insist on the importance of constructing a parallel community of striving souls in which a much more egalitarian mode of interaction, founded in loving brotherhood, should prevail. Even when evoking fatherhood as a model for understanding political and spiritual leadership, Puritans thought in terms of "nursing fathers" whose duty it was to nurture their offspring. The concepts of stewardship and of covenant that played so important a part in their theology had profound implications for their understanding of parental authority, which centered on mutual trust and responsibility, not absolute right. Winthrop and his allies inherited a social and political discourse that was explicitly familial, but then shifted the focus of that familial discourse from paternal authority to fraternal covenants. Indeed New Englanders achieved to a remarkable extent what their brethren in England tried and failed to accomplish during the so-called

Puritan Revolution: the townsmen of Providence were by no means indulging in empty hyperbole when they declared that their "body politic" was a "democracy, or popular government."[76]

Early eighteenth-century evangelists saw it as their mission to reinvigorate spiritual faith in the colonies, restoring an emotional intensity that they believed had disappeared from religious life in recent decades. As with any movement committed to reviving past values, the evangelicals depicted their seventeenth-century forebears in ways that suited them, and the parallels they drew were sometimes more convenient than accurate. But one of the characteristics that seventeenth-century Puritans and eighteenth-century evangelicals clearly did share was their egalitarian sensibility. Privileging the authenticity of spiritual rebirth over intellectual knowledge, professional standing, or social status, the revivalists were perceived—quite correctly—by many contemporaries as posing a serious threat to a culture founded upon hierarchy and deference. We should, of course, beware of overstating the egalitarianism of a movement that relied in large part on personality cults surrounding charismatic preachers such as Jonathan Edwards and George Whitefield. But the spiritual power of these individuals derived from their individual and emotional appeal, not their intellectual, professional, or social credentials. Just as the enemies of seventeenth-century Puritanism had understood its revolutionary potential, so too did the critics of eighteenth-century revivalism. And at the center of that revolutionary potential lay the ethos of fraternal love.

The impassioned and egalitarian spirit of eighteenth-century evangelical religion proved iconoclastic not only in the Northern colonies but also in the Anglican culture of the South, where self-control and the careful management of personal interactions had become crucial to a segregated and hierarchical planter society. Baptist congregations that sprung up throughout the South during the decades prior to and following the Revolution rejected explicitly the ethos of hierarchy, deference, and self-distancing that had come to characterize gentry culture. The contrast between Anglican services and Baptist meetings manifested vividly the gulf between these two versions of Protestant faith. Anglican services, decorous and ritualized, took place in increasingly elegant churches where the seating arrangements reflected social distinctions within the local community: churchgoers of humble rank entered first and then watched as the gentry arrived in splendor to take their seats at the front for the liturgical performance that would follow. Baptist meetings were much less formal in structure and spirit, convening in simple buildings, perhaps a barn, or even an open field. Brethren at worship were often divided by gender but not social status. They engaged in rituals of love that united them, whatever their secular rank, as brothers and sisters in Christ: they kissed each other, washed each other's feet, and shared deeply felt emotions. Evangelical communities of faith challenged even the color lines that had hardened in early eighteenth-century colonial society: a spiritual fellowship that involved emotional empathy and physical affection between black slaves and free whites of whatever social status was radical indeed.

Methodists were less iconoclastic than Baptists in matters of authority and retained an episcopal structure, but they were in other respects remarkably egalitarian. Francis Asbury insisted that itinerant preachers follow his example in setting aside the trappings of gentility, dressing in simple clothing and living austere as well as grueling lives: "We must suffer with if we labor for the poor," he declared. Asbury eschewed liturgical formality in favor of spontaneity and emotional exuberance. The preachers who worked under his watch included men of little or no formal learning who articulated the gospel in straightforward, accessible, and earthy language that resonated with ordinary folk. In common with Baptists, they placed great stress upon an emotional fellowship that transcended distinctions of social status.[77] Evangelicals by no means constituted a majority faith in the pre-revolutionary South: no more than ten percent of mid-eighteenth-century Virginians belonged to an evangelical congregation. Yet as growing numbers of defectors from the Church of England joined evangelical communities (in 1769, there were seven Baptist churches in Virginia; just five years later, there were fifty-four), the challenge that such congregations posed to hierarchical assumptions was abundantly clear to contemporaries.[78]

The egalitarian tone of these three movements and their emphasis upon affective association played an important role in shaping the political upheavals and transformations that Americans experienced during the second half of the eighteenth century. The willingness of evangelicals to challenge established institutional authority and to separate from what they saw as corrupt, unawakened, and therefore illegitimate churches to form purified communities of their own provided a powerful precedent for political protest against British policies and eventually the Declaration of Independence. The notion of voluntary association between fellow believers, so crucial to Puritans and evangelicals, would become the basis for populist revolution.[79] We should beware of overstating the impact of that egalitarian spirit as the new nation took shape. Structures of hierarchy and patriarchal values proved remarkably resilient, most obviously, but not only, in the slave-owning South.[80] Yet as contemporaries recognized, whether they liked it or not, the new nation had embraced principles that were far removed from traditional conceptions of authority.[81]

The rhetoric of free and fraternal association that played such a key role in that revolutionary process laid great emphasis upon emotional affinity. "Let us cherish and cultivate sentiments of brotherly love and tenderness among us," declared a letter to the *Pennsylvania Gazette* in 1774. "While we unite as brethren," urged a patriotic sermon two years later, "let us also love as brethren."[82] That ethos of loving brotherhood, long since embraced by Puritans and evangelicals, now combined with the eighteenth-century culture of sensibility to produce a conception of nationhood held together by affective ties. In 1792, the *Vermont Gazette* declared that loving friendship between "souls congenial" would enable "sacred union, bound by the cement of refined affection, founded on virtue."[83] Historians often highlight the connections between revolutionary principles and Enlightenment thought. Significant though these connections were, we should also pay close attention to the immediate religious context from which revolutionary ferment erupted, that is, evangelical revivals and their language of affective association. The culture of evangelical religion and that of sensibility differed in many regards, but they did converge in their mutual stress upon loving sympathy. During the decades following Independence, sympathetic friendship would become enshrined as one of the informing principles underlying republican society. Celebrations of brotherly love now played a key role in a larger ideological project that reimagined the American family in ways appropriate for a new republican nation. Male friendship thus acquired profound social and political significance. In the next chapter we will meet "a band of brothers" who fought together in defense of the new nation: the aides-de-camp in the Continental army. And then we will examine the social and political roles that patriots carved out for loving male friendship in the early republic.

CHAPTER FOUR

"A Band of Brothers"

Fraternal Love in the Continental Army

I T WAS NOVEMBER 23, 1780, and the Marquis de Chastellux was finally going to meet George Washington. Chastellux had wanted to do so ever since his arrival in North America that summer, as a general with the French military forces that had come to fight alongside American revolutionaries in the War of Independence. After spending several months in Rhode Island, he had traveled southward to join the Marquis de Lafayette, commander of the French army, in New Jersey. The American army was encamped a few miles away at Totowa Falls, and Chastellux hoped that Lafayette would "present" him to General Washington. On reaching the French encampment, the marquis was delighted to learn that Lafayette had just left for Washington's headquarters and that he was to rendezvous with him there. One of Washington's aides-de-camp agreed to show him the way. When the two men arrived at the farmhouse where the general and his officers were staying, Chastellux saw Lafayette "conversing in the yard with a tall man" of "noble and mild countenance." This turned out to be Washington, who greeted Chastellux warmly and took him inside, where Chastellux "found the company still at table, although the dinner had long been over." Washington introduced him to "Colonels Hamilton and Tilghman, his secretaries and his aides de camp, and Major Gibbs, commander of his guards." Chastellux noted with interest that the commander-in-chief referred to these men as "his family" and that other Americans also used that word to describe Washington's "aides-de-camp, adjutants, and other officers attached to [him]." Food soon arrived, and the general's "family" stayed at table to keep him company. Chastellux was struck by the genial atmosphere that Washington seemed to inspire: "The goodness and benevolence which character-ize[d] him" were "evident in all that surround[ed] him." It seemed to

Chastellux that the "sentiment" displayed by American officers toward their commander was based in "profound esteem for his virtues and a high opinion of his talents."[1]

Chastellux caught a glimpse that evening of an intimate band that formed, in more ways than one, the heart of the patriot army. General Washington's aides-de-camp lived and worked together as a tightly knit group of young men whose tasks included secretarial functions, the gathering of intelligence, interpreting (to facilitate communication with their allies in the field), and representing Washington on special missions.[2] The commander-in-chief referred habitually to his staff as a "family" and to his aides as "the gentlemen of the family."[3] The aides also conceived of themselves in familial terms, bound to each other by fraternal love and a collective devotion to the patriot cause, the latter embodied in their military father. John Laurens, for example, often referred to his fellow officers as "brother aides" and to the staff that surrounded Washington as "the general's family." Richard Meade concluded a letter to Alexander Hamilton by asking him to pass on his "sincerest esteem to the lads of the family." And Hamilton himself ended a letter to James Duane, his mentor in the legal profession, by sending "most affectionate respects" from "the General and family," to which Duane responded with "respectful compliments" to "all the family."[4]

As Chastellux observed, the aides-de-camp were attached to their commander by a blend of affection and respect. John Laurens, describing a celebration in 1778 to mark the new alliance with France, noted that the general "received such proofs of the love and attachment of his officers as must have given him the most exquisite feelings." The young man wrote in a subsequent letter that as time passed, Washington's "conduct" of the war only deepened the "love and esteem" that he felt for him. Laurens, the eldest son of a wealthy family based in Charleston, South Carolina, was clearly not seeking an alternative father figure to compensate for lack of warmth between himself and his biological parent. His letters to Henry Laurens—a merchant, rice planter, and leading political figure during the revolutionary period, serving as a delegate to the first Continental Congress and as president of the second—were peppered with expressions of love and affection. "I tenderly embrace you," he wrote. "I have barely time, my dearest friend and father, to say that my heart overflows with gratitude at the repeated proofs of your tender love." But just as he loved and revered his father, so Laurens "love[d] and esteem[ed]" Washington. He made no secret of this and clearly trusted that his father would accept without resentment his expansive conception of love, loyalty, and kinship.[5]

The language that Laurens and his fellow aides-de-camp used in their correspondence with each other was tender and demonstrative. "All the lads embrace you," wrote Hamilton to Laurens, and "remember you as a friend and a brother." In one letter he told Laurens that Robert Harrison, James McHenry, and Caleb Gibbs had asked him to "put you in mind of the place you have in their hearts." In another he wrote, "Meade says God bless you." And at the end of yet another, he told Laurens that "all the family" sent "their love," in which "join[ed] the General and Mrs. Washington." He added significantly: "what is best, 'tis not in the style of ceremony but sincerity." Their use of familial terminology and of affectionate language was, in other words, neither perfunctory nor merely ceremonial, but genuine and meaningful.[6] The Continental army was by no means the only military force in which officers characterized their affection for one another in terms of loving brotherhood, but the significance of that affection and the fraternal language used to describe it varied greatly from one time and place to another, depending on the larger social, political, and cultural context in which the war was taking place. As we will see, what made this particular "band of brothers" distinctive was the remarkable symmetry between their articulation of loving camaraderie and a new conception of political identity that emerged during the imperial crisis, then evolving into a potent vision for republican citizenship in the 1780s and 1790s.[7]

For Washington as for his aides, "friendship," personal "attachment," and "sentiments of the purest affection" operated in tandem with "love to our country." The general was convinced that they would win their war for Independence just as long as they were "linked together in one indissoluble bond" that combined "esteem, admiration, and love." Washington enjoyed receiving "affectionate" letters from his aides and was clearly happy to reciprocate, expressing in fulsome language his own "affection" for comrades in arms and indeed "every sentiment of friendship." He did so "with a pleasure which friendship only is susceptible of." The commander-in-chief wrote that it was his appreciation of a man's "public character," combined with the "happiness" he derived from "private friendship" with him, that aroused "the feelings of [his] heart." "Impressions of esteem and attachment" were, he declared, symbiotic and "ripened" together.[8]

In common with other eighteenth-century male friends, Washington's "brother aides" felt a deep sense of responsibility to foster virtue in each other; that shared commitment to moral integrity would then inform the spirit of their public service. Writing to Richard Meade, John Laurens described their "unbounded and inviolable attachment" as a "bright flame" that "kindled" their "virtues." Laurens wished Alexander Hamilton "pleasure moral and physical" in winter quarters and finished one letter with the benediction, "be as happy as you deserve," a touching expression of faith in his friend's merits. Hamilton responded with a similar blend of affectionate trust and exhortation. "Do justice to my regard for you," he declared. Hamilton noted in another letter to Laurens that they had "the same interests, pains, pleasures, [and] sympathies." As the aides-de-camp strove together for the patriot cause, their personal virtues would combine with the sympathetic understanding that developed between close friends to inspire them. Washington and his officers took, then, an established conception of sentimental, high-minded friendship and turned it into a military ethos.[9]

It would be misleading to suggest that members of Washington's military household always maintained an exalted tone in their relations with one another. Indeed, the camaraderie enjoyed by the aides-de-camp was at times quite scurrilous and puerile. In May 1779, McHenry was apparently too busy to write to Laurens, in part because of "public business" but also because he was "engaged in writing an heroic poem of which the family are the subject." Hamilton told Laurens that Harrison had "a distinguished place in the piece": "His sedentary exploits are sung in strains of laborious dullness. The many breeches he has worn out during the war are enumerated, nor are the depredations which long sitting has made on his [arse] unsung." Harrison's poem also "celebrate[d] our usual matin entertainment, and the music of those fine sounds with which he and I are accustomed to regale the ears of the fraternity," presumably an allusion to their performative breaking of wind. But alongside moments of sophomoric exhibitionism, there was also a cozy confidentiality between the young men. "You shall hear much," Tench Tilghman promised

McHenry, "when we fill the sociable bunks, where all is under the secure lock and key of friendship."[10]

The loving and supportive relationships that developed between officers in the Continental army was by no means limited to Washington's immediate staff. General Nathaniel Greene treasured the "mutual sympathy" that bound patriot warriors to one another and the solace it provided in times of sorrow or loss. When Greene was worried about his wife, who had fallen ill, one of his fellow officers consoled him in "so sympathetic a tone" that his "soul mellowed" and his "grief" became more manageable. That same day, another officer received news that one of his children had died, and the two men found "relief from the pointed sorrow by mutual sympathy and mixed melancholy." They went for a walk "in the dusk of the evening," discussing "the excellence of friendship and the transitory state of human affairs" ("how necessary," Greene wrote, "the former was to carry us comfortably through the voyage of life"). At one point the bereaved father was "bathed in tears," but they both "returned to the company with a calmer spirit." The letters that patriot officers wrote to one another were often suffused with the language of sentimental friendship. A young officer named Ephraim Douglas rejoiced that he had "the sympathetic heart of a sincere friend" and so could "feel" the "distresses" of those to whom he was "powerfully attached." Lieutenant-Colonel Isaac Sherman declared that he and his fellow officers were bound to each other by "ties of friendship" and "those fine and delicate feelings which ever distinguish the generous and manly soul." He characterized the patriot soldier—who aspired to "honor and glory," "the happiness of his country," and "the grateful applause of his fellow citizens"—as a "man of feeling," driven by "sentiment" and "affection."[11]

The premium that officers placed upon sensibility became very clear when Major John André, aide to British general Henry Clinton, was captured and condemned to death as a spy. The prisoner's blend of refinement, good cheer, and seemingly heartfelt candor in the days leading up to his execution in October 1780 won the admiration of many observers at Camp Tappan, including his guard, twenty-six-year-old New Englander Benjamin Tallmadge, who considered André to be "a young fellow of the greatest achievements," "so genteel, handsome, [and] polite a young gentleman" that any "court of ladies" would have acquitted him. André "endeared himself" to Tallmadge by "unbosom[ing] his heart" and sharing with him "almost every motive of his actions." As a result, Tallmadge "sincerely pitied" him and indeed was so moved by the prisoner's spirit of "fortitude" and "cheer" on the day of his execution that he "was obliged to leave the parade in a flood of tears."[12]

Tallmadge was by no means the only person present at André's execution to shed a tear. Richard Meade reported that he also wept for the condemned man, "a rare character" whose conduct "from the time of his capture to his last moment" was "such as did honor to the human race" and whose fate "aroused the compassion of every man of feeling and sentiment." Hamilton wrote that the prisoner carried himself at the scene of his execution with "a composure that excited the admiration and melted the hearts of the beholders." He praised the young man for his "becoming sensibility": in addition to "a peculiar elegance of mind and manners, and the advantage of a pleasing person," the prisoner's "sentiments were elevated and inspired esteem; they had a softness that conciliated affection." André's "character, firmness, and manly behavior," wrote another observer, inspired "tender feelings of humanity and sympathy for a fellow creature." Army chaplain Abraham Baldwin wrote that the spy's death aroused "the tenderest feelings of the most lively sensibility," and military surgeon James Thacher struck a similar chord: "The heart of sensibility mourns when a life of so much worth is sacrificed."[13]

Responses such as these reflected not only the perceived qualities of the spy himself but also the susceptibility of his patriot captors to refined feeling. Lafayette described Hamilton's account of André's death as "a masterpiece of literary talents and amiable sensibility," his praise capturing neatly the combination of genuine feeling and performance of sensibility that had become so important a part of the manhood exemplified by Washington's aides. Not all commentators agreed with these flattering characterizations of the spy, but even they appreciated the delicate sensibilities of those who had perhaps been taken in: one critic, while regretting that even "a distinguished American soldier" (presumably Hamilton) had determined to "emblazon" the spy, then softened his implicit criticism of the soldier in question by noting that the "virtues" imputed to André "existed nowhere but in the sympathetic and generous breast of the writer."[14]

Though officers such as Hamilton and Meade could reach out with "amiable sensibility" even as they sympathized with a stranger and traitor whose behavior seemed honorable and heartfelt, most of their "feeling and sentiment" was reserved for members of their own military band. The ties of affection that bound Washington's staff together as a self-styled family sustained them throughout the war, the stress and loss that it inflicted, and their separation from a more conventional family life. Yet their feelings for one another became a mixed blessing when they clashed with other demands and priorities. This became particularly clear when Laurens was captured by the British at Charleston in May 1780 and taken to Philadelphia. His military "family" was understandably eager to secure his release, but as Washington explained in a letter to Laurens, he could not abandon his policy of "exchanging officers in the order of their captivity," not even to accommodate personal feeling. "Nothing but the principle of justice and policy which I have religiously adhered to," he assured his aide, "has prevented my every exertion to obtain your release and restoration to a family where you will be received with open arms by every individual of it," "none with more cordiality and true affection" than Washington himself. Hamilton apparently tried to persuade the general that Laurens could with "propriety" be given preferential treatment, "on the score of [his] relation to the Commander-in-Chief," but Washington and his brother aides felt that "the rigid rules of impartiality oppose[d] [their] wishes." Meanwhile, Laurens was not shut up in a prison, but "on a parole limited to the state of Pennsylvania." Hamilton and "the lads" wondered—rather naively—if Laurens could persuade his captors to let him visit his "family" in New Jersey. "If you can," he urged, "hasten to give us a pleasure which we shall relish with the sensibility of the sincerest friendship."[15]

When Laurens complained later that year that the other aides-de-camp were not writing to him, Hamilton responded that he had "conveyed [his] reproof to the lads." They sent back a message via Hamilton that they had thought he was writing on their behalf, "as the secretary of the family." Hamilton recognized that Laurens must feel isolated and frustrated by his removal from the center of patriot operations: "I know what you must suffer," he wrote, "to have your hands tied up at a crisis so important as the present." But Laurens also missed his "brother aides" and felt hurt by what he saw as their failure to communicate with him. Hamilton urged Laurens not to misinterpret that silence: "Writing or not writing to you," he declared, "you know they love you and sympathize in all that concerns you." When Laurens remarked that it was dangerous for him as a prisoner to write about any political or military topic since his correspondence was surely vetted, Hamilton responded that Laurens should not hesitate to compose letters just because "private affairs" were the only safe ones to mention. "Remember," he wrote, "that you write to your friends." Hamilton left no doubt as to his sympathetic instincts when he wrote, "Indeed, my Laurens, I often realize your situation."[16]

Though Washington "and all the lads" sent "their love," it would not have surprised anyone in the general's "family" that it was Hamilton who actually wrote to Laurens on a regular basis, or that the other officers assumed he would be the conduit for "sympathy" between them and their imprisoned brother. "I have more of the infirmities of human nature than the others," Hamilton told his friend, "and suspect myself of being biased by my partiality for you." Just as the men we encountered in previous chapters tended to have one or two friends with whom they were especially intimate, so this was true of Hamilton. His particular friend was John Laurens, and the two young men clearly loved each other deeply. They met for the first time in 1777. Both had abandoned their studies in order to fight for the patriot cause. Hamilton had been enrolled as a student at King's College (now Columbia University) in New York; he initially fought with his pen as a pamphleteer before signing up in 1776, soon afterward fighting several battles at the head of an artillery company. In March 1777 he joined Washington's staff as an aide with the rank of lieutenant general. Laurens had been studying law across the Atlantic in London; after returning to the newly independent States in January 1777, he accompanied his father to Philadelphia, where the Continental Congress was to meet. He then traveled on that summer to join the patriot army in New Jersey. A month later, after making a name for himself at the Battle of Brandywine, he also was promoted to the rank of lieutenant general and became an aide to Washington. Henceforth Hamilton and Laurens lived and worked in close proximity until early 1779, when Washington granted Laurens a leave of absence to join the patriot forces in his home state of South Carolina, which was bracing to defend itself against the British. In common with other devoted male friends, Alexander and John now committed their love to paper as they sought to sustain themselves and each other through the hardship of separation. A few months after John left headquarters, he wrote in a letter to Alexander that their separation was a torment to him: "How many violent struggles I have had between duty and inclination—how much my heart was with you, while I appeared to be most actively employed here." Two years later, he sent a moving plea: "Adieu my dear friend; while circumstances place so great a distance between us, I entreat you not to withdraw the consolation of your letters. You know the unalterable sentiments of your affectionate Laurens."[17]

For his part, Alexander had not anticipated how much he would miss his friend: "I hardly knew," he wrote, "the value you had taught my heart to set upon you." He lamented that he now had only words to communicate the warmth of his feelings: "I wish, my dear Laurens, it might be in my power, by actions rather than words, to convince you that I love you." What Hamilton meant exactly by "actions" is unclear. Was he referring to those little acts of kindness that mean so much between friends and loved ones? To physical affection? To something more than that? A nineteenth-century editor of Hamilton's correspondence may have suspected the latter: he wrote in pencil at the top of this letter's first manuscript page, "I must not publish the whole of this." Some of Hamilton's words have been crossed out, presumably by that same editor, and are now impossible to decipher. Alexander ended his letter by lamenting that this was currently "the only kind of intercourse" that he could have with John. Here again his use of language was ambiguous, perhaps deliberately so. At a remove of over three centuries, we should beware of leaping to potentially anachronistic readings of sentences such as this: after all, contemporaries used the word "intercourse" to denote spending time with someone; it did not necessarily imply sexual intimacy. Yet it is clear that Alexander had been used to expressing his love for John in ways that were now denied him and that words were proving an inadequate substitute.[18]

However challenging it may have been for Hamilton to articulate in a letter the depths of his feelings for Laurens, he applied himself to the task with characteristic flair. One of his more striking solutions was to mimic a specific literary genre of the late eighteenth century that was laced with romantic titillation, sexual danger, and the threat of scandal. He took as his inspiration seduction and abandonment narratives in which unscrupulous rakes would ensnare the hearts of innocent young ladies, lure them into premature intimacies by promising to marry them, and then disappear from the scene, leaving the women in question bereft of their virtue, socially humiliated, and emotionally crushed.[19] The seduced and abandoned women who figured in these narratives had often been renowned for their virtuous chastity and their determination not to lose it; this was all part of their appeal to the aspiring seducer. Alexander now depicted his situation as analogous to that of a seduced damsel: "Indeed, my friend, it was not well done. You know the opinion I entertain of mankind, and how much it is my desire to preserve myself free from particular attachments, and to keep my happiness independent of the caprice of others. You should not have taken advantage of my sensibility to steal into my affections without my consent." The line between jesting satire and heartfelt analogy is difficult to draw here, and Hamilton may well have intended it to be so. Since joining Washington's staff, Hamilton had cultivated a reputation for "gallantry"—an ambiguous word beloved of eighteenth-century libertines that denoted both courtly attention to young ladies and sexual adventurism. He was apparently well-known at headquarters for his aggressive pursuit of women: when Martha Washington observed the antics of an oversexed tomcat that cruised the encampment in search of female mates, she named him Hamilton. But the young man now repositioned himself, presumably with self-conscious irony, as the innocent object of another man's affection, depicting his friend as having taken advantage of his "sensibility" to establish an emotional power over him "without [his] consent." Discussions of libertinism in the American press sometimes acknowledged that male rakes had themselves been "seduced" into a life of debauchery by male friends, a process that placed them in a temporarily passive and implicitly feminine role. But Hamilton was comparing himself much more explicitly to a seduced woman whose emotional well-being and reputation now depended upon her lover's sense of honor.[20]

Having lost his "free[dom] from particular attachments," Alexander offered forgiveness on condition that John proved himself a worthy and faithful lover. "But as you have done it and as we are generally indulgent to those we love," he wrote, "I shall not scruple to pardon the fraud you have committed, on condition that for my sake, if not for your own, you will always continue to merit the partiality which you have so artfully instilled into me." Yet several months later, he complained that his friend was proving stereotypes of male infidelity to be well founded: he had received only one letter from John since his departure. Alexander now compared himself to "a jealous lover": "When I thought you slighted my caresses, my affection was alarmed and my vanity piqued. I had almost resolved to lavish no more of them upon you and to reject you as an inconstant and an ungrateful ———." In Alexander's mind, their situation was at least analogous to that of lovers. His decision to invoke a literary genre that dwelt on sexual danger is striking and suggestive. Was Alexander hinting that physical expression of the love he shared with John might lead them into peril? Was his adoption of this genre in letters to John his own version of John Mifflin's relation to James Gibson (via his journal) of a dream about drifting away from the harbor's safety, naked in a fragile vessel with his beloved?[21]

In the letters that Alexander wrote to John, references to friendship, love, courtship, and marriage interwove with ironic humor and multilayered ambiguity. At the time of their separation, Alexander was still a bachelor, but John had already married an Englishwoman named Martha Manning. John and Martha met while John was studying law in London and married in 1776 after conceiving a child together. Early the following year, John returned home to join the Continental army and left his wife behind, eight months pregnant. A few years later Martha traveled with their infant daughter to meet her husband while he was on a diplomatic mission in France, but he had already embarked for North America by the time she arrived; the young father would die in battle shortly before the end of hostilities and so would never meet his daughter. Some historians have suggested that wife and child "occupied little space in John's thoughts."[22] Yet Alexander evidently thought otherwise. Letters arrived from Martha soon after John left headquarters for South Carolina in the spring of 1779, and Alexander sent them on. Like other eighteenth-century friends, he felt confident that he could, through the power of sympathy, understand John's feelings: "I anticipate," he wrote, "by sympathy the pleasure you must feel from the sweet converse of your dearer self in the enclosed letters."[23]

Yet immediately following this apparently heartfelt acknowledgment of the love that bound John to his wife, Alexander launched into a waggish discussion of his own marital ambitions that suggested a rather sardonic attitude toward the entire enterprise of marriage. He asked his friend to keep his eyes peeled for possible candidates in South Carolina and provided him with a playful sketch of the woman he had in mind:

She must be young, handsome (I lay most stress upon a good shape), sensible (a little learning will do), well bred (but she must have an aversion to the word *ton* [a French word meaning manners or breeding that had recently become fashionable in the new republic, apparently to Hamilton's disgust]), chaste and tender (I am an enthusiast in my notions of fidelity and fondness), of some good nature, a great deal of generosity (she must neither love money nor scolding, for I dislike equally a termagant and an economist). In politics I am indifferent what side she may be of; I think I have arguments that will easily convert her to mine. As to religion a moderate stock will satisfy me. She must believe in God and hate a saint. But as to fortune, the larger stock of that the better.

Alexander urged John to bear in mind that he had "no invincible antipathy to the maidenly beauties" and that he was "willing to take the trouble of them upon [him]self," thus reaffirming his reputation as a gallant both able and willing to pleasure the ladies. Alexander suggested that his friend should feel free to take out an advertisement in the newspapers on his behalf, which would doubtless produce "many competitors" who would "be glad to become candidates for such a prize as I am." John could "give an account of the lover—his *size*, make, quality of mind and *body*, achievements, expectations, fortune, etc [Alexander's emphases]." He trusted that John would "no doubt be civil to [his] friend" and "do justice to the length of [his] nose." His references to "size," "body," and "nose" (presumably a surrogate for another of Alexander's well-proportioned appendages) assumed an easy and ribald familiarity between friends who shared, to borrow Tilghman's words, "sociable bunks" in cramped quarters. Yet beneath the humor, it also assumed a depth of intimacy that made John uniquely qualified to sing Alexander's praises.[24]

Having shifted from posing as a besotted and vulnerable damsel to a touching expression of "sympathy" with his friend's love for an absent wife and then to a playful and eventually rather scurrilous discussion of his own marital prospects, Alexander drew back and finished his letter by asking, "What could have put it into my head to hazard this jeu de follie[?]" His answer once again careened between jest and expressions of sincere feeling as well as between the subjects of marriage and loving friendship: "Do I want a wife? No—I have plagues enough without desiring to add to the number that greatest of all; and if I were silly enough to do it, I should take care how I employ a proxy. Did I mean to show my wit? If I did, I am sure I have missed my aim. Did I only intend to frisk [to frolic or jest]? In this I have succeeded, but I have done more." What Alexander had succeeded in doing, beyond indulging his taste for "frisk-[ing]," was to prolong the sense of being with John that he got from writing to him: "I have gratified my feelings by lengthening out the only kind of intercourse now in my power with my friend."[25]

Alexander adopted a barely less sardonic tone on the subject of women when he wrote a year later, in June 1780, to inform his friend that he was now engaged to Elizabeth Schuyler, the second daughter of Major General Philip Schuyler, a trading magnate with extensive holdings along the Mohawk River and around Albany. In earlier letters to John, he had depicted their own relationship in language that evoked the dangers of freedom prior to marriage as innocent women opened their hearts to perhaps unscrupulous suitors, but he now depicted marriage itself as the renunciation of freedom. "Have you not heard," he wrote, "that I am on the point of becoming a benedict? I confess my sins. I am guilty. Next fall completes my doom. I give up my liberty to Miss Schuyler." Alexander's description of his bride-to-be was not exactly the romantic tribute that one suspects she herself would have been happy to read: "She is a good hearted girl who I am sure will never play the termagant; though not a genius, she has good sense enough to be agreeable, and though not a beauty, she has fine black eyes—is rather handsome and has every other requisite of the exterior to make a lover happy." Yet Alexander assured his friend that he was a "lover in earnest," even though he did not "speak of the perfections of [his] mistress in the enthusiasm of chivalry." And he had every intention of proving himself a loving and devoted husband: "I intend to restore the empire of Hymen and that Cupid is to be his prime minister."[26]

Elizabeth Schuyler was by no means the first woman to attract Alexander's attention as a potential match. At the dances organized for officers of the Continental army and their French counterparts, he had flirted with several highly eligible young ladies from the local gentry, including Catherine Livingston, daughter of New Jersey's governor, William Livingston (whose friendship with classmate Noah Welles was discussed above in chapter two). Alexander's correspondence with Miss

Livingston was avowedly a performance; indeed, he told her that he needed her help in settling on which of the several roles at his disposal he should adopt in writing to her. When Alexander heard that she had "a relish for politics," he offered his services as "a political correspondent" but would "not consent to be limited to any particular subject." In addition to "perform[ing] the part of a politician and intelligencer," Alexander also anticipated "amorous transports." He declared proudly that he was "renowned for gallantry" and, should she wish to "make excursions in the flowery walks and roseate bowers of Cupid," he could promise to "entertain" her "with a choice collection of the prettiest things imaginable." Alexander asked if she was "of a romantic or discreet temper as to love affairs." Some women wanted to be addressed as "one of the graces, or Diana, or Venus, or something surpassing them all," while others were "content with being a mere mortal" and wanted their lovers to behave "like one [in] his sober senses." Once he knew her "taste," he would "regulate" himself accordingly.[27]

When Miss Livingston replied several weeks later, by which time Alexander was apparently "almost out of patience and out of humor," he showed her response to "a gentleman of our family" (in other words, one of his fellow aides-de-camp) who declared that "none but a goddess" could have "penned so fine a letter" and that henceforth Alexander must write to her "in the style of adoration." But Miss Livingston had evidently opted for sobriety, expressing "an invincible aversion to all flattery and extravagance." Bearing this in mind, Alexander wrote, he would not fear that "a Quixote capable of uttering himself perfectly in the language of knight-errantry" could "ever be able to supplant me in the good graces of a lady of your sober understanding." He declared that he wrote "at the risk of being anathematized by grave censors for dedicating so much of my time to so trifling and insignificant a toy as woman; and, on the other hand, of being run through the body by saucy inamoratos who will envy me the prodigious favor, forsooth, of your correspondence. So that between the morose apathy of some and the envious sensibility of others, I shall probably be in a fine way. But ALL FOR LOVE is my motto."[28]

Alexander had already acknowledged, then, in his letters to Catherine Livingston that there was more than one way to love a lady. When he turned his attention to Elizabeth Schuyler, the gallantry of earlier flirtations gave way altogether to a less affected, more earnest tone. "I love you more and more every hour," he declared. "The sweet softness and delicacy of your mind and manners, the elevation of your sentiments, the real goodness of your heart, its tenderness to me, the beauties of your face and person, your unpretending good sense and that innocent simplicity and frankness which pervade your actions; all these appear to me with increasing amiableness and place you in my estimation above all the rest of your sex." It was in part what Miss Schuyler lacked that attracted him to her, inspiring in Alexander a depth and sincerity of love quite unlike anything he had felt for any other woman. As his description of her to John Laurens suggests, Elizabeth Schuyler was in certain respects less than dazzling. But what this meant to Alexander becomes much clearer in a letter that he wrote to her sister Margarita, characterizing Elizabeth as both less and more than the archetypical and coveted lady of fashion, often referred to as a "belle":

> [S]he has none of those pretty affectations which are the prerogatives of beauty. Her good sense is destitute of that happy mixture of vanity and ostentation which would make it conspicuous to the whole tribe of fools and foplings as well as to men of understanding so that as the matter now stands it is very little known beyond the circle of these. She has good nature, affability, and vivacity unblemished with that charming frivolousness which is justly deemed one of the principal accomplishments of a *belle*. In short she is so strange a creature that she possesses all the beauties, virtues, and graces of her sex without any of those amiable defects which from their general prevalence are esteemed by connoisseurs necessary shades in the character of a fine woman.

In a letter to Elizabeth, Alexander wrote that those in his circle who "railed at love as a weakness" and "laughed at it as a phantasie" were now "compelled to acknowledge its power." Even the "most determined adversaries of Hymen" among his friends could "find in her no pretext for their hostility." Alexander claimed that he himself had been one of those "adversaries," but that Elizabeth had "overset" his "wise resolutions" to avoid marriage and "transformed" him from "a professed contemner of Cupid" into "the veriest inamorato you perhaps ever saw." In a rather odd confession, he wrote that he had "tried in vain, if not to break, at least to weaken the charm," but she "maintain[ed]" her "empire" over him: "In spite of all my efforts and after every new one I make to draw myself from my allegiance, my partial heart still returns and clings to you with increased attachment. To drop figures, my lovely girl, you become dearer to me every moment." The military gallant expressed wonderment that "a little nut brown maid" such as this could have conquered his affections. But just as John Laurens had successfully laid siege to Alexander's affections, so now had Elizabeth Schuyler. Indeed, Alexander found himself "from a soldier metamorphosed into a puny lover."[29]

Just as Alexander and John drew pleasure and emotional support from their correspondence, so too did Alexander from "the sweet effusions of tenderness" that his "dearest girl" sent him. "My Betsey's soul speaks in every line," he rhapsodized, "and bids me be the happiest of mortals. I am so and will be so." In August 1780, he wrote that he was awaiting "impatiently" the arrival of her father along with "a letter from my charmer": "I long to see the workings of my Betsey's heart, and I promise myself I shall have ample gratification to my fondness in the sweet familiarity of her pen." He envisaged that pen as a brush with which she could "paint" for him "her feelings without reserve." Alexander wrote that she filled his thoughts by day and that at night he met with her "in every dream." It was, he wrote, her "sweetness" that preoccupied him. Whereas in his letters to Catherine Livingston he had bragged about his reputation for "gallantry" and offered to "meet [her] in whatever path [she] dare[d]," he now set aside the innuendoes of the uniformed tomcat and invited Elizabeth, in her "tender moments of pillowed retirement," to "deliver" her "soul" up "to love and to me—yet with all that delicacy which suits the purity of her mind and which is so conspicuous in whatever she does."[30]

As with other young men whom we met in previous chapters, Alexander saw his courtship of Elizabeth Schuyler and his love for male friends as complementary ventures of the heart that all involved—male and female—could share in, appreciate, and encourage. Richard Meade was with Elizabeth when she opened one of her fiancé's letters and he reported back to his friend the "apparent marks of joy" with which she received it. It was "from circumstances like these," wrote Alexander, that "we best discover the true sentiments of the heart," in this instance witnessed vicariously through one of his close male friends. On another occasion, Alexander was in the midst of writing to Elizabeth when Richard arrived in the room: "[He] interrupts me," he told Elizabeth, "by sending his love to you." Meanwhile, Alexander made no secret of his closeness to John Laurens. In July 1780, he wrote to his fiancée that he was hoping to see "my Laurens" on the boundary between Pennsylvania and New Jersey. That October he told her that he "expect[ed] in a few days to go to Philadelphia for a day or two": "I shall there see my friend and make him participate in my good fortune by giving him a picture of my mistress."[31]

When Alexander became engaged, he took care to impress upon John that his love for his wife would in no way lessen his devotion to the new republic or to John himself. "In spite of Miss Schuyler's black eyes," he wrote a few months before the wedding, "I have still a part for the public and another for you." Alexander wrote that he wished his friend's capture had not prevented him from "be[ing] witness" at "the final consummation," a rather ambiguous term for the wedding that conflated public ceremony with what followed in private. He also assured John that his bride "already love[d]" him. Alexander added playfully that the affection between his bride and Laurens was to be respectable and chaste: "She loves you *a l'americaine,* not *a la francoise.*" It seems quite clear that Alexander intended to alleviate any concern on his friend's part that their intimate friendship might become a casualty of Alexander's marriage. He ended this particular letter by declaring, "Let friendship between us be more than a name."[32]

Yet Alexander himself worried in letters written during his courtship of Elizabeth Schuyler and following their marriage that his feelings for her were becoming all-consuming. "I love you too much," he declared in a compliment that barely shrouded his anxiety. "You engross my thoughts too entirely to allow me to think anything else." Alexander was evidently concerned that marital devotion might prove a dangerous rival to other claims, including those of public service. He reported in another letter to his fiancée that Richard Meade was planning to consult a widow whom he was courting about "the propriety of quitting the service." He hoped that this lady would set his own Betsey "an example of fortitude and patriotism." Alexander had apparently already promised "to conform to [Elizabeth's] wishes" on this subject and "persist[ed] in this intention." "I know," he wrote, "you have so much of the Portia in you that you will not be outdone in this line by any of your sex, and that if you saw me inclined to quit the service of your country, you would dissuade me from it."

But he then added a little more doubtfully, "It remains with you to show whether you are a Roman or an American wife." Persuading patriots to serve their country in the armed forces had proven a challenge throughout the War of Independence. Alexander now suggested that American women were at least partly to blame because they inspired in their menfolk a doting affection that overrode a sense of civic responsibility.[33]

Once married, Alexander's own resolve to remain in "the service of [his] country" began to falter. In September 1781, he promised his wife that they would soon be reunited "with the assurance of never more being separated." "Every day confirms me," he wrote, "in the intention of renouncing public life, and devoting myself wholly to you. Let others waste their time and their tranquillity in a vain pursuit of power and glory; be it my object to be happy in a quiet retreat with my better angel." Alexander wrote to Richard Meade in March 1782 that he was becoming "entirely domestic" and "los[ing] all taste for the pursuits of ambition": "I sigh for nothing but the company of my wife and my baby." He declared that only "ties of duty" kept him "from renouncing public life altogether." Meanwhile, John Laurens was becoming worried, evidently with some justification, that Alexander might quit the army and retire from public life. According to John, his friend's newfound devotion to family life was responsible for this danger. "Your private affairs cannot require such immediate and close attention," he protested. "You speak like a *pater familias* surrounded with a numerous progeny." He wrote to Alexander that he "would not wish to have [him] for a moment withdrawn" from military service unless he went into Congress and assumed high office within the new government.[34]

When Alexander declared that, "in spite of Miss Schuyler's eyes," he still had room in his heart "for the public" and for John Laurens, he envisaged that his love for his wife, his love for his male friend, and his love for the republic would work together in a triangular symbiosis, sustaining rather than competing with each other. Yet family life and his love for Elizabeth did become a rival to public service, at least in the minds of Alexander and his fellow officers. His love for John, on the other hand, as for other members of the general's military family, did not pose any such danger. Alexander's relationship with John had its intimate and private moments: "My ravings are for your own bosom," he wrote in one letter. But it always functioned within and served a larger context: John's value as a friend and as a patriot were always entwined in Alexander's mind and heart. As John prepared to engage on the battlefield in the spring of 1780, Alexander sent this benediction: "My dear, I am sure you will exert yourself to save your country; but do not unnecessarily risk one of its most valuable sons. Take as make care of yourself as you aught for the public sake and for the sake of your affectionate A Hamilton."[35]

When Alexander wrote in August 1782 to tell John that he had been appointed a delegate to the Continental Congress, he looked ahead to the end of the war and the role that they would play together in the new republic: "Peace made, my dear friend, a new scene opens. The object then will be to make our independence a blessing. To do this we must secure our union on solid foundations; an herculean task and to effect which mountains of prejudice must be leveled! It requires all the virtue and all the abilities of the country. Quit your sword, my friend, put on the toga, come to Congress. We know each other's sentiments, our views are the same: we have fought side by side to make America free, let us hand in hand struggle to make her happy." The two friends would join together, hand in hand, to secure the nation's happiness. To do so required not only "all the virtue and all the abilities of the country" but also the sensibility exemplified in loving male friendships such as theirs. The emotional and sympathetic power of such relationships would enable virtuous collaboration in the new republic: "We know each other's sentiments," wrote Alexander, "our views are the same." He ended his letter with the words, "yours for ever." Tragically, John was killed in a skirmish with the British two weeks after the date on which Alexander wrote; it is unlikely that the letter would have reached John in time for him to read his friend's words.[36]

Alexander's expressions of grief in the aftermath of his friend's death illustrate movingly the combination of qualities that had attracted Alexander to him. Consider this extract from his letter to Nathaniel Greene, who commanded the Southern army: "I feel the deepest affliction at the news we have just received of the loss of our dear and inestimable friend Laurens. His career of virtue is at an end. How strangely are human affairs conducted, that so many excellent qualities could not ensure a more happy fate? The world will feel the loss of a man who has left few like him behind, and America of a citizen whose heart realized that patriotism of which others only talk. I feel the loss of a friend I truly and most tenderly loved, and one of a very small number." The loss that Alexander felt was due not only to John having been a dear personal friend but also an "inestimable" one: his "career of virtue" was "at an end." His qualities would be mourned by the world, by his fellow citizens of the United States, and by his personal friends, none more so than by Alexander himself. Robert Hayne, a U.S. senator from South Carolina, would declare in a eulogy to John Laurens that "[t]he love of his country controlled every other feeling of his heart." Yet it was equally true that Laurens and his officers were inspired to love their country by feelings of the heart, including their feelings for one another. His virtuous career had a national and even global significance in the minds of those who supported the revolutionary cause, yet the qualities that made him a patriotic hero were fostered and sustained by intensely personal and heartfelt connection to close friends, especially Alexander Hamilton. In a letter to Lafayette, Alexander wrote that John had "fallen a sacrifice to his ardor in a trifling skirmish in South Carolina." It was "ardor" that had driven Laurens, and it was his "ardor" that won Hamilton's heart. "You know how truly I loved him," he wrote.[37]

What path the friendship between Hamilton and Laurens would have taken if the latter had not been killed in battle, whether the intensity of the emotional bond between them would have persisted over the years, whether and in what terms they would have hankered for each other if circumstances had led them to settle at a distance from each other, we will, of course, never know. But another aide-de-camp in the Continental army, William North, did not fare well emotionally following the end of the war because, as he acknowledged quite openly, he missed the men to whom he had become so close. William North and Benjamin Walker had been assigned as aides-de-camp to the Baron Friedrich von Steuben, a Prussian career soldier who played a crucial role in improving discipline within the Continental army. The three men worked and lived together for roughly two years until Walker's transfer to Washington's staff in 1782. North and Walker were both clearly devoted to Steuben: "We love him," wrote North, "and he deserves it for he loves us tenderly."[38] This was despite the frustrations caused by Steuben's quite spectacular recklessness with money, which became an ongoing source of anxiety and embarrassment to the young men around him as they sought to hold off the Baron's creditors and tried in vain to rein in the Baron's expensive tastes. "I sometimes wish I had never seen or never loved the Baron," Walker declared in a letter to North. "If he makes his friends happy by his goodness and amiable qualities, he also makes them miserable by his want of management and misfortunes." But as North wrote, Steuben's "thousand acts of kindness," "his goodness of heart," and "numberless other amiable qualities" eclipsed all his defects: "We both love the Baron and should love him if his foibles were a thousand times greater than they are."[39]

The three men remained close throughout the years between the end of the war and Steuben's death in 1794. Steuben's letters to his former aides were affectionate and demonstrative. He addressed North as "my dear, dear Billy." "I embrace you heartily," he wrote, "and remain inviolable your true and affectionate friend."[40] Like Washington, Steuben was often characterized by contemporaries as a paternal figure; in common with his commander-in-chief, the baron saw his relationship with his aides in familial terms.[41] Indeed, in his final will, Steuben made North and Walker his "adopted children" and his heirs. In his account of the baron's funeral, North wrote of his good fortune in having been "one on whom for fifteen years [Steuben's] eyes had never ceased to beam with kindness."[42]

North's relationship with Walker, his brother aide, was loving and tender. Writing just over a decade after the end of the war, he recalled the intimacy that they had enjoyed together. Walker had apparently supplanted another officer, James Fairlie, in North's affections. North wrote that he felt this for the first time one night at Camp Tappan. "When I began to love you, I know not," he declared, but "the first motion of disregard to Fairlie I remember—'twas at Tappan—I lay on straw with one blanket." Exactly how intimate they became that night as North "lay on straw with one blanket" or on subsequent nights it is impossible to tell, but what mattered to the two young men was the emotional bond that they formed and then sustained over many years despite their physical separation. "I think of you frequently," wrote North, "I shall not forget you—I shall not—and when I remember you, I remember a friend who is very dear to me."[43] In another letter he described their friendship as "among the choicest" of the gifts for which he owed God his thanks: "Friendship such as I feel for you, the Baron, and one or two more binds us more closely to each other than any other tie."[44] North acknowledged that he often wrote to his friend despite his not having any specific news to impart: "I cannot let a post go without writing you, though I should have nothing to say." But the real purpose of these letters was, of course, to reaffirm the bond between them: "I don't know that I have anything in particular to say to you," he wrote in a 1796 letter, "and therefore conclude not to write anything more than that I am as much as ever your friend."[45]

Following their return to civilian life, North and Walker both married and became devoted fathers. In common with other male friends we have encountered, North and Walker made no effort to keep their friendship hidden or separate from their new familial commitments and indeed visited one another with their families; Polly North and Molly Walker were evidently very fond of each other and often had their husbands include brief messages or felicitations in the letters that passed back and forth between the two men. North, who had settled with his wife on a farm near Duanesburg, New York, constantly urged Walker and his wife to visit: "You know we have room and victuals and drink and heart to offer." Indeed, he urged Walker to relocate so that they could become neighbors and regular companions: "I wish we could all live together, Ben!" The two former aides sought to integrate two versions of elective kinship: marriage to a woman and friendship with a man. In a moving letter about the death of his little daughter in 1812, North told Walker that his "dear child" had referred to him "by no other appellation than Uncle Walker." This was hardly surprising to North: "Do we not feel," he declared, "that we are brothers[?]"[46]

North clearly treasured his continued friendships with Walker and Steuben, but an affectionate correspondence, occasional visits, and dreams of becoming close neighbors left him hungry for more. North made no secret of the fact that he missed the camaraderie of his fellow officers and that nostalgic memories were no substitute for the real thing. He avowed himself discontented and restless. "My wife is the best woman possible," he wrote to Steuben, "but I am not happy . . . I shall come to New York, kiss you and Ben, to go Boston [to] comfort my old mother, and return here to drudge on." Though avowedly "not the best of husbands," he would "endeavour to be as good as I can." The problem was not that North's marriage was loveless or floundering. Indeed, he suggested in a letter to Walker that his marriage had grown more rather than less loving as the years passed, and he evidently believed the same to be true of his friend: "Our heads had more to do in our marriages than our hearts, our hearts have now more to do in the business than our heads—we began by esteeming and end with loving—I believe the women went on the same way. I am sure neither my wife [n]or I loved each other half so well a year ago as we do now."[47]

Yet the love that had grown between North and his wife was insufficient to compensate for the loving friendships that he missed so much, and he evidently felt guilty that such was the case. One evening in November 1792, North became drunk and wrote to Walker in his cups. He had been trying to drown his sorrows in some port given him by Walker: "The first glass I drank formally to the health of my wife and little children—I wish I could have only thoughts of them when I drank it, but Walker, his wife (I love her, Ben, for her own sake) and the Baron crowded into my mind and the Devil could not put them out again." His military brothers and father would not give way to his marital household, even though North evidently felt that they should do so. With "every glass" that he drank, "the whole squad . . . cheek by jowl brought themselves alongside of my wife and children." The images of those whom North loved and who loved him jostled for attention in his port-addled heart, but he felt cut off from them all: "At the third glass I cried, 'tis damned hard, I felt I was alone." As he wrote this letter, he drank "another glass of wine, not to all the saints in heaven, but to all those on earth whom I love—so God bless you."[48]

North became increasingly preoccupied by feelings of loss and isolation. "During forty years," he wrote, "I have not found more than three or four men to love sincerely—two of which I have lost and the other [Walker] lives at a hundred miles distance." Following the death of Steuben and then that of another much beloved friend, North felt more and more alone: "It is comfortless to be left alone in a desert," he declared in one of his letters to Walker. In another he wrote, "Our number lessens, let us draw together—one of us will soon drop—let it be him who can bear the loss of the other with least fortitude."[49] Following the death of his wife and several of his children, North hankered even more intensely for the company and support of his friend: he wrote that he was "alone, sick with anxiety and fear and grief without a friend to help." Polly's death had been a bitter blow: "I have lost," he wrote, "infinitely lost." That another close friend from the army, William Eustis, was also sick added to his "fears" for the future. "I wish it was possible that we could meet," he declared, "it would be something in this miserable world to meet once more—we shall soon one of us see the other no more." North also wished that they could all "be sure of meeting and knowing each other" again in a life to come, but on this subject he had his doubts: "Everything is dark—yet there must be God and he must of necessity be merciful."[50]

North's feelings for Walker remained intense even as their wartime camaraderie became an increasingly distant memory. Their correspondence did lapse for a period in the early 1800s following their disagreement over a piece of legislation making its way through the U.S. Congress. But when North wrote to reestablish communication with Walker, he made it very clear that he still loved him: "My dear friend, for so I shall continue to think and believe and feel that you are, notwithstanding the silence which has reigned between us for so long a time that I don't know whether one or two years have passed without my writing to, certainly without being written to by you. You have never been for a month out of my mind, [and] I have wished to write." North continued to reach out across the miles, comforting his friend in times of disappointment or bereavement. When Walker's wife died in 1817, North's letter of condolence captured with simple eloquence the emotional affinity that still bound them to one another: "There is nothing to be said, my dear friend, but there is enough to feel." In common with other male friends, North lamented that the written word could not express in full what he felt or provide the support that he wished he could give in person: "To tell your friend whom you love in a letter what you feel for him—how can it be done[?]—what is it worth if done [?]—I could embrace you, Ben, and I could weep with you in silence over your griefs—but on such a subject one who feels cannot write." Yet however frustrating and upsetting it was to have feelings for a friend that could not be expressed directly, North preferred to suffer than to close his heart or deny his capacity for emotional empathy: "I thank God," he wrote, "that I can and do feel for myself and for those who are dear to me."[51]

Contemporaries were well aware that Continental army officers described themselves as "brothers" in a "family" that was tight-knit, loving, and supportive. New England dramatist Royall Tyler addressed this sense of kinship among patriot officers in *The Contrast,* a play first performed in April 1787 at the John Street Theater in New York City. Colonel Manly, who has just arrived in New York, declines an invitation to "see the city" with a foppish character named Billy Dimple, even though the latter is "known to almost every family in town," on the grounds that he has business to attend to and that his own "family" will "be anxious to hear from [him]." Maria, a young lady with secret designs on the officer, concludes from this remark that he must be married and so asks him, "How did you leave your lady, sir?" But Charlotte, Manly's sister, assures Maria that it is "only an odd way he has of expressing himself." Colonel Manly himself goes on to explain: "I call my late soldiers my family. Those who were not in the field in the late glorious contest, and those who were, have their respective merits; but, I confess, my old brother-soldiers are dearer to me than the former description. Friendships made in adversity are lasting; our countrymen may forget us, but that is no reason why we should forget one another." Indeed, Colonel Manly is in New York "to solicit the honorable Congress, that a number of my brave old soldiers may be put upon the pension-list, who were, at first, not judged to be so materially wounded as to need the public assistance." He is there, in other words, to take care of his "family."[52]

When officers referred to themselves as fellow members of a military family, they conferred on their relationships with one another a meaning and status that paralleled those of a domestic household. As we have already seen, the family served in early American society not only as the basic unit of social identity but also as a fundamental point of reference for understanding any kind of relationship.[53] In the past, familial imagery had been used most commonly and conventionally to evoke the authority exercised by fathers and husbands, but American revolutionaries were much more interested in the ties of brotherhood. In a manifesto issued by George Washington in 1778 on behalf of the Continental army, the general declared that patriots "invite[d] all nations to mutual friendship and brotherly love." The commander-in-chief's choice of words was deliberate and part of a larger rhetorical strategy that had taken shape during the decade preceding Independence. As early as 1768, faced with a parent country that had confounded their expectations and trust, John Dickinson envisaged "a band of brothers" joined in "righteous contest," "cemented by the dearest ties" and "that sympathetic ardor which animates good men confederated in a good cause." Six years later, another opponent of British policies also envisaged "patriots and heroes" joined as "a band of brothers."[54]

As Americans became disenchanted with the British government and its insistence that colonists defer to imperial authority, they had to find a language that would express and legitimize an alternative vision for political engagement. They inherited a social and political discourse that was explicitly familial and, to be more specific, patriarchal. Just as Puritans and evangelicals had taken a familiar, familial discourse and adapted it to suit their new version of spirituality, shifting attention from the relationship between the father and his household to that between brothers, from a vertical to a more horizontal kind of relationship, so too did the patriots. Meanwhile, they reimagined fatherhood itself in ways consistent with a more egalitarian model for society. Washington would embody that new version of fatherhood, while the "brother aides" who worked under him in the Continental army embraced the spirit of "mutual friendship and brotherly love" that patriots hoped would inspire and define their Revolution.[55]

Throughout the years of unrest that preceded the Declaration of Independence, opponents of the new taxes and other measures emanating from London characterized the relationship between Britain and its North American colonies in familial terms. They wrote of "the tenderness" that "a maternal state" should show toward "her dutiful children." They wanted the king to behave "like a tender, kind, benevolent father." And they protested their "unbounded affection" for "His Majesty's royal person and family."[56] On some occasions they referred specifically to George III and his responsibilities as father of his people; at others they argued that England itself should behave like a nurturing mother. They also described in more gender-neutral terms the "parental" love and nourishment that they felt was their due from the imperial metropolis. During the early decades of the eighteenth century, Americans had rediscovered a strong emotional attachment to the British monarchy. That neo-royalist sensibility, purged of any association with the hated and deposed Stuarts, depicted the monarch's benevolent love for his subjects as holding the empire together in much the same way that the sun's gravitational force enabled the physical world to cohere. Indeed, it was loyalty to the monarch, conjoined with Protestant faith, that gave the colonies of North America a sense of common identity with the British.[57]

Yet the version of parenthood now put into practice by the British government struck many colonists as downright abusive. As John Adams put it, "filial affection" for "England as their mother-country" transformed into "indignation and horror" as it became clear that their mother, far from being "a kind and tender parent," was "a cruel Bedlam, willing, like Lady Macbeth, to 'dash their brains out.'" Adams was referring to a scene in Shakespeare's play in which Lady Macbeth tells her husband that she would sooner, while her "babe" was "smiling in [her] face, have plucked [her] nipple from his boneless gums and dashed the brains out" than abandon their resolution to win the crown by murder. For Britain as for Lady Macbeth, the imperatives of dominion eclipsed those of natural affection. The depiction of imperial policy as a horrifying violation of parental love expressed the protesters' sense of outrage and betrayal as they viewed the crisis through a familial lens.[58] John Dickinson depicted the colonists as "filled with grief and anxiety," asking, "Where is maternal affection?" Adams adopted a more sarcastic tone: "Such were the bowels of compassion," he declared, "such the tender mercies of our pious, virtuous, our moral and religious mother country towards her most dutiful and affectionate children!"[59]

In the earlier phases of the crisis, critics of imperial policy had avoided direct or personal attacks on the king. They blamed repressive measures on members of Parliament and corrupt ministers who were apparently misinforming and misleading their monarch. They attacked the government collectively as an abusive parent, but chose to assume that the king as father was not implicated. Even the radical wing of the resistance movement—an expanding constellation of activist cells that called themselves, significantly, the Sons of Liberty—proclaimed their loyalty to George III as well as to the constitution: following a centuries-old tradition of deflecting blame for unpopular policies away from the monarch onto evil counselors, they denounced George III's ministers, the members of Parliament, and also officials in North America whose task it was to enforce new legislation, but not the king himself. Protesters located sovereignty in the person of the monarch, not in Parliament, and they now trusted that their "King and Father" would save them from Parliament's abusive actions.[60]

Nonetheless, in attacking those who supported or carried out unpopular policies, protesters used language that made abundantly clear their equation of imperial repression with parental abuse. Men such as Andrew Oliver, Boston's stamp tax collector, and Thomas Hutchinson, lieutenant governor of Massachusetts in the 1760s and then governor in the early 1770s, were "parricides of their country" and "the murderers of their own children and families."[61] The word "parricide" was used to signify not only murder of a father but also treason against one's country, and it was in this latter sense that protestors deployed it against supporters of royal policy. They did so with what must have been self-conscious and bitter irony, since the "parricides" acted in the name of their royal father. Hutchinson had throughout his years of public service depicted himself as "a father of his people."[62] Hutchinson was actually opposed to the Stamp Act and, in a paper laying out his objections, had questioned the sincerity of Britain's "parental affection to the colonists." But opponents of imperial policy now turned the paternal role that Hutchinson had assumed against him, condemning him for having betrayed his responsibilities as a father. Americans who defended imperial policy became not only surrogate parental abusers but also destroyers of their own colonial brethren and of themselves in what James Otis depicted as a crazed orgy of violence: he characterized one apologist for the new legislation coming out of London as displaying "the rage, malice, and fury of an Orestes, tearing out the bowels of his mother, stabbing his sister, killing his own sons and daughters, and plucking out his own eyes."[63]

Yet it was the "parricides" themselves who ended up being murdered, at least symbolically. Demonstrations orchestrated by the Sons of Liberty often included the hanging in effigy of George III's officials in North America. These ritual executions borrowed heavily from Guy Fawkes Day, an annual celebration in England of the thwarted plot by Catholic conspirators in 1605 to blow up the Houses of Parliament. The eighteenth-century North American version of this festival burned the pope instead of Guy Fawkes himself: local craftsmen would create an effigy of the Holy Father which they then carried through the streets on a cart; the pope was usually accompanied by the devil, while alongside the cart pranced little boys dressed up as demonic imps. It was no coincidence that supporters of imperial policy were thought to be plotting the imposition of Episcopalianism, seen by many Americans as an authoritarian faith one step away from popery; nor was it coincidental that the pope was customarily referred to as a father. The demonstrators of the 1760s were appropriating ritual traditions used previously to enact the symbolic murder of a father figure whose authority was, from a Protestant perspective, utterly fraudulent and inspired by the devil.[64]

Colonial attacks on the king as a father, at first oblique and displaced onto his representatives, became much more frank and direct in the final phase of the crisis. By 1774, protesters such as Josiah Quincy of Massachusetts were decrying the king's claim to be a loving parental figure as utterly spurious. Quincy referred sardonically to George III as "that generous prince, styled the father of all his people," who was "solemnly consigning" the colonists to "ruin, misery, and desperation," even as they still clung to their "love for a parent king." The king might be "styled" a father, but this was not the kind of parent that any child would want to have. Quincy urged patriots to "form a band of brothers" who would become the "Bruti and Cassii" of American history. (Brutus, the adopted son of Caesar, had joined with Cassius and other conspirators in assassinating Caesar.)[65]

When George III refused to receive, let alone read, the Olive Branch Petition of July 1775, it was impossible to deny any longer that he was aware of and approved the policies enacted in his name. This unleashed a deluge of bitter resentment and vitriol against the king, which Thomas Paine harnessed to spectacular effect in *Common Sense*, published in January 1776. Paine argued that monarchy could be justified neither by "rights of nature" nor by "the authority of scripture" and that "in every instance" monarchy was "the popery of government." He equated hereditary succession, which conferred political power through familial inheritance, with original sin: "As in the one all mankind were subjected to Satan," so "in the other" sovereignty rested with potentially "foolish" and "wicked" rulers who had nothing but their parenthood to recommend them. Hereditary monarchy was not only "absurd" but also "evil" and "poisoned" any country in which it took root. England's line of succession, Paine reminded his readers, went back to William the Conquerer, "a French bastard" who established himself as king at the head of an army and "against the consent of the natives," "in plain terms a very paltry rascally original." The latest incumbent, George III, was a "hardened, sullen-tempered Pharoah" whose "pretended title of FATHER OF HIS PEOPLE" was a travesty: no father who deserved the appellation could so "unfeelingly hear of [his children's] slaughter and composedly sleep with their blood upon his soul." According to Paine, terms such as "parent or mother country" had been "jesuitically adopted by the [king] and his parasites, with a low papistical design of gaining an unfair bias on the credulous weaknesses of our minds." If Britain was indeed "the parent country," then "the more shame upon her conduct."[66]

The Declaration of Independence said almost nothing about Parliament's usurpation of power or the designs of manipulative advisers, concentrating instead on a litany of abuses allegedly devised by George III himself, whose "character" was "marked by every act which may define a tyrant." Many of the demonstrations, processions, and public rituals that accompanied Independence included some form of ritual regicide, or rather, patricide. The violence with which Americans turned on George III reflected the trust they had placed in him, now exposed as tragically misplaced, as well as their faith in the ideal of a nurturing and responsible father, also utterly confounded by recent events. As patriot soldiers returned from their defeat of the British troops at Concord in April 1776, they shot bullet holes through the royal insignia that adorned public buildings and tavern signs: the king had betrayed his people and so he must perish. A few months later, public readings of the Declaration of Independence throughout the newly independent States were accompanied by the parading, burning, and burial of the king in effigy. George III's portrait, his initials, and other royal insignia were torn from public buildings and consigned to the debris of revolution. The erstwhile father of his people was dead and the children would now come into their inheritance.[67]

Allegations of parental abuse during the imperial crisis reflected a very different perspective on parenthood from that espoused by supporters of absolute monarchy. Defenders of government policy in the British press made abundantly clear their expectation of filial submission by the colonists, describing England as a "mother country" that was "entitled to the support of her colonies, as a parent to the obedience of her children." Those who opposed the new taxes evidently "want[ed] to throw off all dependence and subjection." Accusations of ingratitude pervaded British condemnations of colonial protests: "hot headed vote[s]" and protests in the streets, through which colonists sought to "bully . . . their King, and the august council of the mother country," demonstrated their "want of gratitude" and must arouse "the resentment of every considerate man."[68] Yet on both sides of the Atlantic, parenthood and the prerogatives associated with it had undergone a fundamental reevaluation during the first half of the eighteenth century; its meaning and implications were now bitterly contested. Given that contemporaries were accustomed to thinking about political authority in familial terms, changing conceptions of parenthood inevitably had an impact on political life.

Eighteenth-century Americans had absorbed a new philosophy of child rearing that shifted attention away from the absolute prerogatives of parents and their duty to quell unruliness in their children, emphasizing instead parental responsibility and the conditionality of a child's obligation to obey parental demands. John Locke's treatise on education, published in 1693, had a seminal influence on this reevaluation of parenthood. Locke argued that reason and affection were more effective than coercion and fear in establishing and maintaining parental authority: the former inspired respect and esteem, the latter servility and resentment. According to Locke, a nurturing parent deserved to be obeyed and revered; an abusive parent did not. Along with this reassessment of parenthood, Locke's contractual theory of governmental authority and, at a more mundane level, the increasing exposure of ordinary folk to economic contracts in the commercialized society of the eighteenth century made Americans more and more inclined to understand and assess relationships in terms of mutual responsibilities. The revival of royalism in the early eighteenth century and of a reverence for "sacred majesty" did not imply that the monarchy could once again demand unconditional obedience from its subjects. The king might embody sovereignty, but his right to act as sovereign rested upon his benign and responsible use of his position as parent of the nation.[69] Indeed, James Otis condemned as "horrid blasphemy" the assertion that laws enacted by the crown were "nothing else but the will of him that hath the power of the supreme father." As far as he was concerned, kingship did not carry with it any absolute authority derived from God, the ultimate father.[70]

Meanwhile, a combination of other factors, some common to both sides of the Atlantic and others more specific to North American circumstances, had also weakened parental authority in the colonies. The Enlightenment's elevation of nature and happiness over convention and duty led to a greater stress on the importance of emotional compatibility and fulfillment in marriage. One consequence of this was that young people were less and less inclined to consider their parents' wishes in forming personal relationships. As the land in densely settled communities was divided and subdivided from generation to generation, it became increasingly difficult for parents to provide their children with adequate plots on which they could settle in homes of their own. Parental authority based on control of inheritable land was thus undermined by population pressure. By the early eighteenth century, many young American adults reached maturity in communities that no longer had enough land for the rising generation to settle on and so moved either to the peripheries of existing communities or farther west. This dramatic shift in settlement patterns stretched and in some cases snapped the ties of kinship as parents, children, and other relatives no longer lived in close proximity to each other. The range of wealth and social status in newly established settlements on the edge of the colonies was much narrower than on the eastern seaboard, creating communities in which a hierarchical conception of society had much less credibility. The difficulties involved in maintaining control over an increasingly mobile population, along with the growth of large market towns and seaports that made possible a degree of anonymity and personal freedom inconceivable in a small town or village, all contributed to the emergence of a society much less orderly and deferential than before. The ritual patricide that accompanied the Declaration of Independence thus dramatized a process that had been underway for many decades.[71]

Many eighteenth-century commentators pointed to a decline in respect for authority throughout the colonies. Children and young adults in particular were becoming increasingly unruly and disobedient. Far from being "overawed by their parents," youngsters in North America gave "very little" evidence of "subordination." "Implicit obedience to old age," declared one observer, did not figure among "their qualifications." "Surely it is happy our laws prevent parricide," declared a particularly bitter father, "or the devil that moves to this treatment would move [my son] to put his father out of the way." When a Lutheran minister in late eighteenth-century Philadelphia requested proof of parental consent from young couples who wanted to marry, they "insist[ed] on their capacity and right of choosing for themselves." The minister wrote that these young people found his request "odd," since they had "no idea of parental authority."[72] At the end of the century, John Adams wrote in a letter to his son Thomas that "the source of revolution" had been "a systematical dissolution" of "family authority."[73] The tone of his letter was somewhat facetious, but like many facetious remarks, this one was not entirely frivolous. Citizens of the new republic had by no means abandoned completely their respect for paternal authority or their willingness to express filial affection. Yet a significant shift had taken place. Given their recent experience of what they saw as abuse by a royal father, patriots now wanted to construct for themselves a new kind of family and a new kind of father. The fond reverence articulated by many late eighteenth-century Americans toward George Washington, so often referred to as "the father of his people," exemplified a reformed and thoroughly republican filiopietism. Washington may have become a paternal figure to many contemporaries, but he was revered because of his personal qualities and the admiration that they inspired; he was a father by choice and acclamation, not hereditary right. Americans would unite as siblings under an enlightened father, not as dependent subjects but as free citizens who felt a common affection for their loving parent, who had guided them into adulthood as they freed themselves from the tyrannical patriarch and abusive father, George III.[74]

As Thomas Paine set about undermining automatic deference to patriarchal figures, so he invoked fraternal love as a new foundation for legitimate political and moral association. Americans, he wrote, "claim[ed] brotherhood with every European Christian and triumph[ed] in the generosity of that sentiment." Sentiment also played a key role in Paine's impassioned address to Americans. The title of his pamphlet, *Common Sense*, was multivalent: it referred not only to the basic and readily comprehensible principles on which its argument was constructed but also to Americans' common capacity for sensation, which in the eighteenth century implied emotional feeling as well as physical perception. Paine appealed to the "feelings" and "hearts" of his readers. "The cause of America," he declared, was "the concern of every man to whom nature hath given the power of feeling." The colonies had united against their oppressors in an "unexampled concurrence of sentiment." As "friendship," "affection," and "kindred" with Britain "expire[d]," so a new family—a brotherhood of feeling friendship—would be born. Americans must set aside their divisions and "each of us hold out to his neighbor the hearty hand of friendship." The new society that Paine envisaged would be bound together by "the chain of mutual love." And the "good citizen" on whom the republic would depend had "the warm ardour of a friend," animated by "the heart that feels."[75]

Paine was not the first of those advocating outright rebellion against British authority to depict patriots as men of feeling. Americans who sought to justify taking up arms deployed a rhetoric that melded political protest and military bravado with the culture of sensibility and brotherly love. In 1774, Josiah Quincy described those who opposed British policy as armed with "memories and feelings, courage and swords—courage that shall inflame their ardent bosoms, till their hands cleave to their swords, and their swords to their enemies' hearts." These were men of "feeling," united as much by their "sympathetic ardor" for each other as by the mighty cause of freedom. Thomas Jefferson wrote that Americans, when "pressed with wrongs at the point of a bayonet," had responded with their "hearts," not their "heads," and that it was the emotional integrity of their response that had enabled them to withstand the British redcoats. He described the relationship that colonists had previously enjoyed with the British in terms of "brotherly love" that united them in "bands of amity." Yet a series of repressive measures had escalated into acts of betrayal that dealt "the last stab to agonizing affection": "Manly spirit," he declared, "bids us to renounce for ever these unfeeling brethren." Jefferson made a pointed comparison between the "unfeeling" British and their more susceptible brethren in North America. The colonists' capacity for "warmth of affection" would now be redirected as patriots joined together to fight for their freedom, bound to one another in loving and virtuous friendship.[76] Jefferson and his fellow revolutionary John Adams ended up on opposite sides of the party conflict that came to dominate national politics during the closing years of the century, yet whatever else they may have disputed, Adams did agree with Jefferson's emphasis upon emotion and sensibility as crucial components of what made Independence possible. "The real American Revolution," Adams would later declare, consisted of "radical change in the principles, opinions, sentiments, and affections of the people."[77]

When Washington and the principal officers of the Continental army gathered for a farewell meal in New York on December 6, 1783, the occasion was described in the press as a testimonial to the "sensibility" and "feeling" that had characterized the patriot forces and enabled their victory. "The passions of human nature," declared one account, "were never more tenderly agitated than in this interesting scene." When Washington told his officers that he took leave of them "with a heart full of love and gratitude," his words "produced extreme sensibility" along with "warm expressions and fervent wishes from the gentlemen of the army, whose truly pathetic feelings it is not in our power to convey to the reader." The tone of this farewell was far from unique: that summer General Robert Howe had declared in a final address to his troops that their parting was painful to "his feelings as a man." "Sympathies have been excited, affections impressed, and friendships established" that "time, absence, or accident shall never wipe away." He felt confident that "those of similar feelings" would understand that his "sensibility upon this occasion" was "too big for utterance."[78]

Many of the officers who had participated in that heartfelt fraternity during the war now sought to sustain its spirit into the postwar period. Alexander Hamilton was a founding member of the Society of the Cincinnati, established in 1783 and named for a Roman who twice set aside his private life and pursuits to defend his republic on the battlefield. Hamilton and other leading figures in the War of Independence founded the society in part as a way to put pressure on Congress to pay the Continental army's officers, whose salaries were several years in arrears. But the society's constitution also stressed the need to commemorate the "mutual friendships formed" in the army. One of the officers who proposed the formation of such a society "said that it was unhappy that such a band of friends and brothers should be separated, perhaps never to meet again." Army surgeon William Eustis later recounted that "the Society grew naturally out of the affections of the officers from a desire to perpetuate their friendships." And Philadelphia's Cincinnati declared that their friendships "should be as immutable as they [were] sincere."[79]

Later that same decade, Hamilton and other supporters of the proposed United States Constitution set out to persuade fellow citizens that their new republic was sufficiently unified in character and sentiment that a strong overarching government was both justifiable and feasible. As they did so in a series of newspaper articles that became known as the Federalist Papers, they invoked the same trinity of friendship, love, and virtue that had suffused the correspondence between Hamilton and his "brother aides" during the war. The United States comprised "one united people," "a band of brethren, united to each other by the strongest ties" and "similar sentiments" that "prevailed among all orders and denominations of men among us." The Federalists appealed explicitly to a sense of family that combined "connections of blood, of friendship, and of acquaintance." Such feelings of kinship "embrace[d] a great proportion of the most influential part of the society": "Hearken not to the unnatural voice which tells you that the people of America, knit together as they are by so many cords of affection, can no longer live together as members of the same family . . . Shut your hearts against the poison which it conveys; the kindred blood which flows in the veins of American citizens, the mingled blood which they have shed in defense of their sacred rights, consecrate their union, and excite horror at the idea of their becoming aliens, rivals, enemies." Hamilton and his allies called on Americans to foster that "community of interests and sympathy of sentiments of which few governments have furnished examples" but which they could now exemplify. According to the Federalists, "a well-ordered political society" was enabled by the "moral magnetism" of those who cultivated "social passions" and "the best feelings of the human heart." One Federalist essay that appeared in the *Pennsylvania Gazette* coupled "federal sentiments" with the "man of sensibility," whose sense of loving identification with "his country" was "entwined with every fibre of his heart."[80]

A principal source from which that "community of interests and sympathy of sentiments" would flow was loving male friendship. During the first quarter-century of Independence, hundreds of articles and poems that appeared in newspapers throughout the new nation stressed the social as well as personal benefits of intimate and sentimental friendships between men. These encomia, which played a central part in public conversation about the moral character of the new republic, often described male friendships in familial terms. Fraternal love, which religious radicals in the seventeenth and eighteenth centuries had placed at the center of their blueprint for spiritual community, now became a key component in republican ideology. As we will see, that ideology envisaged a republican family in which enlightened paternalism, marital friendship, and loving brotherhood would unite, inspire, and sustain virtuous citizens. It is to that vision of the United States that we now turn.

CHAPTER FIVE

"The Overflowing of Friendship"

Friends, Brothers, and Citizens in a Republic of Sympathy

O N MAY 1, 1794, reported the *Pennsylvania Gazette*, Philadelphians gathered in a civic festival to celebrate "the alliance between the sister republics of the United States and France." Those in attendance toasted "the great family of mankind" and expressed their hope that "distinction[s] of nation and of language" would in time "be lost in the association of freedom and of friendship, till the inhabitants of the various sections of the globe shall be distinguished only by their virtues and talents." Setting aside "the luxury of aristocracy," the citizens of both republics would labor to build a world in which "the rights of man shall become the supreme law of every land, and their separate fraternities be absorbed in one great democratic society comprehending the human race." Meanwhile, all "unfortunate victims" of "tyranny" who sought "asylum" in the United States would "find in every American a brother and a friend."[1]

According to President Washington, this spirit of loving friendship and brotherhood was essential to the well-being and even survival of the fledgling republic. In his 1796 Farewell Address, Washington declared that "fraternal affection" would quell the "jealousies and heart burnings" of "party" and "faction," replacing these destructive "passions" with "love," "affection," and "every sentiment which ennobles human nature." The president's entire speech was suffused with affective language: Washington offered his "counsel" not as thoughts but in the form of "sentiments," "actuated" by "fervent love" for his country and "free government—the ever favorite object of my heart." He spoke as "an old and affectionate friend" who urged upon his fellow citizens that they continue in their quest to create a republic of "sentiment" that would redirect "the usual current of the passions." He prayed that heaven would bestow on Americans "the choicest tokens of its beneficence," first and foremost of which was that "union and brotherly affection may be perpetual."[2]

The tone that Washington adopted in his Farewell Address accorded well with an emerging vision of the republic that American writers invoked with almost messianic enthusiasm in the closing decades of the eighteenth century—even though, or perhaps because, that vision was belied at almost every turn by the factious vitriol of political life in the new nation. When Jefferson urged his fellow citizens in his 1801 inaugural address to "unite with one heart and one mind" in "harmony and affection," he echoed a quarter-century of political discourse that expounded and celebrated the notion of an affective republic.[3] This model for republican democracy combined a democratized version of family values with an emphasis on the social dividends yielded by sentimental friendship: it reaffirmed a shift in attention away from patriarchal authority and toward a brotherhood of choice, reflecting the egalitarian spirit of the new republic; at the same time, it politicized sentiment and sympathy as a basis for constructive identification and collaboration between citizens.

⚘

Sentimental friendship took on a particular and profound significance for Americans in the last quarter of the eighteenth century. Their post-revolutionary understanding of friendship was rooted in a conception of sympathy and its relationship to broader social identity that was borrowed from moral philosophers associated with the Scottish Enlightenment. These philosophers—including Francis Hutcheson, David Hume, and Adam Smith—exerted a powerful influence over the development of social and political thought in the new republic. Not only was their work widely read by educated Americans, but their ideas also percolated through to less privileged citizens via hundreds of essays and poems that appeared in late eighteenth-century newspapers and magazines. As we will see, these homilies addressed in more accessible terms the subject of friendship. Few were explicitly political, but their message had far-reaching social and political implications. Their authors translated into vivid and accessible prose the moral and social ethos promoted by philosophers of the Scottish Enlightenment. That ethos became, at least for a brief period, the animating spirit of republican ideology.[4]

Scottish thinkers argued that the recent emergence of a commercial society enabled a new form of friendship that would in turn lay the foundation for a moral and harmonious society. The key to this transformation was that impersonal forces of the market and new bureaucratic entities would now perform functions hitherto fulfilled by personal relationships. Previously, they argued, a primary function of friendship had been to collaborate in getting things done. As Adam Smith put it, "the necessity of the situation" had created and shaped these relationships. But now personal friendships could be based on personal compatibility rather than calculations of interest, "arising not from a constrained sympathy, not from a sympathy which has been assumed and rendered habitual for the sake of conveniency and accommodation; but from a natural sympathy, from an involuntary feeling that the persons to whom we attach ourselves are the natural and proper objects of esteem and approbation." That an understanding of friendship as a form of alliance or patronage was giving way to an emphasis on emotional attachment becomes clear in Samuel Johnson's midcentury definition of a friend as "one who supports you and comforts you while others do not," as someone "with whom to compare minds and cherish private virtues." This had profound implications for society as a whole, since disinterested affection would become the driving force for individual relationships, which would then set a very different tone for civic engagement.[5]

Love between friends and the sympathy that underlay this purified version of friendship would expand into a more comprehensive benevolence as personal relationships nurtured qualities that in turn enabled individuals to become better citizens. Hutcheson argued that although all of humankind lived "under natural bonds of beneficence and humanity toward all," each individual had "more special ties to some of [his] fellows." Like gravitation, benevolence "extend[ed] to all bodies in the universe" but "increase[d] as the distance [was] diminished" and was "strongest when bodies come to touch each other." Its primary orientation was, in other words, immediate and personal. Yet that benevolent instinct, nurtured through "special ties," would then express itself, albeit in attenuated form, as "beneficence and humanity toward all." Each of us felt "obliged by the natural feelings of our hearts, and by many tender affections," to exercise that universal "beneficence." Thus, "the strong ties of friendship, acquaintance, neighborhood, [and] partnership" were "exceedingly necessary to the order of human society." Writing in a similar vein, Hume declared that "sympathy" with the "sentiments" of those with whom we have "a more particular connection," though always stronger than that we felt for those "remote from ourselves," would foster an enlightened sociability based on the "intercourse of sentiments," a free-flowing and mutual benevolence that would transcend and reconcile otherwise distinct interests.[6]

Scottish theorists placed great importance on the role played by sympathy in promoting social benevolence: this was "the secret chain between each person and mankind." They became convinced that sympathy with the feelings and needs of others was not an automatic reflex but an effort of the imagination that needed to be cultivated: because "we have no immediate experience of what other men feel," declared Adam Smith, "it is by the imagination only that we can form any conception of what are his sensations." According to Smith, we had to "place ourselves in his situation," "enter as it were into his body," and "become in some measure the same person with him" so as to "form some idea of his sensations, and even feel something which, though weaker in degree, is not altogether unlike them." By imagining oneself as another and by incorporating into oneself a "copy" of another person's "sensations"—by "changing places in fancy," as Smith put it—one could transcend the self without negating or abandoning self, creating communities of reciprocal feeling and benevolence. Scottish theorists were advocating that friendship be detached from an interest-based social calculus and then reattached to a new calculus based on the binding power of emotional attachment. Friendship would remain useful and productive, but its utility and productivity would now be primarily affective: the emotional ties that developed between friends would reverberate throughout society as a driving principle of civic engagement. Sympathy, defined by Adam Smith as "fellow-feeling with any passion," would become the basis for sociability and moral order.[7]

Philosophical works such as Smith's *Theory of Moral Sentiments* and David Hume's *Treatise of Nature* as well as sentimental novels such as Samuel Richardson's *Pamela* and *Clarissa* promulgated a new social theory in which sentiment and sympathy enabled a peaceable, moral society. As economic transformation and increasing geographical as well as social mobility made it more and more difficult to think of society as an organic and stable entity, so the power of sympathy, fueled by sensibility, would provide a new means to create a sense of community. Alert to the possibility that some critics might equate the embrace of sentimental instincts with a debilitating effemination, Smith emphasized that "sensibility to the feelings of others, so far from being inconsistent with the manhood of self-command, [was] the very principle upon which that manhood is founded." Real men were, in other words, men of feeling. It was, furthermore, through their embrace of sensibility that men became good citizens. Smith argued that sympathetic sensations guided moral judgment, since "we either approve or disapprove of the conduct of another man according as we feel that, when we bring his case home to ourselves, we either can or cannot entirely sympathize with the sentiments and motives which directed it." Smith defined the man of virtue as he who had mastered the art of reciprocal sympathy, combining "command of his own original and selfish feelings" with "sensibility both to the original and sympathetic feelings of others." Richardson's novels, which proved enormously influential on both sides of the Atlantic, associated moral integrity with sensibility: nurturing the human potential for emotional affinity would enable the triumph of generosity and virtue over selfish appetite—within personal lives and in society at large.[8]

Educated Americans were well aware of this tendency among contemporary moral and social theorists to identify feeling, especially shared feeling, as the foundation for social order and a principled public life. Take, for example, Daniel Webster, whom we met in chapter two: Webster equated "the enjoyment of friendship" with "the cultivation of the social feelings of the heart." When John Mifflin wrote that "life seem[ed] to stagnate unemployed in friendship," he recognized that friendship was itself a worthy form of employment. This was not just a source of personal pleasure but also a vocation with broader implications and benefits. The notion that society could cohere and prosper through the agency of benevolent instincts—felt individually and then transfigured through personal relationships into a social principle—became increasingly commonplace by the eve of the Revolution. Colonial society and politics might be wracked by dissension and vitriol, but contemporaries insisted that it did not need to be that way. Nathaniel Greene was convinced that a "principle of attraction" united the "spirits and minds of men" in "communities, friendships, and the various species of society." And according to Hamilton, it was an understanding of "each other's sentiments" that would enable friends to work together in the service of their new nation. Individual friendships would foster social instincts through the power of sympathy and a universalized spirit of benevolence. The latter, declared a New England clergyman in 1753, was "the single principle that constitutes and preserves all the peace and harmony, all the beauty and advantage of society." It was "the cement and support of families, of churches, of states and kingdoms, and of the great community of mankind."[9]

That faith in a linkage between personal friendship, the spirit of benevolence, and social harmony acquired particular significance for American statesmen in the late eighteenth century as they faced the challenge of creating a united nation out of disparate colonies, cultures, and interests. Once Independence was won and the common enemy vanquished, how would they cohere as a nation? And how would citizens of the new republic, no longer bound by ties of loyalty and deference to a monarch, be inspired to think in terms of the common good instead of their own individual, partisan, or sectional interests? The answer seemed to lie in the Scottish philosophers' theory of social benevolence. Enlightenment thinkers in general argued that humankind was naturally sociable, affectionate, and benevolent. That human society so rarely exhibited these qualities was due to unnatural impediments. The American Revolution provided a unique opportunity to sweep these away. Freed of the artificial obstacles to natural affection created by monarchy and its attendant culture of dependency, the natural flow of benevolence would suffuse society and in turn transform politics. "Society," declared Thomas Paine in *Common Sense,* "promotes our happiness positively by uniting our affections." John Quincy Adams declared in 1793 that "the soft control of mild and amiable sentiments" would "unite in social harmony the innumerable varieties of the human race," enabling "the long expected era of human felicity" to begin "its splendid progress."[10]

One of the fundamental assumptions underlying this optimistic vision of the future was that the individual could not function in isolation: both personal and collective well-being depended upon emotional affinity between citizens. The ideal of the independent yeoman farmer, free to think and act uncorrupted by dependence upon others, worked alongside this commitment to emotional interdependence. Eighteenth-century Americans did not equate independence with a disconnected or atomized individualism but instead understood it as a freedom from dependence that would liberate citizens to sympathize and collaborate with one another. The spirit of benevolence fostered by individual friendships would infuse social relationships in general; that broader transformation would, in turn, enable an enlightened political culture to emerge and sustain itself. Republican ideology envisaged, then, a public discourse alchemized by the purifying genius of loving friendship.

Jefferson's emphasis upon sentimental feeling in his justifications for revolution (mentioned at the end of the previous chapter) was clearly entwined with his economic, social, and political vision for the new nation. Jefferson held that men were corrupt not by nature but as a result of corrupt institutions: in a free and representative democracy that abolished exclusive privileges and ensured equal rights, men would not invade the rights of others, because they would recognize that they had the same interests, just as in an unimpeded market society men would see that they each had identical interests as producers and consumers. Government, so often used by the few to limit opportunities for the many, would be utilized not to restrain or control but to release individual potential. Jefferson wanted to create an environment in which men could pursue their natural instincts, which would as a matter of course create a virtuous and benign society. Instead of excluding the poor from full citizenship because of their dependence upon others, Jefferson sought to make them independent by increasing dramatically the proportion of Americans who owned their own land. A program of territorial expansion and the end of repressive institutions—such as monarchy, aristocracy, and established religion—would enable the liberation of mankind from shackles of its own making, freeing men to develop their natural benevolence. The unprecedented penetration of the market throughout the newly independent States in the closing decades of the eighteenth century and the lack of rigid social distinctions in the new republic, at least among free whites, made it possible to contemplate Smith's model for free exchange between individuals on an even playing field as a basis for nation building.[11]

American statesmen of the early republic disagreed fundamentally on many issues. It is particularly striking, therefore, that thinkers as antagonistic in their views and priorities as Hamilton and Jefferson both laid emphasis in their writings upon the importance of sentiment and affection. Their elaborate blueprints for moral, social, political, and economic development were assuredly not the stuff of everyday conversation in the new republic, but the ethos of sympathetic and sentimental friendship that played such an important part in these theories did become familiar even to Americans who had no claim to membership in a privileged and erudite elite. The broad dissemination of that ethos depended in large part on a medium that had recently emerged as a major force within American society, the newspaper, which now became a principal purveyor of republican values. A recurring theme within this ephemeral literature was loving, sympathetic friendship and its beneficent power, conveyed in score upon score of poems and essays that translated into vivid and accessible language this strand of eighteenth-century moral, social, and political philosophy. That evocation of a republican brotherhood in which love between individuals would inspire a common sense of purpose and mutual responsibility would play a central role in the fledgling republic's attempt to craft for itself a new conception of social identity and political citizenship.

✑

The American Revolution coincided with a massive increase in literacy rates and the rapid proliferation of ephemeral print, including newspapers. Widely available not only in large cities and seaports but also in smaller inland communities, newspapers were often read aloud in taverns and at home to those who could not read for themselves, which extended their reach to many Americans who were not technically literate but who could access printed matter via literate neighbors and family members. Eighteenth-century newspapers printed not only news and announcements of local, national, and international significance but also advertisements and items intended to entertain and improve. The latter didactic category addressed a broad range of topics, from the debate over inoculation to the fate of seduced and abandoned young women in an age of increasing sexual freedom. One subject that cropped up again and again in newspaper items during the last quarter of the century was that of friendship and the immeasurable blessings it bestowed upon individual lives and also society as a whole.[12]

Essays and poems on the subject of friendship, that "greatest sweetener of human life," were staple items in late eighteenth-century newspapers. According to their authors, "a sure friend, a tried friend," who became "as the one half of your own soul," was "the best panacea heaven ever sent on earth for human afflictions." The "seeds of friendship," they explained, were "planted in every human heart": "There is a gentle tender fibre that runs from heart to heart, conveys the feelings of one to another, and produces a mutuality of pleasures and of pains." That emotional conduit was "the source of human felicity . . . from whence the meandering streams of pleasure sweetly glide from heart to heart."[13] To rest confident in "the constant love" of "a firm and virtuous friend," declared the *Massachusetts Spy*, was "the superlative happiness of every rational being," "our paradise here below," "the wine of life and the source from whence flows our greatest happiness." *Dunlap's American Daily Advertiser* assured its readers that every man craved another "whose soul beats in uniform with his own, and whose corresponding form of manners strongly invite to the most pleasing attachment." According to the *Connecticut Gazette,* he who found such a friend experienced the "noblest ardor of the soul."[14]

Identifying someone who could qualify as that special friend was—or should be—a crucial part of becoming an adult. The *Newburyport Herald* recommended that as soon as a young man "commence[d] an actor on the theatre of human life," he should seek "one among the crowd of his acquaintance whose sincerity, whose sensibility and whose sympathetic feelings distinguish[ed] him as formed for the peculiar and honorable office of a friend," someone "in whom he may safely confide, and whose benevolent affections are ever alive to the feelings of humanity." Friendship, these authors assumed, along with the emotional support that it provided, was a fundamental need in each and every man. Once he found that friend, "all the anxieties of fortune vanish[ed] and his soul overflow[ed] with a profusion of joy." Friendship would "smooth the path of life and render less miserable the tempestuous days of adversity." Ideally, "early attachments" would "ripen" into "the firmest, manly friendship" so that the "bosom confidant" of youth became "a lifelong source" of "our most happifying enjoyments." An item printed in the *Massachusetts Spy* celebrated one such friendship: "You and I, my friend, have found great changes; but hitherto we have much reason to congratulate ourselves that nothing has intervened to prevent that harmony, that sympathy of souls, which has so long continued, and which I trust shall continue to the end of life."[15]

These authors emphasized the yearning for sentimental intimacy and sympathetic support that brought men together as friends. Every man craved "the sympathetic affection of the soul." He wanted "someone who, from benevolence of disposition and sensibility of soul," could "sympathize with him," "a friend whose clay is replete with softness and refinement, whose understanding is strong and enlarged, and whose heart is faithful," with whom he could enjoy "affectionate interviews," nestled "in the retired bower of friendship." The qualities nurtured by friendship were those of emotional refinement. According to one publication, sensibility was the "moral polish of the feeling heart." "The best dispositions," declared another, "usually have the most sensibility." The *Providence Gazette and Country Journal* assured its readers that a friendship "without sentiment" was nothing but "a name" and "a shadow." True friends were "bound" to one another by "sweet sensibility" and "mutual sympathy." Indeed, the greatest blessing bestowed by friendship was its "sympathizing power."[16] One particularly vivid essay exemplified this idealization of male friendship and its tone of unabashed sentimentality:

> Tell me ye of refined feelings—have you ever found pleasures equal to those derived from friendship? What can be more delightful to the eye of benevolence than the prospect of a connection where the sentiments and affections are sweetly united? Picture to yourself, reader, two young men mutually bound by a sacred friendship—a friendship established upon the experience of years. See them with interlocked arms walking the pleasant grove, reciprocally breathing forth, without reserve, the sentiments of their bosoms! Observe the essence of benevolence glowing on their cheeks, and the gleams of participated ecstasy sparkling in their eyes. View them sweetly seated at the enchanted shrine of their goddess—friendship—unbosoming every sensation, and even mingling heart with heart! Notice them saluting each other after being separated for a season by the calls of interest— with what cordiality—with what emotions of joy—with what exquisite delight they embrace.

Reminiscent of the afternoons that John Mifflin spent with Isaac Norris and James Gibson in their Philadelphian pear grove, this and other passages like it celebrated "the silken cord of friendship" as a source of sweet, sentimental, and even rhapsodic personal happiness. "Pardon me," concluded the author, "ye sons and daughters of sensibility, for thus vainly attempting to portray a picture so far beyond the power of the most descriptive pen!"[17]

As we have seen, classical culture and its reverence for love between men provided an important source of inspiration for pre-revolutionary friendships. That continued to be the case throughout the decades following Independence. Officers in the Continental army modeled their devotion to one another quite self-consciously on classical ideals. Hamilton copied into an artillery pay book for 1777 the following extract from Plutarch's biography of Spartan legislator Lycurgus: "Every lad had a lover or friend who took care of his education and shared in the praise or blame of his virtues and vices." The young officers compared themselves to ancient heroes such as Damon and Pythias, who risked death for one another as an expression of their loving friendship. Damon, condemned to death by Dionysus of Syracuse, asked permission to return home and settle his affairs before being executed. His friend Pythias volunteered to take his place as a hostage until he returned, under sentence of death should Damon fail to do so. When the day of execution arrived, Damon appeared just in time to save his friend, who then declared his intention to die with him, inspiring Dionysus to pardon Damon.[18]

A 1790 issue of the *Worcester Magazine* retold the story for American readers who might not have received a classical education. According to this version, Pythias spent his time as a hostage dreading the prospect of having to watch his beloved friend perish: "O leave me not to die the worst of deaths in my Damon." Hoping to escape that heartrending fate, he urged the gods to delay Damon's return until through his own death he had "redeemed a life a thousand times of more consequence, of more value, than my own." Damon was just as eager to save his friend. On arriving just in time to release Pythias from his fatal bond, Damon declared, "You are safe, you are safe, my friend, my beloved friend, the gods be praised, you are safe. I now have nothing but death to suffer, and I am delivered from the anguish of those reproaches which I gave myself for having endangered a life so much dearer than my own." Pythias, "pale, cold, and half-speechless in the arms of his Damon," declared that he could not live without his friend: "Fatal haste! Cruel impatience! What envious powers have wrought impossibilities in your favour? But I will not be wholly disappointed. Since I cannot die to save you, I will not survive you."[19]

This rendition of the classical story paid close attention not only to the nobility and profound love that bound the two friends but also to the reaction of Dionysus to their mutual devotion. It was not unusual for stories about friendship on both sides of the Atlantic to include a figure of authority whose moral character underwent transformation for the better as a result of the example set by loving friends such as Damon and Pythias. In this version of the story, the king declared as he pardoned Damon that he had previously considered "virtue, friendship, benevolence, love of one's country, and the like . . . as terms invented by the wise to keep in awe and impose upon the weak." But in granting Damon his life, Dionysus declared that the two friends had "borne unquestionable testimony of the existence of virtue" and of "sacred friendship." In a postrevolutionary context, the moral rehabilitation of a monarchical figure such as Dionysus would have had a particular significance for American readers: some father figures such as Washington exemplified of their own accord the qualities of enlightened fatherhood; others, like Dionysus, would reform as a result of the moral example set by sentimental friendship. The republican family had a place of honor for fathers, but they must embrace the spirit of affectionate benevolence embodied by Washington (or at least by the public's perception of Washington) and acquired by Dionysus.[20]

It was no coincidence that this retelling of the Damon and Pythias myth stressed the linkage between "virtue, friendship, benevolence, [and] love of one's country." According to late-eighteenth-century newspapers, sentimental friendship had public as well as personal implications: it fostered a capacity for mutual feeling that would then flow outward and transform society as a whole. "It is like a crystal fountain," declared one editorial, "uncontaminated at its source, issuing its stream along the vale and over the fertile mead, which makes the flowers in spontaneous order spring and flourish, and the valleys smile with pleasing blossoms, uniting fragrance over the wide expanse." Friendship was "a distinct and peculiar species of that general benevolence" with which the virtuous man was "actuated toward all mankind." It "dilate[d] the heart," "animate[d] to the practice of all the social virtues," and united humanity through "fraternal love." From friendship emanated "each ray of social happiness." In common with Scottish theorists such as Adam Smith, these authors argued that sympathetic instincts were natural but had to be nurtured with self-conscious deliberation. If society was to prosper and become truly civilized, it was essential that its members "cultivate intimate friendships; that they mutually sympathize with the misfortunes of each other; and that a passionate show of affections [be] promoted."[21]

When newspapers pronounced that "virtuous friendship" was "the source of everything that is great, good and excellent on earth," they had in mind the specific social and political needs of the new republic. Having repudiated their loyalty to the monarch and the accompanying culture of deference which, for good or ill, had given colonial society some sense of coherence and common identity, citizens of the newly independent United States would need to find another form of social and political cement to hold their republic together. Naked self-interest would not suffice, as the *Newburyport Herald* explained: "Where the members of society are cemented together by interest only, the social connection will dissolve whenever this motive is out of view, and the advantages resulting from such a union will be but mercenary: in such a connection jealousy and suspicion will exert themselves on every occasion; mutual hatred and animosity will sap the foundation on which the fabric of felicity is erected, and every malevolent passion unite its influence in subjecting mankind to wretchedness and misery." Recent events seemed to justify that grim prediction. Bloody dissension over the cause of Independence soon gave way to no less deeply felt divisions over the political and economic problems of the 1780s. The acrimonious debates over recommendations made by the constitutional convention in 1787 and the vicious political strife of the 1790s appalled many contemporaries. In 1800, the *South Carolina State Gazette* quoted "an American gentleman of rank and respectability now in Europe" who apparently dreaded returning to his "native country" because of the "party bitterness and rancour, such a boiling of foul and malignant passions, apparently growing worse from day to day there."[22]

The antidote to this poison, most commentators agreed, was civic virtue, an altruistic spirit that would inspire citizens to rise above partisan or selfish impulses as they engaged with public issues. Political thinkers argued that public and private virtue were closely intertwined, that a man who was morally upstanding in his personal life would prove a worthy citizen, and that friendship had a crucial role to play in nurturing virtue among American citizens. "Pure friendship," declared the *New Hampshire Gazette,* had "virtue for its guide and mutual happiness for its object." "That which makes one friend assured of another," declared the *Windham Herald,* "is the knowledge he has of his integrity. The sureties he has for him are his good disposition, his truth and constancy." One author defined friendship as "a sweet attraction of the heart towards the merit we esteem, or the perfections we admire," which produced "a mutual inclination between two persons to promote each other's interest, knowledge, virtue, and happiness."[23] The sympathetic power of loving friendship, that "cement of refined affection," would nurture men's nobler instincts so that they would be willing to set aside narrowly conceived self-interest in favor of mutual needs that they shared with and recognized in each other—thus the title of the *Worcester Gazette*'s retelling of the Damon and Pythias myth, "Disinterested Friendship." The word "disinterested"—which pervaded political discourse in the early republic—signified for contemporaries not a lack of interest or emotional investment but the transfiguration of self-interest through sympathy with others for whom one felt deeply. This model of friendship insisted that those who feared passion should distinguish between passions that were dangerous and those that yielded constructive, beneficent results: "Let the votaries of apathy and malignity cry down the passions," proclaimed one contributor, "still there is a principle of disinterested affection in the human heart."[24]

The spirit of friendship, that "endearing tie, which binds the willing soul, and brings along her chastest, strongest, and sublimest powers," would thus become the "firm cement of the world." The *South Carolina State Gazette* declared that friendship was "parent of union" and "foe to fell discord." Its "fond embrace" would prove "constant" against "raging winds inclement" and "impending storms." And the implications of that "fond embrace" were far-reaching. The *Newburyport Herald,* which had lamented the fate of a world in which "the members of society are cemented together by interest only," foresaw a very different future if mankind was "held together by the bonds of love and friendship": "How different the scene, all is harmony and concord—all is happiness and peace. Society wears a pleasing aspect and like the system of the universe rolls on through the varied paths of life in the most harmonious order."[25]

Ironically, these authors pointed out, it was a particular version of narcissism intrinsic to these friendships that enabled them to rise above the personal and become a redemptive social force. In order for loving friendships to blossom, "a coincidence of sentiment" was indispensable. "We admire in another what is peculiarly characteristic in ourselves," declared *Dunlap's American Daily Advertiser,* "and finding respected the same propensities, and the same failings, we are led to contract an intimacy, and insensibly to grant a portion of our esteem."[26] Early modern depictions of friendship across the Atlantic had emphasized the appeal of the friend as "another self," the relationship between friends creating "one soul in two bodies."[27] Post-revolutionary American commentators made sure that their readers appreciated this feature of loving friendship: they were being asked not to become selfless but to embrace self in others. Friendship was "a mirror, which between two minds reflects alternately its own pure image, and removes the barrier 'twixt each other's sentiments." It was that recognition of self in another that inspired friends to love: "We, in some sort, love ourselves in our friend" and "make a joint offering to benevolence and self-love." The love of oneself in another would, then, inspire friends to transcend a narrow conception of self-interest that saw self and other as inherently antagonistic. It would prompt the realization that furthering the interests of others did not necessarily mean disregarding oneself. Loving oneself in another and appreciating others at least in part because one saw oneself in them laid the basis for "mutual benevolence" through "an entire conformity of sentiment" as "the disinterestedness of love" worked in symbiosis with "the cement of gratitude."[28]

In order to achieve "an entire conformity of sentiment," friends must be compatible in social and economic status as well as in temperament. Commentators argued that "equality of rank and fortune" was "not only favourable, but even necessary, to a pure and uninterrupted friendship," since any dependence of one friend upon another would prove an obstacle to "the free easy intercourse of friendship."[29] As sympathy depended upon commonality in "rank and fortune," so it served to articulate not only a shared capacity for feeling among literate, educated friends but also the differences between them and less "refined" men. Indeed, the language of sentimental friendship, which now became a crucial component of republican discourse, was self-consciously exclusive in its insistence upon "refinement" (based in part on social rank) as a prerequisite for sympathetic fraternity. Eighteenth-century moral philosophers had argued that only relationships freed from calculations of interest could provide the basis for genuine benevolence and an enlightened sociability. That notion of disinterested affection as a prerequisite for responsible civic engagement was ambiguous in its implications for democracy among white Americans in the early republic. In the hands of those who feared mob rule, the argument that only those who were truly independent had the freedom to avoid choices based on obligation justified the exclusion of all but men of independent property from full citizenship; for more radical thinkers, that same argument helped to justify expanding landownership so as to create a nation united by a fundamental similarity in interests, which in turn would produce mutual sympathy and regard.[30]

Meanwhile abolitionists invoked brotherhood between all men as a justification for emancipation and the admission of former slaves into full citizenship. "Am I not a man and a brother?" asked the kneeling African man in the image that served as an emblem for abolitionists on both sides of the Atlantic at the end of the eighteenth century. Benjamin Banneker, a free black astronomer who became internationally famous for the almanacs he produced during the 1790s, declared, "We are all of the same family," and asked white Americans (quoting from Job 16:4) to "put your soul in their souls' stead": "Thus shall your hearts be enlarged with kindness and benevolence towards them." According to Banneker, "sympathy and affection" could transcend distinctions of race and social status. Quaker abolitionist John Woolman also urged his readers to empathize with African slaves so as to "make their case ours." Woolman acknowledged that their "present situation" was so degraded that there was "not much to engage the friendship or move the affection of selfish men." Nonetheless, those "who live[d] in the spirit of true charity" could surely "sympathize with the afflicted," even those "in the lowest stations of life." White and black Americans belonged, after all, to a "general brotherhood." Black petitioners in Connecticut also declared in 1779 that all nations and races were "kindred" and "of one blood."[31]

Yet despite this appropriation of sympathy and the rhetoric of an all-encompassing brotherhood in the cause of emancipation, most of those who already enjoyed membership in civil society had no intention of expanding their conception of fraternity to include even landless whites, let alone Africans. Indeed, given the gulf in "rank and fortune" between propertied whites and less privileged Americans, the logic of a social ethos based upon sympathetic commonality seemed to preclude such a move. That ethos might encourage a sense of fraternity within the privileged white male elite, but it also fostered paternalistic condescension to those who had not been deemed worthy of admission to civil society. And so it should not surprise us that while abolitionists adopted the rhetoric of brotherhood to bolster their cause, advocates of slavery turned increasingly to a loving and beneficent paternalism in order to characterize and justify the institution. Contemporary accounts celebrated Washington not only as the new nation's father but also as parent to his slaves. By presenting the emotional bonds that tied the president to his people as parallel to those which bound him to plantation slaves, eulogists handily downplayed, or even erased, the coercion intrinsic to slavery. Yet there was, of course, an important difference between these two variants on the American family: unlike free white children, who could grow up to become independent adults, their decisions and behavior inspired but not coerced by the sage counsel of a benign national parent, slaves were depicted as permanently childlike and so in need of an ongoing and directive paternal oversight incompatible with independent adulthood.[32]

Regardless of how one defined the parameters of this new national brotherhood, republican ideology endowed personal friendship and its encouragement of virtue with a broad social and political significance. The qualities that made a good friend would also make a good citizen. Indeed, friendship acted as an apprenticeship for civic virtue, as a bridge between individual happiness and social responsibility. Each individual had "particular tenderness" for those to whom he was bound "by the ties of blood, love, or friendship," but also "owe[d]" a more expansive sort of "affection" to "all mankind, as being all members of one family, of which God [was] the creator and father." Friendship animated that more general "affection" which brought members of society together by awakening "that interest which mankind take in the good of one another in general." The true friend combined the qualities of "father," "mother," and "brother": he encapsulated and then universalized the familial through a caring and redemptive bond that would inspire citizens, united in loving fraternity, to build a new and expansive republican family in which love and sympathy bound them in willing service to the mutual good. Individual love would, then, blossom into "a more refined, a more universal love of mankind." Personal friendship, which incorporated "all the social affections," would foster "public and private happiness," undoing the "contentions and animosities" which could otherwise poison "parishes, towns, counties, and commonwealths." Its influence would "effectually eradicate the spirit of division, dispel discord, and introduce harmony and happiness in all our circles and societies through this pleasant land."[33]

Seen from this perspective, the cultivation of friendship became the first duty of a virtuous citizen: "Surely no one can withhold a hand from endeavouring to save his country, when it can be done in a way so consistent with, and promotive of, his own happiness." Two years prior to Independence, the *Newport Mercury* had declared that "mutual affection, friendship, and public spirit" would save the colonies from "miserable oppression." Now it was "the duty of every good citizen to endeavor that urbanity and friendship should pervade the community in which he dwells." The "sympathy of friendship" would produce "an upright and expanded heart," which was the fundamental prerequisite for a good citizen: "Upon this foundation the strongest and most beautiful super-structure may be raised." The magnanimity born of "brotherly friendship" would inspire citizens to "yield our opinions, and make the will of the majority the will of the whole."[34] The *Continental Journal* had declared in 1778 that true liberty was "liberty restrained in such a manner as to render society one great family, where everyone must consult his neighbor's happiness as well as his own."[35] The key words here are "as well as": from this perspective, selfishness must give way not to selflessness but rather to mutuality in a "manly submission" to one's loving obligations within "one great family." Those obligations melded self-interest with altruism. A "true republican" was "pledged" to "be no man's who [was] not his," giving "assistance for assistance; zeal for zeal; friendship for friendship." No wonder, then, that the *Pennsylvania Gazette* declared friendship to be "the glory of society and the boast of republicanism."[36]

&

Male friendship was not the only human bond capable of encouraging the "social virtues" so essential to the well-being of a republic. Just as the friends we met in earlier chapters believed that loving relationships with men could flourish alongside marriage to a woman, so the articles on friendship that appeared in newspapers during the final decades of the century depicted these two forms of relationship as yielding similar dividends—personal, social, and political. Each conferred happiness and comfort, each provided moral guidance and support, and each had a meliorative influence upon the general character of the men involved. Just as male friends had a responsibility to encourage each other's higher instincts, so wives were bound by a similar duty. Embracing the axiom that "public good must grow out of private virtue," these essayists held that wives could further the "public good" by nurturing their husbands' capacity for virtue, sensibility, and sympathy. The love of a good woman for her husband, like that of a good man for his friend, would promote "the happiness of individuals and of society."[37]

According to these essays and poems, marriage should be considered a form of friendship. Indeed, it was essential that husband and wife become friends if they were to enjoy a happy and lasting marriage. One author advised that couples should take "great care" in choosing a mate to ensure "that friendship be the foundation of love." This would "cement the harmony between the sexes." There could never be "any steady or lasting happiness in a married state," declared another, without "a mutual esteem and friendship of the strongest and noblest kind." This particular author stressed that "friendship and esteem" relied upon "principles of reason and thought," which would counteract the "changeable, transient, and accidental" nature of "love considered merely as a passion." But a marital love that incorporated the exercise of reason and a commitment to virtue did not need to be cold or bloodless. Postrevolutionary authors held that depth of feeling was just as essential to marriage as to male friendship. Hamilton described marriage as "a state which, with a kind of magnetic force, attracts every breast to it, in which sensibility has a place."[38] According to the *Independent Gazetteer*, husband and wife should enjoy "a gentle and mild sympathy, producing a reciprocal and lively friendship" that would "brighten in its worth, beauties, and excellencies" over the years, "unmingled joys springing from a mutual affection." Such feelings might prove "gentle and mild" rather than torrid, but they were nonetheless heartfelt. "United by the indissoluble ties of mutual congeniality," their "affections" would "beat in union" in "their reciprocal tenderness and concern for each other." Marriage could provide "the basis and the cement of those numberless tender sympathies, mutual endearments and interchanges of love" that fostered "morality" and "happiness." A marriage that was "happy" combined, then, "all the pleasures of friendship."[39]

Just as the benign influence of virtue played a crucial role in any worthwhile friendship between two men, the same was true of marriage: the woman's emotional and moral qualities would win her husband's heart and inspire him to a life of personal and public virtue, complementing the impact of male friendship on her husband's moral character. "Female beauty," declared one author, was "insipid and spiritless" unless "adorned by virtue," which attracted "as with magnetic force" and transformed "admiration" into "the warmth of esteem and friendship." Marital friendship, averred another, "when directed by virtue and sensibility," dispersed "the clouds of error that we are led into from the delirium of sense alone," and fostered "a softness of attachment founded upon the consciousness of internal merit." The esteem in which husbands held their wives, combined with feminine charm, would enable women to exercise a "happy influence" over their menfolk. According to a piece printed in the *Continental Journal*, "the smiles and endearments of the female sex" not only "compensated" men for "the cares and vexations" of "the world" but also "spur[red] men onto industry, that they may be better enabled to endear themselves to, and by the acts of generosity and kindness, win the love of women." Another essay published in the same newspaper argued that marriage made a man "more beneficent and less selfish." It "improved, refined, and exalted" his "natural affection;" it "humanize[d] his heart for others." Marriage was, in short, "an excellent school of virtue to men."[40]

Contemporaries argued that women had a crucial role to play in ensuring that male citizens of the new republic embodied civic virtue. As mothers, they should raise their boys to be morally upstanding and generous spirited citizens; as wives, they must ensure that their husbands remained so. "You have not only an interest in being good for your *own* sakes," declared the *American Magazine: "Society* is interested in your goodness—you polish our manners—correct our vices—and inspire our hearts with a love of virtue." Another author declared in a piece entitled "On the Virtues of Women" that it was "in their power to give either a good or a bad turn to society, and to make men take whatever shape they think proper to impose." Women exerted this influence not only within the home but also at genteel venues such as salons and public assemblies. These were not political events in any formal sense and yet often included conversation and negotiation on political subjects; women could elevate the tone of political discussion at such gatherings and thus have a significant impact on public life without themselves becoming active participants in organized politics.[41] But women would shape the character and moral tone of political discourse first and foremost as friends to their husbands, instilling men with the qualities required to make them worthy and effective citizens of the new republic. Foremost among those qualities were sympathetic engagement and a commitment to virtue. As we have seen, contemporaries assumed that the exercise of sympathy in personal contexts would foster social benevolence and civic virtue. Though both sexes were expected to cultivate a capacity for affection and sympathy, women had a special role to play in modeling a benign sensibility and encouraging that temperament in their menfolk. It was a wife's emotional power as "queen of every gentle passion, tender sympathy and love" that made it possible for her to exercise this benign and far-reaching influence. The "mutual love and friendship" that a husband experienced with his wife would "ennoble" him, "produc[ing] much good in the world" as it "render[ed] him more civilized and compassionate abroad." Virtuous love between husband and wife would, then, generate "the happiness of social virtue."[42]

In a cultural climate that characterized women as guardians of moral virtue, it is hardly surprising that some writers depicted marital friendship as more effective in encouraging virtue than friendship between men simply because a woman was involved. These authors claimed that marital love was "friendship raised to its highest pitch" and "the highest instance of human friendship."[43] According to a piece printed in the *Connecticut Courant,* "social virtues" and "sentimental feelings" were "commonly the offspring of mixed society." Men became "polished and refined . . . in proportion to the time spent in the conversation of their women" and "less so as they neglect[ed] and despise[d] them." This particular author claimed that nothing promoted "the happiness of individuals and of society" so much as "constant efforts to please" and that these were "in a great measure only produced by the company of women." Another argued that friendships tended to work best if there was a distinction in temperament between the two friends and that this was easier to achieve between a man and a woman since "the dispositions of one sex" were "qualified by the proper perfections of the other." It was preferable that there be "on the one side a little more judgment, and on the other a little more sensibility; and the parties should be conscious of each other's perfections." Thus the two friends would "make up a complete character together, rather than two alike perfect and distinct ones." According to a poem that appeared in the *Independent Journal,* male friendship would always be lacking in one crucial ingredient that grew out of friendship between a man and woman. A man could have "pleasing converse" with men whose friendship gave him "comfort" and "calm" in both "heart" and "mind," but the company of a "fair" and "pleasing" woman would soon give rise to "sensations" that affected him in much the way that "kindling" would a fire: it was "love" and the man's "desire" to "have her by [his] side" that made men so eager to please and that in turn gave women their power as moral guides.[44]

Yet none of these arguments appear to have achieved general acceptance in the closing decades of the eighteenth century. A deluge of essays and poems that appeared in print during those years paid tribute to the loving devotion of male friends and the joy that men experienced in providing one another with emotional companionship, solace, and moral support, undermining any claim that men were much more eager to please when dealing with women and therefore more likely to become pleasingly virtuous. Though descriptions of friendship between men used the word "love" less frequently than did private communications between male friends, their celebration of the "ardor" that such men felt for each other, locating their "attraction" to each other in the "heart" or "bosom," left little doubt that these were intense and heartfelt relationships. The notion that friendship worked best if the two people involved had contrasting temperaments was contradicted by the many commentators who argued that friendship worked best "between persons of exactly similar qualities and dispositions." One piece defined friendship as "an affectionate union of two persons, nearly of the same age, the same situation in life, the same dispositions and sentiments, and, as some writers will have it, of the same sex." The author clearly agreed with this latter body of opinion, declaring that "the friendship of Achilles and Patroclus in Homer, of Nysas and Eurylas in Virgil, and of David and Jonathan in the Sacred Writings, show how strong an attachment may be formed by two persons of the same sex." This particular author was writing for the *Lady's Magazine and Musical Repository,* but evidently felt that female readers could draw inspiration from "the brightest examples" of friendship, regardless of whether those involved were men or women.[45]

The claim that an ideal friendship combined a woman's "sensibility" with a man's "judgment" accorded well with the increasingly prevalent notion that men and women were quite distinct in physical and temperamental makeup. But even at the end of the eighteenth century that trend toward gender differentiation had by no means eclipsed an older paradigm that emphasized the similarities between men and women. Sensibility was, contemporaries agreed, "one of the most shining virtues," and a woman who lacked sensibility "scarcely deserve[d] the name of woman."[46] Yet Robert Bell's circulating library used a bookplate that appealed to "sentimentalists, whether ladies or gentlemen."[47] Though women as mothers and wives were clearly accorded a distinct role as purveyors of virtue and sensibility within the early republic, they were not perceived as having a monopoly in this regard, since male friends had a parallel role to play in the fostering of moral benevolence and civic virtue: this was, then, by no means a gender-exclusive endeavor. Some of the men we met in the first two chapters of this book clearly took the view that a man could incorporate characteristics associated with femininity: they celebrated the fusion of gender attributes as an important part of what made a man worthy as a friend, and by extension a better husband and citizen. In a striking gesture that exemplified the ways in which male and female could be combined or even conflated, Thomas Jefferson included on his wife's gravestone a quotation from the lament that Achilles delivered over the body of his beloved friend Patroclus: "Nay if even in the House of Hades the dead forget their dead, yet will I even there be mindful of my dear comrade."[48] Most discussions of friendship that appeared in late eighteenth-century newspapers treated friendships between men and those between husband and wife as virtually indistinguishable. Either they described friendship in gender-neutral terms or they used the same vocabulary and turns of phrase for both kinds of friendship. There was, argued one author, "an indescribable sympathy betwixt the hearts of friends" that was "not confined to hearts of different sexes, felt between a man and a maiden in the pleasing transports of mutual love": "it pervade[d] the hearts of all the human race."[49]

Friendship, exulted late eighteenth-century newspapers, whether between a married couple or two men, was "the crown of all our felicities" and "the perfection of our natures." There was hardly any mention of friendship between women in these articles, probably because the focus of interest was so often the impact of friendship on the male character and the public implications of that beneficent influence. A friendship between women that nurtured moral character would, of course, have a constructive impact on their capacity to foster in turn their menfolk's potential for sensibility and virtue, but newspapers did not discuss this connection.[50] They focused instead on marital and fraternal friendship, both of which were crucial to fostering civic virtue, the mainstay of the new republic. Just as the patriarchal family had served as a model for the hierarchical structure of early modern society, so now a conceptualization of the family that focused on companionate friendship and the ties of sensibility became an indispensable foundation for republican citizenship and political engagement.[51] Within the conventional family, women presided as the architects and guardians of virtue. But as Washington's aides-de-camp had made abundantly clear in their correspondence with one another, there was more than one kind of family and more than one kind of love. The conventional family would play a central role in sustaining personal and public virtue, once it had been made fit for republican society by the reinvention of the father and the insistence that marriage take the form of a friendship that was characterized, at least rhetorically, by a spirit of sympathetic reciprocity. But loving male friends would also nurture and sustain moral integrity in each other. Recall Alexander Hamilton's conception of his three fundamental relationships—with his friend John Laurens, with his wife Elizabeth Schuyler, and with "the public"—as a symbiotic trinity of heartfelt and high-minded devotion. The cultivation of virtue—personal and civic—was a *homosocial* as well as *heterosocial* enterprise, achieved not only through the benign ministrations of wives and mothers but also through the "fraternal sympathy and ardor" that bound male friends to one another.[52]

Given the importance of sympathetic friendship to late eighteenth-century republican ideology, learning how to assess potential friends became a pressing concern. If a citizen was to become and remain virtuous, he must choose his companions wisely. As the *New-York Daily Gazette* put it, "He will neither choose his friend at a gaming-table, nor his wife in a brothel." As loving and virtuous friends, men could inspire each other to become worthy citizens; but as dissipated rakes, they could seduce men and women alike into lives of self-indulgence and depravity, undermining the moral capacity of their companions with ghastly and far-reaching consequences. Male libertines figured in late eighteenth-century moral parables and essays as profoundly dangerous characters who devoted themselves to sensual gratification instead of seeking out "real solid qualities" and lasting pleasure, both of which had "their source in the heart and in the social affections."[53]

Men and women alike must protect themselves from such creatures, lest they become not only corrupted themselves but also malign influences in their own right. Women must reject the temptations offered by libertine suitors, who sought to ensnare them, rob them of their honor, and then abandon them to degradation. According to narratives of seduction and abandonment, fallen women often ended up in the streets as prostitutes, purveyors of vice and disease. No longer fit to serve the nation as guardians of virtue, they now became agents of physical and moral pollution. Just as the republican wife and mother had her foil in the infectious whore, so the loving and virtuous male friend had his foil in the depraved and corrupting libertine. And just as the dereliction of a woman's duty to inspire virtue had public and political implications, so young men who embraced a libertine sensibility would corrupt not only themselves and their friends but also the republic.[54] Associates in depravity made a mockery of friendship and its exalted purpose. "The wicked" might join together in what they pleased to call "a society of friends," declared the *Windham Herald,* but in reality they were "not friends, but confederates in guilt."[55] Hamilton's depiction of himself as a seduced and betrayed damsel in relation to his male friend reflected not only the fluidity of gender roles in premodern transatlantic culture but also the vulnerability that men as well as women could feel as they negotiated matters of the heart. Seduction narratives enabled men as well as women to experience vicariously the dangers posed by rakish libertines without actually succumbing to their pernicious influence.[56]

Royall Tyler dramatized the dangers that rakes could pose to men and women alike in his 1787 play *The Contrast.* Billy Dimple, once a promising and "ruddy youth," has become a "polite beau," an "odious," "unmanly," and "depraved wretch," his "only virtue" a "polished exterior." Dimple is eager to conquer the affections of a young lady named Maria, but she is much more interested in Colonel Manly, a "grave" and "solid" gentleman whose "anti-gallant" heart is "replete with the noblest sentiments." Modeling himself on "our illustrious Washington," Manly speaks "the language of sentiment," while his eyes radiate "tenderness and honour." Maria yearns for "manly virtue," which appeals more to her "delicacy and sentiment" than do Dimple's "frivolous manners, actuated by the most depraved heart." Having read many sentimental novels, she is well aware of the dangers posed by rakish admirers who seduce and then abandon the susceptible objects of their passing interest. Maria contrasts "the good sense of her books" with "the flimsiness" of Dimple's love letters and wants nothing to do with him. Dimple, meanwhile, has more than one potential victim in mind. He hopes to seduce the virtuous Colonel Manly into a life of dissipation by "pretend[ing] to be struck by his person and address," and then "endeavour[ing] to steal into his confidence." Manly does "experience a thrill of pleasure" on hearing Dimple's flattering remarks about "those brave men" in the army who have "suffered so much in the service of their country," but "the superiority of his sentiments" enables him to see through Dimple's advances and reject them.[57]

That Tyler depicted Maria as able to withstand Dimple's attempts at seduction because she had spent so much time immersed in sentimental novels would not have surprised those attending his play. Though some critics argued that novels filled young women with romantic notions, making them more vulnerable than before to men such as Dimple, others were more optimistic about the genre's likely impact. They insisted that novelistic depictions of the dangers posed by male libertines, along with didactic essays and cautionary stories printed in newspapers and magazines, forewarned and forearmed young women so that they could conduct themselves with due regard to their own safety. According to the author of "Reflections on Gallantry," the most effective weapon against the threat posed by libertines was better education for women, cultivating their "sensibility" and "imagination" so as to value "talent" and "virtue." That education would take place not only through formal tutelage but also through the reading of cautionary tales. Women would then be drawn to men with "elevated sentiments." Those who chose husbands for their "real solid qualities" would "know true pleasures, of which frivolous beings see only the shadow." Once these "enlightened" wives were "penetrated with that delightful sentiment which arises from virtue," there would "unfold the latent seeds of all the virtues." Because men were "naturally inclined to court the good graces of the fair" and because many women seemed to value "enervated minds absorbed in trifles," young gentlemen felt "obliged to degrade and vilify themselves in order to please." But when faced with "enlightened" women, they would respond by cultivating their undoubted capacity for "elevated sentiment." The two sexes, "instead of mutually corrupting," would "inspire each other" and "reciprocally enhance the value of each other." Love would no longer be corrupted into "a gross instinct," but would "be composed of all that can fill delightfully the entire capacity of the soul, of all that is most delicate in pleasure; the most tender friendship, the most satisfying confidence, and the most pleasing esteem."[58]

Meanwhile, essayists encouraged young men to seek out male companions whose sensibility and moral integrity would make them worthy friends. Discussions of male debauchery often claimed that men who gave way to corrupt impulses did so against their better instincts: the rake was "dissolute rather from fashion than inclination." The *New-York Daily Gazette* argued that "by far the greater part of our weaknesses and vices" resulted from "ill-judged example": "Our follies and our miseries proceed not so much from depravity of nature and propensity to vice as from an injudicious choice of a model. Gay and inconsiderate; unshielded by experience against the allurements of vanity, and the fascinations of bad examples; a young man is particularly disposed to admire, to applaud, and to imitate whatever pleases his imagination." This argument could and sometimes did become an insidious alibi that depicted men as enslaved to their foibles and so not wholly culpable. But it also held out the hope that men could be saved from moral corruption if they fell into the hands of companions who would nurture their potential for virtue. The *Gazette* was convinced that "the mind of man" was "by nature benevolently inclined" and that a "tacit confession of the superiority of virtue" would surely draw most youths back to "the society of the virtuous." Some contemporaries urged young ladies to try their hand at reforming rakes, using their charms to seduce these wretches into virtuous domesticity; others placed their faith in the redemptive influence of high-minded male friends, who would guide the misdirected back to the path of virtue. Even he who succumbed temporarily to less wholesome influences ("more from the silly dictates of vanity than from the strong impulse of appetite") would in good time "disengage himself from the unworthy attachment, and return with rapture to the paths of manly prudence, and to the bosom of honorable friendship."[59]

Male citizens of the new republic could develop their capacity for sentiment, sympathy, and virtue not only in the context of individual friendships but also through larger and sometimes formally structured fraternities. The growth in popularity of such organizations during the eighteenth century—from religious support groups in Boston to Benjamin Franklin's self-improvement societies in Philadelphia to the rapidly expanding network of Masonic lodges—manifested a new male culture of affective association. In the early decades of the century, young New Englanders had joined together in all-male groups designed to nurture morality and faith through mutual stewardship and spiritual companionship. Youths in Charlestown, Massachusetts, formed a devotional group in 1703 "for our assistance in the designs of early piety and for the prevention of the snares which we are exposed unto or are in danger of being entangled in by evil company." Another group of young men that met in Boston's North End sought "to avoid those temptations and abandon those courses that by sad experience we find our youth to be exposed or inclined to." And in 1719, a group of Harvard students established a religious society through which they hoped "to avoid all those temptations and allurements to evil which we are in danger to meet with." They also promised to "live in peace, love, and unity with one another." Franklin, who perhaps not coincidentally migrated from Boston to Philadelphia as a teenage boy, gathered a group of aspiring young tradesmen into "a club for mutual improvement" that started to meet on a weekly basis in 1727. These young men were keen to acquire knowledge of current developments in science and philosophy as well as debating skills and a sheen of urban sophistication that would assist them in their professional endeavors, but they were also firmly committed to promoting the virtuous behavior of group members through mutual moral stewardship.[60]

As members of these groups, young men who were still subject to the authority of their fathers or (in the case of apprentices) their masters could nonetheless assume adult roles and responsibilities. They regulated their own moral behavior and in so doing operated independently of any supervision by ministers or parents. The young men in Charlestown committed themselves in a covenant akin to that of the local church to watch over each other and to "admonish" those who strayed from the path of righteousness, suspending errant brethren from the society until they showed "visible signs of repentance." Their counterparts in the North End of Boston agreed that any member who "live[d] scandalously and prove[d] a discredit to the meeting or a dishonor to religion" would be expelled. And the Harvard students promised that when they witnessed "unbecoming" behavior within their group, they would "reprove" each other "with all meekness, love, and tenderness." Older New Englanders, including and especially ministers, encouraged these ventures, worried as they were about the strength of spiritual commitment among younger New Englanders in an increasingly diverse colonial society that seemed to be losing its original sense of moral commitment. But these were fraternal rather than paternalistic endeavors, modeled on principles of self-governance: they not only supplemented the family and church as sites for spiritual guidance but also encouraged a conceptualization of moral influence and association that was horizontal rather than vertical.[61]

Though the young adults who formed support groups at Harvard and in the North End committed themselves to a series of principles and goals, their communities of mutual stewardship were much less formal than those that took form within Masonic lodges, a network of fraternal societies that originated in England but rapidly spread across the Atlantic and throughout the British colonies of North America during the early decades of the eighteenth century. Freemasons envisioned themselves as "a society of friends, linked in a strong bond of brotherly love" and committed to "the advancement of humanity and good fellowship." They sought to encourage enlightened learning, religious devotion, moral virtue, and social benevolence. North American Masons hoped that the love they felt for one another would provide an antidote to the divisions and tensions that poisoned colonial society. Faced with "a monstrous diversity of religious tenets, a mad contention about little honours, a furious clashing in worldly interests, and an unchristian enmity between rival families," the combination of which was "rending the very bowels of society in pieces," colonial society desperately needed to find a means "whereby men merely as men might be conjoined as friends and brethren, notwithstanding a disagreement in any particular principles." The answer, Masons argued, lay in the "brotherly love" that blossomed in their lodges and that would foster a "universal love" that comprised in equal parts virtue and benevolence. One celebration of the order proclaimed that love, "the cement of souls and bond of perfectness," was the only "healing" force that could "keep any society whatever from being dissolved." Happily, declared another, that spirit of "brotherly love" was "the foundation and cap-stone, the cement and glory, of this ancient and honourable fraternity."[62]

Yet despite these worthy goals, not everyone welcomed the proliferation of lodges throughout the colonies. Newspaper satirists attacked the order for its pomposity, its exclusivity, and its secret rituals. There seems also to have been considerable suspicion regarding the rhetoric of love so prominent in Masonic discourse. A series of attacks published at mid-century contrasted the order's proclaimed ideals with what critics claimed to be a much less wholesome reality, that of sodomy and sadomasochism. An anti-Masonic piece printed in the January 7, 1751 issue of the *Boston Evening Post* was accompanied by a drawing that showed one Freemason hammering a "trunnel" (tree nail) into a brother's backside. Another piece referred to the enthusiastic use of enemas by a brother apothecary to ease the pain of fellow members suffering from constipation. And yet another claimed that one lodge chose its master by testing his ability to withstand having his "posteriors" beaten. Masonic brothers were apparently "cemented" to one another in more ways than one; they used their "friendly arms" not only to engage in innocent embraces but also to "flog," "lash," and "trunnel" each other's backsides, "those hemispheres of love."[63] Such references had connotations for eighteenth-century readers that are not immediately obvious to us today. Colonial newspapers often linked sodomy and other forms of homoerotic behavior to foreign corruption, urban vice, and the seamier aspects of transatlantic commercial enterprise. Sodomy, these publications implied, was fundamentally un-American. Attempts by satirists to associate early Freemasons with sodomy went hand in hand with their mockery of the brotherhood for its aristocratic pretension: both enabled critics to equate the Freemasons with a decadent and corrupt imperial culture that Americans increasingly sought to contrast with their own more straightforward and allegedly wholesome way of life.[64]

And yet by the end of the eighteenth century, freemasonry and its celebration of brotherly love had become the epitome of respectable American manhood. When George Washington, acting as first president of the United States, dedicated the Capitol in 1793, he wore a Masonic apron. Placing a silver plate on the cornerstone of the new building, he then filled it with the Masonic symbols of corn, oil, and wine. The text engraved on the plate noted that the ceremony was taking place in "the thirteenth year of the American republic" and "in the year of Masonry 5793."[65] Washington's decision to wear Masonic vestments at this momentous ceremony and his explicit association of the state with Masonic insignia would not have surprised contemporaries, given the prominent place that freemasonry by then occupied in the public rituals and rhetoric of the new nation. This remarkable transformation was made possible in part by the order's more inclusive membership policy in the aftermath of the Revolution, which made it seem more compatible with the democratic rhetoric of the new nation. But even more significant was that it had come to be seen as a key component in the fostering of civic virtue, so crucial to the survival of the republic. Freemasons would create in their lodges across the fledgling nation temples of brotherly love, dedicated to the promotion of moral affection, mutual benevolence, and thus national redemption. The Masons had argued from their first appearance that their loving fraternity would foster "universal love" and so exercise a far-reaching and beneficent influence over society as a whole, but that argument became much more powerful in the context of post-revolutionary rhetoric about the importance of civic virtue and social affection. Masonic love would "cement together the whole brotherhood of men, and build them up an edifice of affection and love." No longer the butt of ribald satire and suspicion, freemasonry had become the corporate quintessence of loving, virtuous, and redemptive brotherhood. The Masonic order, declared George Washington, taught "the duties of men and citizens." It was "a lodge for the virtues."[66]

Just as patriots had joined together as loving brothers in what the *Continental Journal* called "one great family," Masons conceived of themselves in much the same terms, as elective kinfolk. The order fostered an "artificial consanguinity" that had "as much force and effect as the natural relationship of blood." Just as "children of the same family" had "generally a tender affection for each other," so "the term brethren" could be used by lodge members who, "though destitute of any ties of consanguinity, [were] nevertheless tied together in the bonds of strict friendship." Members would "expand [their] hearts for all the offices of humanity" by creating communities of love and commitment modeled on the family: "by a voluntary association with all parts of the family into which [they] enter[ed]," they would develop feelings for each other "such only as exist in every kindred." Though their order had an explicit internal hierarchy, the fundamental ties that bound Masons to one another were fraternal, that is, horizontal. "Masonry thus makes brothers of us all," declared one panegyric to the order, "and binds our hearts together forever."[67] It was no coincidence that many officers in the Continental army became Masons: the order not only gave them a sense of common identity—transcending their disparate geographical and social origins—but also expressed that affinity in familial terms, replicating in a more formal setting the individual expressions of fraternal love through which officers created for themselves a network of elective kinfolk that would sustain them through the perils of the war.[68]

A Mason was characterized by "the ardor and constancy of his affection." One enthusiast rejoiced in the delicious blends of "song, sentiment, and social-loving mirth" that "inspire our hearts," so that "three times three thousand thrills of generous sensations possess our bosoms, vibrating to the remotest pulsations of sensibility." Membership in the order offered "the indulgence of all the innocent passions, and all the incentives of generous affections." Caught up in "a numerous train of exquisitely pleasing sensations," they would "unbend in social glee, catch the sweet sympathy of pleasure, and share it with fullness of soul."[69] Those who became brothers in "the grand temple of love" would develop their potential for sensibility and benevolence, blossoming into an improved version of manhood through the support and example of fellow members. Masons found themselves surrounded by men "who possess[ed] congenial hearts, mutual good dispositions and propensities, and reciprocal esteem and love." In common with late eighteenth-century newspapers, they depicted "brotherly love" as based in a mutuality that recognized self in others: "The animating and connecting principle is self-love, which seeks its own good in that of its fellow creatures." Bound by "vows of eternal amity in a most sacred, intimate, and endeared alliance," Masons made "the prosperity of each individual the object of the whole" and "the prosperity of the whole the object of each individual."[70]

Just as individual friendships promoted personal happiness and laid the foundation for a virtuous citizenry, so the same was true of freemasonry. Not only did it "produce the greatest comfort to individuals," but it also "augment[ed] the happiness of society" by "directing the natural propensities of the human soul, the love of pleasure and the love of action, to their noblest ends." Masons proclaimed that their fraternity would serve the nation as a "nursery of virtue" and as "the school of all the virtues." Their characterization of the order as a "nursery" was highly significant, given the latter's feminine connotations. Republican ideology saw the nurturing of virtue in young boys as a maternal enterprise, but what would happen to men once they became adults? As we have seen, republican wives were expected to reinforce in their husbands the moral precepts instilled into males at an early age. But the rhetoric surrounding freemasonry suggests a belief that men could also exert a redemptive influence upon each other as adults through fraternal love and affection. An anonymous "lady" writing from Worcester, Massachusetts, declared that the order would "level the masculine character of the other sex with the feminine softness of ours." In common with other versions of sentimental friendship, freemasonry would help men to cultivate within themselves "feminine" qualities that would make them better men and thus better citizens.[71]

Freemasonry was, then, "a moral institution intended to promote individual and social happiness." Its "cultivation of unity, brotherly love, and benevolence" within its lodges would encourage "social and benevolent affections," prompting men to "do their duty in society." Their "mutual endearments of brotherhood" would become "a bulwark of union": by "harmoniz[ing] the passions and perfect[ing] the virtues of individuals," Masons would "embellish the state of general society, and bind together in the same amities and interests the whole family of mankind."[72] Masons saw themselves as operating on personal, local, national, and universal planes. By "promoting peace, unity, and concord among the brotherhood of men, and binding them all together by the indissoluble bonds of affection and love," Masonic fellowship would end "all strife and contention on the earth; injustice, and oppression, and cruelty, and rapine, and murder, and war, and rebellion, and tyranny would cease." They would banish "the evil effects of discord and contention," including "the horrors and distresses of civil war," establishing in their place "the happy effects of unity, love, and mutual benevolence, flourishing and diffusing the serenest joy and happiness."[73] The impact of Masonic love would spread outward from "nearest connections" to "others more remote":

Friend, parent, neighbour first it will embrace,
Our country next, and next all human race.

When advocates for the fraternity spoke of "comprehensive benevolence and universal virtue," they used the words "comprehensive" and "universal" quite literally: they aspired to a "great circle of fellowship throughout the world," united in "the unceasing duties of morality, religion, and virtue."[74] Masons sought nothing less than "to cultivate the humane and sociable propensities of the heart, and to diffuse the blessings of unity, concord, and peace through the world." Freemasons wanted to reconstruct "the whole family of mankind" as a "brotherhood of men," joined in loving friendship and committed to "render[ing] man amiable and friendly to man."[75]

       $\mathscr{O}$

Freemasons positioned their crusade to transform the world within an explicitly religious context. They stressed that brotherly love, "a leading, fundamental, and comprehensive principle" in their lives, was also one of God's fundamental commandments: love of the heavenly father was "the first and greatest commandment of all," but "the love of our neighbor" was its twin, and together these two loves constituted "the sum total of religion."[76] Masons saw their order as pursuing the same goals as Christianity and sought to ally whenever possible with religious figures and institutions. Some sectarians distrusted Masons, in part because they saw the order as a rival claimant to individual loyalties and in part because they abhorred its trans-denominational sensibility.[77] But many of the public orations praising freemasonry in the late eighteenth century took the form of sermons delivered by ministers who saw the fraternal lodges as natural allies: these preachers held that the spirit of social affection intrinsic to freemasonry was also "the distinguishing attribute of the Deity" and "the spirit of true religion." "No grace or virtue" was "so often inculcated in the Bible as this," declared the Reverend Zabdiel Adams in his sermon marking the establishment of a new lodge in Lancaster, Massachusetts. And Simeon Howard, pastor of the West Church in Boston, quoted from Romans 13 in a sermon addressed to that town's Masonic lodge: "He that loveth another hath fulfilled the law." According to these sermons, the "object" of freemasonry was "to make man the visible image of the INVISIBLE ARCHITECT." Those who "love[d] fervently as Christians and as brethren," embracing the spirit of their faith and of the Masonic order, would be friends forever, "hereafter admitted to the society of the Perfect in the Temple not made with hands, eternal in the Heavens!"[78]

The spirit of this post-revolutionary alliance between freemasonry and Christianity was avowedly ecumenical.[79] Its mission was to overcome the artificial distinctions that divided humanity and to convince people that they "all belong[ed] to the same great family," "knit together" by "brotherly love." According to a 1788 oration delivered at a Masonic gathering in New Jersey, Jesus had urged his followers to forsake a "confined" spirit of love in favor of a "comprehensive" love that embraced all of God's creation: "Let not your idea of brother be confined to those who are the children of Abraham, but extend your benevolence to all men; for you are all descended from the same father; you all belong to the same great family; and if you walk in the ways of righteousness, you are all heirs of the same immortal inheritance. In this comprehensive view we ought to understand the doctrine of brotherly love." Though Christian "brethren" had a particular affinity with fellow members in "the household of faith," just as Masons had a special loyalty to and love for one another, the conception of "family" promoted in these addresses encapsulated "the whole human race." By emulating God in universal love, men would prove themselves "to be his children." Masons and Christians had the same fundamental objective, to join individuals together as "brethren" and so to reconstitute "mankind in general." The spirit of this endeavor would transform personal, social, and political relationships, "making persons not only good husbands and wives, but good rulers and subjects, citizens and neighbours."[80]

Meanwhile, newspaper essayists also insisted that religious faith, loving fraternity, and social affection could—indeed must—sustain each other. "We are all the children of one kind and indulgent Father," declared one author: "We ought therefore to be affectionate towards each other; to promote mutual happiness in this world, and to assist one another in obtaining the smiles of Heaven, and the friendship of God." Friendship was, averred other contributors, a "boon of heaven," "a holy thing," modeled on "friendship of that refined complexion which angels feel towards each other."[81] Such relationships served personal, social, and spiritual ends:

> Then as our hands in friendship join
> So let our social powers combine
> (Ruled by a passion most divine)
> Friendship with our Creator.

According to this sacralized version of the republican ethos, it was loving empathy within the community of the faithful along with a devotion to moral virtue that would create worthy citizens and sustain the new nation. Washington declared in his 1796 Farewell Address that "religion and morality" were "indispensable supports" for "all the dispositions and habits which lead to political prosperity" and that "virtue, or morality," aligned with "fraternal affection," was "a necessary spring of popular government." As the *Vermont Gazette* declared, "sacred friendship" enabled "souls congenial" to enjoy "sacred union, bound by the cement of refined affection, founded on virtue."[82]

It is hardly surprising that discussion of loving brotherhood in the new nation was so often framed in religious language. As the nation's founding fathers developed plans to ensure social and political order in the new republic, they drew on a dazzling array of theories developed by European philosophers, by no means all of which placed religious principles at the center of their arguments. But the version of republican ideology that reached most Americans through speeches, sermons, and newspaper articles allotted a central place to religious sensibility. Its blend of loving fraternity, social affection, and religious faith owed a significant debt to the spirit of pre-revolutionary evangelical revivals. This is not to suggest that there was any clear correlation between support for the revivals and support for the patriot cause or any particular version of republican ideology. But the revolutionary crisis did unfold in the context of religious ferment unleashed by recent evangelical "awakenings." As readers will recall, revivalists had placed at the very center of their social theology a conception of brotherly love that laid the foundations, however unintentionally, for a post-revolutionary ethos of sentimental friendship.[83]

Quaker conceptions of loving friendship were also well attuned to the spirit of sympathetic brotherhood that pervaded post-revolutionary rhetoric. It was entirely fitting and perhaps no coincidence that in the early 1770s—as Americans denounced their abusive parent across the Atlantic and began to envision for themselves a future as brothers within a new, more just, and loving family—colonists had the opportunity to read the recently published sermons of Quaker itinerant John Woolman. According to Woolman, those who closed their hearts to Christ were characterized by a "narrowness" and "selfish spirit" that saw people as having distinct and opposed interests, whereas those inspired by "divine love" embraced "mankind universally" and could "sympathize [even] with strangers." Woolman argued that once people recognized their common identity, they would find true "fellowship one with another" and so "dwell together in unity." Inspired by "brotherly feeling," "sympathy," "tenderness of heart," "pure inward feeling," and "ardent longings" for "the spreading of his kingdom amongst mankind," they would build a just society with "the way opened for a harmonious walking together." The parallels between this argument and attacks on the "unfeeling" British government for its failure to treat American colonists as "brethren" (described toward the end of the previous chapter) cannot have escaped contemporary readers. By no means all supporters of the Revolution would have sympathized with Woolman's application of these broad principles to causes such as the abolition of slavery. But his vision of a harmonious society held together by "brotherly sympathy" accorded well with the credo embraced by the architects of Independence.[84]

Readers today are more likely to associate brotherly love with Quakerism or Philadelphia (the city in which Quakers exerted most influence) than with freemasonry, yet in the late eighteenth century it was the Masonic order that most effectively positioned itself as the epitome of brotherly love and as the model for an affectionate, virtuous, and godly republic. Masons arranged for the publication of sermon after sermon that depicted their version of family values as entirely consonant with the national welfare and God's will. Their fraternity was "not natural [that is, based on blood kinship] but purely elective, depending upon choice." Merging the feelings and loyalties of "friend and brother," it was modeled on "the friendship of David and Jonathan." There could be "no brotherhood," declared these preachers, "no friendship of the true and noblest kind, but what is founded on the fear of God, and a love to religion and virtue." That love engendered "a union of souls more intimate and endearing than anything else." It also had far-reaching social and political implications. "Fraternal affection," embodied in the Masonic order, would become "a leading, fundamental, and comprehensive principle" in all social relations and "would serve greatly to facilitate the practice of every duty, making persons not only good husbands and wives, but good rulers and subjects, citizens and neighbours." Brotherly love would save the republic and redeem humankind.[85]

W E MIGHT SEEM to have come a very long way from John Mifflin's nostalgic stroll through his neighbor's pear grove, remembering the hours of pleasure he had spent there with his dear friends Isaac Norris and James Gibson. Likewise, the declarations of loving devotion that other male friends penned for one another throughout the eighteenth century might strike us as far removed from affairs of state and the lofty ideals of republican ideology. Today we tend to see personal friendship as just that, personal and private. Yet eighteenth-century friends saw the personal and public as tightly interwoven. Recall Joseph Hooper's 1763 letter to his "bosom friend" Benjamin Dolbeare, in which he celebrated "the overflowing of friendship, that noble passion without which there is no pleasure in society, or enjoyment of those blessings with which we are favored in this life." That vivid phrase, "the overflowing of friendship," evoked the effusion of male love into society at large, ennobling the hearts of all those it touched and inspiring in them a spirit of all-encompassing benevolence.[1]

Early Americans assumed that the structure and well-being of society were determined by the dynamics and tone of personal relationships, especially those between family members and also between close friends who saw themselves as elective kinfolk. Americans influenced by the eighteenth-century culture of sensibility believed that a capacity for sympathetic benevolence, nurtured through the intense feelings that bound friends to one another, would enable a new and enlightened sociability. In the aftermath of revolution, cultural architects appropriated that conception of sentimental friendship for political ends: they envisaged a society informed and inspired by loving, benevolent instincts that citizens of the new republic would nurture in one another through the "sympathetic power" of friendship. Thus, the two young friends envisaged by the *Cumberland Gazette* in 1789—strolling "with interlocked arms" through "the pleasant grove," "the essence of benevolence glowing on their cheeks," and "the gleams of participated ecstasy sparkling in their eyes"—embodied not only the modish man of feeling but also the benign, empathetic citizen without whom the new nation could not prosper. Post-revolutionary Americans trusted that ties of love and affection would hold men such as these together in virtuous fraternity, laying an indispensable foundation for high-minded public collaboration. Male friendships, sustained by intense emotional sensibility and shared moral values, would work in tandem with marital friendship to make a republic feasible. Seen from this perspective, post-revolutionary political philosophy was fundamentally an emotional enterprise, a passionate and romantic commitment of the heart.

The ultimate goal of republican ideology was to enable enlightened collaboration between citizens. Post-revolutionary thinkers argued that in order for republicanism to succeed, citizens had to be independent of deferential ties and arbitrary authority, so that they could work together in freedom and a spirit of mutual trust. The abhorrence of dependency that emerges clearly from late eighteenth-century political writings did not translate automatically or immediately into an exaltation of autonomous individualism. The persistent myth that this did happen—establishing individualism as a necessary and central feature of American identity—is clearly belied by the central role that sympathy played in post-revolutionary discourse. Late eighteenth-century commentators predicted that personal independence (by which they meant both individual freedom and landownership) would enable Americans to experience interdependence as citizens in a new way: this new civic identity would be built not upon ties of patronage and dependence but instead upon fundamental equality and loving sympathy. They articulated that vision as a new version of familial politics that was built on fraternal rather than patriarchal principles.

The rhetoric of sympathetic brotherhood that suffuses late eighteenth-century writings should not blind us to the reality of post-revolutionary politics. As we have seen, that vision of republican sympathy excluded many men and women who were deemed not to qualify as truly free and independent. And even among those who did, the hope that fraternal sentiment would transform society and political life turned out to be utterly quixotic. Just as the ethos of brotherly love embraced by Puritans and eighteenth-century evangelicals failed to prevent rancor and division within the religious cultures that they sought to dominate, in the early decades of the republic effusive tributes to fraternal sympathy were often juxtaposed in newspapers with items that reported and expressed the vitriolic spirit of politics in the new nation. Yet however rancorous and divisive political life may have been in the first decades of Independence, many contemporaries did at least aspire to a different spirit of engagement. Their dream of a republic built upon sympathetic brotherhood may have been quixotic, but they dreamt nonetheless. Tragically, as other historians have shown, even the ideal of generous-spirited collaboration within the civic arena would soon give way to a celebration of individualistic competition and self-interested factionalism, much to the horror of some nineteenth-century observers. It was ironic indeed that ideals of sentimental fraternity, which had played such a central role in the founding period, would now find a refuge on the honorable margins of American political discourse, including and especially within the antislavery movement of the early nineteenth century, which challenged Americans to revisit the principles that had inspired Independence and to rethink in fundamental ways what it meant to be a citizen and a brother.[2]

At the same time that ideals of fraternal collaboration lost their place of prominence within the cultural mainstream, sensibility itself came under increasing attack on both sides of the Atlantic. Eighteenth-century advocates of sensibility, including those who believed that the power of sympathy could play a key role in the triumph of North America's republican experiment, had depicted emotion as operating in close alliance with reason. But critics now portrayed the realm of emotion as not only distinct from but even antithetical to rational endeavor. American apologists for sensibility sought to distinguish between "false" sensibility, which indulged uncontrolled emotions at the expense of all else, and "true" sensibility, in which the exercise of affectionate instincts was inseparable from the cultivation of rational and moral capacities. Yet despite this attempt to defend the social utility and respectability of emotional faculties, the culture of sensibility became increasingly suspect in many quarters.[3]

As sympathy and sensibility underwent an often derogatory reformulation into sentiment and sentimentality, they also became associated primarily with women. In the eighteenth century, a capacity for emotion had been depicted as a desirable and indeed essential character trait for men and women alike. But in the early decades of the nineteenth century, as Americans more and more perceived gender in terms of fundamental differences between men and women, sentiment came to be seen as an attribute that belonged naturally to women. That shift was not entirely negative in its implications for women and indeed gave them a new form of authority. Their much-vaunted emotional instincts provided the basis for moral and religious discernment, which in turn made women fitting guardians of morality, not only within the home but also through their involvement in reform societies that sought to rid the world of moral scourges such as alcohol, prostitution, and slavery. The principle of affective association, so crucial to eighteenth-century male friendships and post-revolutionary political ideology, found renewed life in these nineteenth-century reform movements. But that notion of heartfelt collaboration was now seen as a distinct realm dominated by women, closely bound up with assumptions about women's emotional and moral capacities. Such had not been the case in the late eighteenth century, when Americans were encouraged to think that men and women alike should embrace their potential for feeling empathy, working together to build a world in which sympathetic friendship—among men as well as among women and between members of the opposite sex—could align reason with emotion and provide a middle way between selfishness and self-denial, in which love between friends would become "the glory of society and the boast of republicanism."[4]

Male friendships that were to have played such a crucial role in sustaining republican society would come to be seen as dangerous and subversive. Sentimental and physically affectionate friendships between men remained a legitimate and visible part of American manhood through the early and middle decades of the nineteenth century, as men not only wrote of their love for one another but were also photographed in poses that emphasized the warmth, tenderness, and ease of their camaraderie. Yet such feelings became increasingly problematic as the century drew to a close. The Darwinian notion of struggle as the defining characteristic of a man's life fostered an aggressive masculinity that percolated throughout American society and informed imperialistic policies abroad. That new version of manhood had a spiritual component, as proponents of a "muscular Christianity" diverted attention away from tenderhearted images of Jesus Christ to the dictates of a strident and virile faith. This brave new world had little room for the exhibition of sentimental friendship. Meanwhile, the invention by Freud and other sexologists of sexual orientation as a way to understand human attraction, romantic as well as erotic, had profound implications for the acknowledgment and expression of love between men.[5] The subsequent rise of that paradigm to cultural ascendancy made it increasingly difficult for a man to articulate love for a male friend without being suspected of also having sexual feelings for him. Given the stigma attached to sex between males, the expression of love for another man became very risky. Indeed, the principal categories of sexual identity that came to dominate American culture in the twentieth century—heterosexuality and homosexuality—inhibited men (and not just those who identified as heterosexual) from expressing nonsexual love for other men because their feelings might be misread.

The modern notion of sexual identity has enabled men and women who desire people of the same sex to comprehend and express their feelings in ways that were not previously possible. In that sense it has enabled emotional, physical, and social emancipation. But its implications for nonsexual love between men of any sexual orientation have turned out to be profoundly destructive. Love and lust do sometimes go together, but not always: we can lust without loving, and we can love without lusting. Modern Americans have less difficulty with the concept of lusting without loving, but the idea of romantic love without lust seems to perplex many people (less so if a woman declares that she loves another woman, more so if the persons involved are two men or a man and a woman). The letters and journals from which I have quoted throughout this book allow us to glimpse lives sustained and enriched by emotional ties that today seem elusive and even perilous. Early Americans exalted love between men as a personal, public, and spiritual good. This book is in part an elegy for a world of love, and even the possibility of love, that we have sadly lost—let us hope not forever.

NOTES

Introduction

1. Joseph Hooper to Benjamin Dolbeare, 4 September 1763, Dolbeare Family Papers, Massachusetts Historical Society.

2. Leander [John Mifflin], "Journal, Volume 1st," 12 May 1786–11 November 1786, private collection: 13 September 1786. See chapter 1, note 1 below for further discussion of this journal and its provenance.

3. William Wirt to Dabney Carr, 8 June 1804, 1 April 1810, and to Benjamin Edwards, 2 July 1808, Wirt Papers, Maryland Historical Society.

4. Theorists have challenged the model of sexual orientation from a range of perspectives; many young people in the late twentieth and early twenty-first centuries also reject as artificial the clear-cut distinctions on which the homo/heterosexual paradigm depends, invoking instead a more fluid understanding of sexual desire and identity; meanwhile, some Christian denominations insist that our selection of sexual partners results from moral choice and not an innate drive. Yet the basic assumptions underlying this paradigm remain powerful and indeed predominant within our culture. As classical scholar David Halperin has noted, that modern conception of sexuality poses "a significant obstacle to understanding the distinctive features of sexual life in non-western and pre-modern cultures." See David M. Halperin, *One Hundred Years of Homosexuality, and Other Essays on Greek Love* (New York: Routledge, 1990), 18; and Bruce R. Smith, *Homosexual Desire in Shakespeare's England: A Cultural Poetics* (Chicago: University of Chicago Press, 1991), 10–11. For further discussion of the rise to ascendancy of that modern paradigm and its implications, see epilogue.

5. See Richard Godbeer, *Sexual Revolution in Early America* (Baltimore: Johns Hopkins University Press, 2002), esp. 62–71, 113–14, 190–93.

6. To put it another way, if homosexuality and heterosexuality are categories of self-identification, then there were neither homosexuals nor heterosexuals in the eighteenth century.

7. See Richard Godbeer, "Performing Patriarchy: Gendered Roles and Hierarchies in Early Modern England and Seventeenth-Century New England," in *The World of John Winthrop: Essays on England and New England, 1588–1649,* ed. Francis J. Bremer and Lynn A. Botelho (Boston: Massachusetts Historical Society, 2005), 290–333.

8. See, for example, George Haggerty, *Men in Love: Masculinity and Sexuality in the Eighteenth Century* (New York: Columbia University Press, 1999) and Guido Ruggiero, *Machiavelli in Love: Sex, Self, and Society in the Italian Renaissance* (Baltimore: Johns Hopkins University Press, 2007).

9. Most biographers of Alexander Hamilton, for example, either ignore highly suggestive passages in Hamilton's correspondence with John Laurens or insist that their loving friendship must have been entirely nonsexual. As William Benemann quite rightly points out, while there is "no irrefutable proof that Laurens and Hamilton were lovers," there is "sufficient circumstantial evidence to render indefensible any unqualified pronouncement that they were not" (Benemann, *Male-Male Intimacy in Early America: Beyond Romantic Friendships* [New York: Haworth Press, 2006], xii–xiii). Unfortunately Benemann goes on to claim that other male friendships probably did have an erotic component even when there is no evidence at all to suggest sexual attraction, let alone that sexual relations were taking place. See my forthcoming review of his book in *Journal of the History of Sexuality* 18 (May 2009): 2.

10. Lack of urban development also presents a problem for early Americanists who wish to investigate male-male sexuality: across the Atlantic, major metropolitan centers had already produced urban subcultures for men who desired other men, which then attracted attention from contemporaries; the absence of large cities in North America meant that male-male encounters were more diffuse and elusive. Yet drawing on court records, legal and theological commentaries, private journals and correspondence, articles in newspapers and magazines, and literary works either imported for consumption by Americans or produced in North America, recent historians have produced a rapidly expanding scholarship examining same-sex intimacy in the colonial and early national periods. See Louis Crompton, "Homosexuals and the Death Penalty in Colonial America," *Journal of Homosexuality* 1 (1976): 277–93; Jonathan Ned Katz, *Gay American History: Lesbians and Gay Men in the U.S.A.* (New York: Avon Books, 1976); Katz, *Gay/Lesbian Almanac: A New Documentary* (New York: Harper and Row, 1983); Robert F. Oaks, "Perceptions of Homosexuality by Justices of the Peace in Colonial Virginia," *Journal of Homosexuality* 5 (1979–80): 35–41; Oaks, "'Things Fearful to Name': Sodomy and Buggery in Seventeenth-Century New England," *Journal of Social History* 12 (1978): 268–81; Oaks, "Defining Sodomy in Seventeenth-Century Massachusetts," *Journal of Homosexuality* 6 (1981): 79–83; Alan Bray, "To Be a Man in Early Modern Society: The Curious Case of Michael Wigglesworth," *History Workshop Journal* 41 (1996): 155–65; Richard Godbeer, "'The Cry of Sodom': Discourse, Intercourse, and Desire in Colonial New England," *William and Mary Quarterly* 52 (1995): 259–86; Anne G. Myles, "Queering the Study of Early American Sexuality," *William and Mary*

Quarterly 60 (2003): 199–202; Nicholas F. Radel, "A Sodom Within: Historicizing Puritan Homoerotics in the Diary of Michael Wigglesworth," in *The Puritan Origins of American Sex: Religion, Sexuality, and National Identity in American Literature,* ed. Tracy Fessenden, Nicholas F. Radel, and Magdalena J. Zaborowska (New York: Routledge, 2001), 41–55; Colin L. Talley, "Gender and Male Same-Sex Erotic Behavior in British North America in the Seventeenth Century," *Journal of the History of Sexuality* 6 (1996): 385–408; Roger Thompson, "Attitudes towards Homosexuality in the Seventeenth-Century New England Colonies," *Journal of American Studies* 23 (1989): 27–40; Thomas A. Foster, "Antimasonic Satire, Sodomy, and Eighteenth-Century Masculinity in the *Boston Evening Post,*" *William and Mary Quarterly* 60 (2003): 171–84; and Clare A. Lyons, "Mapping an Atlantic Sexual Culture: Homoeroticism in Eighteenth-Century Philadelphia," *William and Mary Quarterly* 60 (2003): 119–54.

11. David Halperin makes a similar point in his introduction to *Love, Sex, Intimacy, and Friendship between Men 1550–1800,* ed. Katherine O'Donnell and Michael O'Rourke (Basingstoke: Palgrave, 2003), 8–11. Historians such as Lillian Faderman and Carroll Smith-Rosenberg have uncovered a world of female friendship that incorporated a broad range of possibilities for emotional and physical intimacy; see Faderman, *Surpassing the Love of Men: Romantic Friendship and Love between Women from the Renaissance to the Present* (New York: William Morrow, 1981); and Smith-Rosenberg, "The Female World of Love and Ritual: Relations between Women in Nineteenth-Century America," in *Disorderly Conduct: Visions of Gender in Victorian America* (New York: Knopf, 1985), 53–76. Scholars of early America have so far paid scant attention to the emotional and romantic ties that bound men together. For exceptions, see Caleb Crain, "Leander, Lorenzo, and Castalio: An Early American Romance," *Early American Literature* 33 (1998): 6–38, reworked as *American Sympathy: Men, Friendship, and Literature in the New Nation* (New Haven, Conn.: Yale University Press, 2001), chap. 1; and Michael Warner, "New English Sodom," in *Queering the Renaissance,* ed. Jonathan Goldberg (Durham, N.C.: Duke University Press, 1994), 330–58. Anthony Rotundo and Donald Yacovone have both commented on the importance of male friendship in the eighteenth century, though they each focus on the nineteenth; their pioneering and insightful scholarship has been an important source of inspiration for this project. See E. Anthony Rotundo, *American Manhood: Transformations in Masculinity from the Revolution to the Modern Era* (New York: Basic Books, 1993); Donald Yacovone, "'Surpassing the Love of Women': Victorian Manhood and the Language of Fraternal Love," in *A Shared Experience: Men, Women, and the History of Gender,* ed. Laura McCall and Donald Yacovone (New York: New York University Press, 1998),

195–221; and Yacovone, "Abolitionists and the 'Language of Fraternal Love,'" in *Meanings for Manhood: Constructions of Masculinity in Victorian America*, ed. Mark C. Carnes and Clyde Griffen (Chicago: University of Chicago Press, 1990), 85–95.

12. As Alan Bray has pointed out, "[t]he inability to conceive of relationships in other than sexual terms says something of contemporary poverty; or, to put the point more precisely, the effect of a shaping concern with sexuality is precisely to obscure that wider frame" (*The Friend* [Chicago: University of Chicago Press, 2003], 6). Ivy Schweitzer makes a similar point: "Without denying the erotic and sexual potential of friendship," we should recognize that "a very different logic guided its understandings in this period." That logic "enabled an array of social and political relations that critics have frequently overlooked" (*Perfecting Friendship: Politics and Affiliation in Early American Literature* [Chapel Hill: University of North Carolina Press, 2006], 6). For recent scholarship on early modern male friendship, see Bray, *The Friend*, including the author's insightful "Afterword: Historians and Friendship," 307–23; O'Donnell and O'Rourke, *Love, Sex, Intimacy, and Friendship;* Haggerty, *Men in Love;* Raymond Stephanson, "'Epicoene Friendship': Understanding Male Friendship in the Early Eighteenth Century, with Some Speculations about Pope," *The Eighteenth Century: Theory and Interpretation* 38 (1997): 151–70; Bruce R. Smith, *Homosexual Desire in Shakespeare's England: A Cultural Poetics* (Chicago: University of Chicago Press, 1991); David Robinson, "Unravelling the 'Cord Which Ties Good Men to Good Men': Male Friendship in Richardson's Novels," in *Samuel Richardson: Tercentenary Essays*, ed. Margaret Anne Doody and Peter Sabor (New York: Cambridge University Press, 1989); and Eve Kosofsky Sedgwick, *Between Men: English Literature and Male Homosexual Desire* (New York: Columbia University Press, 1985). See also Christopher Craft, *Another Kind of Love: Male Homosexual Desire in English Discourse, 1850–1920* (Berkeley: University of California Press, 1994); Linda Dowling, *Hellenism and Homosexuality in Victorian Oxford* (Ithaca, N.Y.: Cornell University Press, 1994); Robert Aldrich, *The Seduction of the Mediterranean: Writing, Art, and Homosexual Fantasy* (New York: Routledge, 1993); and Richard Dellamora, *Masculine Desire: The Sexual Politics of Victorian Aestheticism* (Chapel Hill: University of North Carolina Press, 1990).

Nineteenth-century Americanists have also written insightfully about male friendship and love during that period. See Anya Jabour, "Male Friendship and Masculinity in the Early National South: William Wirt and His Friends," *Journal of the Early Republic* 20 (2000): 83–111; Yacovone, "'Surpassing the Love of Women'"; Yacovone, "Abolitionists and the 'Language of Fraternal Love'"; Samuel J. Watson, "Flexible Gender Roles during the Market Revolution: Family, Friendship, Marriage, and Masculinity among U.S. Army Officers, 1815–1846," *Journal of Social History* 29 (1995): 81–106; Rotundo, *American Manhood;* Karen V. Hansen, "'Our Eyes Behold Each Other': Masculinity and Intimate Friendship in Antebellum New England," in *Men's Friendships,* ed. Peter M. Nardi, (Newbury Park, Calif.: Sage Publications, 1992), 35–58; Robert K. Martin, "Knights-Errant and Gothic Seducers: The Representation of Male Friendship in Mid-Nineteenth-Century America," in *Hidden from History: Reclaiming the Gay and Lesbian Past,* ed. Martin Duberman, Martha Vicinus, and George Chauncey Jr. (New York: NAL Books, 1989), 169–82; Jeffrey Richards, "'Passing the Love of Women': Manly Love and Victorian Society," in *Manliness and Morality: Middle-Class Masculinity in Britain and America, 1800–1940,* ed. J. A. Mangan and James Walvin (Manchester, U.K.: Manchester University Press, 1987), 92–122; and Drew Gilpin Faust, *A Sacred Circle: The Dilemma of the Intellectual in the Old South, 1840–1860* (Baltimore: Johns Hopkins University Press, 1977).

13. Alan Bray, for example, discusses "dark suggestions of sodomy" in Elizabethan literary representations of male friendship in "Homosexuality and the Signs of Male Friendship in Elizabethan England," in *Queering the Renaissance,* ed. Jonathan Goldberg (Durham, N.C.: Duke University Press, 1994), 40–61 (quotation, 49).

14. See Alan Bray and Michel Rey, "The Body of the Friend: Continuity and Change in Masculine Friendship in the Seventeenth Century," in *English Masculinities, 1660–1800,* ed. Tim Hitchcock and Michele Cohen (New York: Longman, 1999), esp. 80. Bray discusses the emergence of this subculture in *Homosexuality in Renaissance England* (London: Gay Men's Press, 1982), chap. 4; see also Rictor Norton, *Mother Clap's Molly House: The Gay Subculture in England, 1700–1830* (London: Gay Men's Press, 1992). Randolph Trumbach argues that the emergence of the adult effeminate sodomite as a "third gender" had profound implications for the ways in which other men perceived and enacted their own versions of manhood as they sought to distinguish themselves from this new effeminate persona; see his *Sex and the Gender Revolution: Heterosexuality and the Third Gender in Enlightenment London* (Chicago: University of Chicago Press, 1998).

15. See Foster, "Antimasonic Satire," 171–84; and Lyons, "Mapping an Atlantic Sexual Culture," 152.

16. Ezekiel Dodge to Robert Treat Paine, 15 January 1749, in *The Papers of Robert Treat Paine,* 3 vols., ed. Stephen T. Riley and Edward W. Hanson (Boston: Massachusetts Historical Society, 1992), 1:40–41; Thomas Wait to George Thatcher, 15 April 1789, Thomas B. Wait Papers, Massachusetts Historical Society. Michael Warner's essay, "New English Sodom," has alerted us to the impor-

tance of biblical models for male friendship in the context of Puritan New England. David S. Shields reminds us that educated men and women in British America had a lively interest in and were much indebted to classical literature; see his *Civil Tongues and Polite Letters in British America* (Chapel Hill: University of North Carolina Press, 1997), esp. xxi–xxiv.

17. See especially James Daly, *Sir Robert Filmer and English Political Thought* (Toronto: University of Toronto Press, 1979); Susan Dwyer Amussen, *An Ordered Society: Gender and Class in Early Modern England* (New York: Blackwell, 1988); Edmund S. Morgan, *The Puritan Family: Religion and Domestic Relations in Seventeenth-Century New England* (1944; New York: Harper and Row, 1966); John Demos, *A Little Commonwealth: Family Life in Plymouth Colony* (New York: Oxford University Press, 1970); Gordon J. Schochet, *Patriarchalism in Political Thought: The Authoritarian Family and Political Speculation and Attitudes, Especially in Seventeenth-Century New England* (New York: Basic Books, 1975); and Mary Beth Norton, *Founding Mothers and Fathers: Gendered Power and the Forming of American Society* (New York: Knopf, 1996). As Edmund Morgan has shown, intermarriage among those of similar faith created tribal networks that translated assertions of spiritual kinship into flesh and blood (Morgan, *Puritan Family*, chap. 7).

18. See Naomi Tadmor's important book, *Family and Friends in Eighteenth-Century England* (New York: Cambridge University Press, 2001), and also Anne S. Lombard, *Making Manhood: Growing Up Male in Colonial New England* (Cambridge, Mass.: Harvard University Press, 2003), 54.

19. For an interesting example of this conflation in a late medieval English context, see Alan Bray, "A Traditional Rite for Blessing Friendship," in O'Donnell and O'Rourke, *Love, Sex, Intimacy, and Friendship*, 88–89.

20. See Lisa Jardine, "Companionate Marriage versus Male Friendship: Anxiety for the Lineal Family in Jacobean Drama," in *Political Culture and Cultural Politics in Early Modern England*, ed. Susan D. Amussen and Mark A. Kishlansky (Manchester, U.K.: Manchester University Press, 1995), 234–54; Linda Woodbridge, *Women and the English Renaissance: Literature and the Nature of Womankind, 1540–1620* (Urbana: University of Illinois Press, 1984), 237–39; and Elizabeth A. Foyster, *Manhood in Early Modern England: Honour, Sex, and Marriage* (New York: Longman, 1999), 125–30.

21. Anya Jabour, *Marriage in the Early Republic: Elizabeth and William Wirt and the Companionate Ideal* (Baltimore: Johns Hopkins University Press, 1998), 5; Jabour, "Male Friendship and Masculinity."

22. Bray, *The Friend*, 2; see also 6: "The ethics of friendship operated persuasively only in a larger frame of reference that lay *outside* the good of the individuals for whom the friendship was made." Bray argues that during the course of

the eighteenth century Locke's conception of "civil society" began to eclipse an older model of society and politics that interwove public and private; see 212–19, and also Norton, *Founding Mothers and Fathers*, 5, 11. I argue that alongside this new way of thinking an older unified worldview, in which ties of family and friendship informed modes of public identity and action, still had enormous influence in American society throughout the eighteenth century.

23. The increasing predominance of affect within friendship is discussed below in chapter 5. Bray notes that within an early modern frame of reference the practical benefits of friendship ceased to be legitimate if they became a primary and mercenary motivation, rather than part of a mutually caring relationship that included looking after one another's interests (Bray, "Homosexuality and the Signs of Male Friendship," 50–51).

24. This paragraph is indebted to Martha Tomhave Blauvelt, *The Work of the Heart: Young Women and Emotion, 1780–1830* (Charlottesville: University of Virginia Press, 2007); Arlie Russell Hochschild, "Emotion Work, Feeling Rules, and Social Structure," *American Journal of Sociology* 85 (1979): 551–75; and Hochschild, *The Managed Heart: Commercialization of Human Feeling* (Berkeley: University of California Press, 1983). See also Nicole Eustace, *Passion Is the Gale: Emotion, Power, and the Coming of the American Revolution* (Chapel Hill: University of North Carolina Press, 2008), including and especially her thoughtful appendix, "Toward a Lexicon of Eighteenth-Century Emotion" (481–86). For the eighteenth-century culture of sympathy and sensibility, see Janet Todd, *Sensibility: An Introduction* (New York: Methuen, 1986); John Mullan, *Sentiment and Sociability: The Language of Feeling in the Eighteenth Century* (Oxford: Clarendon Press, 1988); and G. J. Barker-Benfield, *The Culture of Sensibility: Sex and Society in Eighteenth-Century Britain* (Chicago: University of Chicago Press, 1992).

25. Caleb Crain and Julie Ellison also highlight the interconnections between male and female friendships; see Julie Ellison, *Cato's Tears and the Making of Anglo-American Emotion* (Chicago: University of Chicago Press, 1999); and Crain, *American Sympathy*, esp. 32. Carroll Smith-Rosenberg, however, argues that the realm of female friendship was "a world in which men made but a shadowy appearance"; Smith-Rosenberg, "The Female World of Love and Ritual," 53.

26. Biological brotherhood could itself become a hostile relationship, especially in families where parental adherence to primogeniture fostered resentment between male siblings. But early Americans saw elective brotherhood as redeeming fraternity in particular as well as male association in general through the power of sympathy. This perspective contradicts the stereotype perpetuated by scholars such as Joan R. Gunderson, who argues that "[a]s men created a competitive culture for themselves (separate from women) in politics, taverns,

and clubs, women sought each other's support and comfort"; Gunderson, *To Be Useful to the World: Women in Revolutionary America, 1740–1790* (New York: Twayne, 1996), 141.

27. Indeed, affective association became an important means through which men created communities of scientific enquiry and also religious faith across national boundaries and vast distances. See, for example, Susan Scott Parrish, *American Curiosity: Cultures of Natural History in the Colonial British Atlantic World* (Chapel Hill: University of North Carolina Press, 2006).

28. I was first prompted to think about the relationship between male friendships and republican sociability by three very different essays, Caleb Crain's "Leander, Lorenzo, and Castalio"; Michael Warner's "New English Sodom"; and Rosemary Zagarri's "Morals, Manners, and the Republican Mother," *American Quarterly* 44 (1992): 192–215. I have also learned much from my encounters with Ellison, *Cato's Tears*, and Schweitzer, *Perfecting Friendship*. Lynn Hunt explores the implications of fraternal imagery for revolutionary politics in *The Family Romance of the French Revolution* (Berkeley: University of California Press, 1992).

29. Israel Cheever to Robert Treat Paine, 27 July 1749, in Riley and Hanson, *Papers of Robert Treat Paine*, 1:58.

Chapter One: "The Friend of My Bosom"

1. Leander [John Mifflin], "Journal, Volume 1st," 12 May 1786–11 November 1786 [hereafter Leander's Journal, 1], 3, 4 September 1786, private collection. I am grateful to Caleb Crain for his generosity in sharing with me a photocopy of this journal. He and I agree—based on analysis of the handwriting, prose style, and content—that this privately owned manuscript journal is in fact the genuine precursor to the second volume of Leander's journal, which is owned by the Historical Society of Pennsylvania (see below). I am also much indebted to Crain's essay, "Leander, Lorenzo, and Castalio: An Early American Romance," *Early American Literature* 33 (1998): 6–38, revised as chap. 1 of Crain, *American Sympathy: Men, Friendship, and Literature in the New Nation* (New Haven, Conn.: Yale University Press, 2001), which contains much information about John Mifflin, James Gibson, and Isaac Norris, along with their families and social circle.

2. Leander's Journal, 1: 4 September 1786.

3. For the use of literary nicknames by genteel eighteenth-century Americans, see Crain, *American Sympathy*, 24; and David S. Shields, *Civil Tongues and Polite Letters in British America* (Chapel Hill: University of North Carolina Press, 1997), 263–64.

4. Mary Dickinson to Isaac Norris, 2 February 1790, Norris Papers, Historical Society of Pennsylvania [hereafter HSP].

5. Deborah Norris Logan to Isaac Norris, 7 August 1783, Norris Papers.

6. Mary Parker Norris to Isaac Norris, 7 August 1784, Norris Papers; Mary Dickinson to Isaac Norris, n.d., ibid.; Mary Parker Norris to Isaac Norris, 3 June 1785, ibid.

7. Isaac Norris to Deborah Norris Logan, 18 April 1784, 5 March 1785, 12 March 1786, Robert R. Logan Collection, box 12, folder 10, HSP.

8. Mary Dickinson to Isaac Norris, n.d., Norris Papers; Mary Parker Norris to Isaac Norris, 12 March, 8 April, 3 June, 28 October 1785, and postscript by John Mifflin at bottom of Mary Parker Norris to Isaac Norris, 22 December 1785, Norris Papers.

9. Leander [John Mifflin], "Journal, Volume 2nd," 12 November 1786–11 May 1787 [hereafter Leander's Journal, 2], bound with Lorenzo [James Gibson]'s Journal and catalogued as James Gibson, "Journal of Lorenzo and Leander" Am. O69, HSP: 3 January 1787.

10. Mary Parker Norris to Isaac Norris, 29 August 1785, Norris Papers; Mary Parker Norris to Charles Thomson, 16 May 1786, Maria Dickinson Logan Papers, HSP.

11. Hannah Thomson to John Mifflin, 26 May, 12 December 1786, manuscript collection, Yi2 7295 F, Library Company of Philadelphia.

12. Leander's Journal, 1: 31 May 1786; 2: 14 March 1787.

13. Leander's Journal, 1: 14, 31 May, 1, 13 June 1786.

14. Ibid., 21, 22 July 1786.

15. Ibid., 26 July 1786.

16. Ibid., 30 August, 3, 4 September 1786.

17. Ibid., 5 September 1786.

18. Ibid., 20, 26 September 1786, and Deborah Norris Logan, *The Norris House* (Philadelphia: Fair-Hill Press, 1867), 1, 6; see also Elizabeth McLean, "Town and Country Gardens in Eighteenth-Century Philadelphia," in *British and American Gardens in the Eighteenth Century: Eighteen Illustrated Essays on Garden History,* ed. Robert P. Maccubbin and Peter Martin (Williamsburg, Va.: Colonial Williamsburg Foundation, 1984), 136–47.

19. Leander's Journal, 2: 23, 24 February 1787.

20. Leander's Journal, 1: 24 September 1786.

21. Joseph Norris to Deborah Norris Logan, 4 February 1786, Robert R. Logan Collection. For Isaac's conversion, see Mary Parker Norris to Isaac Norris, 30 October 1784, Norris Papers, and Leander's Journal, 1: 24 September 1786.

22. Leander's Journal, 1: 23 September 1786; 2: 20 January, 5 April 1787.

23. Leander's Journal, 2: 26 November 1786, 20 January 1787; Mary Parker Norris to Charles Thomson, 15 November 1787, Maria Dickinson Logan Papers.

24. Leander's Journal, 2: 16, 17, 26 February, 2 March 1787.

25. Mary Parker Norris to Isaac Norris, 28 October 1785, Norris Papers; Leander's Journal, 2: 14 March 1787.

26. Leander's Journal, 2: 14 March 1787.

27. Caleb Crain notes that Mifflin's tendency to lecture Gibson about his foibles matches the tone of the narrator in *The Complaint* toward this particular character. It is, of course, possible that Mifflin chose the nickname. See Crain, *American Sympathy*, 25–26.

28. Lorenzo [James Gibson], "Journal," 6 February 1786–1 October 1786 [hereafter Lorenzo's Journal], 4 August 1786, bound with Leander [John Mifflin]'s Journal and catalogued as James Gibson, "Journal of Lorenzo and Leander" Am. O69, HSP; Leander's Journal, 1: 7, 13 September 1786.

29. Leander's Journal, 1: 2 June, 25, 26, 27 July 1786; 2: 12 January 1787. Richard Bushman points out in *The Refinement of America: Persons, Houses, Cities* (New York: Knopf, 1992) that the garden was "an extension of the parlor, a place where polite people walked and conversed" (130).

30. Leander's Journal, 1: 26 August 1786.

31. Ibid., 3, 4, 10 June 1786.

32. Ibid., 12, 13, 14, 18 June 1786.

33. Ibid., 10 November 1786; Leander's Journal, 2: 10, 23 December 1786, 7 March 1787.

34. Lorenzo's Journal, 1 August 1786; Leander's Journal, 1: 16 August, 7 September 1786.

35. Leander's Journal, 1: 27 September 1786.

36. Ibid., 12, 13, 15, 17, 20 May 1786.

37. Ibid., 28 May 1786.

38. Ibid., 29 July, 2 August 1786.

39. Ibid., 13, 17 August 1786; Lorenzo's Journal, 15 August 1786.

40. Leander's Journal, 1: 12 August 1786; 2: 11 May 1787.

41. Leander's Journal, 1: 23, 24, 25, 26 May 1786.

42. Lorenzo's Journal, 14 June, 15 August 1786.

43. Leander's Journal, 1: 24, 25 June, 17 August, 7, 8 September 1786.

44. Ibid., 13, 15 September 1786.

45. Ibid., 15, 21 September 1786; Leander's Journal, 2: 25 December 1786.

46. Leander's Journal, 1: 25, 26, 27 July 1786.

47. Lorenzo's Journal, 27 June, 18, 24, 28 July 1786.

48. Leander's Journal, 1: 29 July 1786; Lorenzo's Journal, 29 July 1786.

49. Lorenzo's Journal, 31 July 1786; Leander's Journal, 1: 31 July, 1 August 1786.

50. Leander's Journal, 1: 1 August 1786.

51. Ibid.; Lorenzo's Journal, 1 August 1786. John seems to have told James, either in this letter or on another occasion, that he resented the time his friend spent with other students. A few days after his return to Philadelphia, John received "an old letter" from James "informing me (and oh! how consolatory) that I need not labor under any apprehensions from him on the score of rivalship" (Leander's Journal, 1: 25 August 1786).

52. Leander's Journal, 1: 2, 3, 4 August 1786; Lorenzo's Journal, 1, 2, 3, 4 August 1786.

53. Lorenzo's Journal, 5, 6 August 1786; Leander's Journal, 1: 8, 10, 15 August 1786.

54. Lorenzo's Journal, 19 August 1786; Leander's Journal, 1: 19 August 1786.

55. Leander's Journal, 1: 20, 21, 22 August 1786; Lorenzo's Journal, 22 August 1786.

56. Nor was it unusual for courting couples to spend the night together, for which custom see Richard Godbeer, *Sexual Revolution in Early America* (Baltimore: Johns Hopkins University Press, 2002), 245–55.

57. Leander's Journal, 1: 1 August, 11 October 1786; 2: 8 April 1787.

58. Lorenzo's Journal, 29, 30 September 1786; Leander's Journal, 1: 29, 30 September 1786.

59. Leander's Journal, 1: 6, 29 October, 1 November 1786.

60. Ibid., 6 October 1786; Leander's Journal, 2: 12, 13, 14, 15 November 1786.

61. Leander's Journal, 2: 29, 30 November 1786.

62. Ibid., 13 February 1787.

63. Ibid., 3 January 1787.

64. Leander's Journal, 1: 22 September 1786.

65. Lorenzo's Journal, 21 August 1786.

66. Crain notes this possibility in *American Sympathy*, 34.

67. John Rhea Smith, "Journal at Nassau Hall," 1 January 1786–22 September 1786: 19 January, 12, 17 August, 4 September 1786, General Manuscripts Bound, C0199, no. 518, Firestone Rare Books and Manuscripts Library, Princeton University.

68. Leander's Journal, 2: 9 December 1786.

69. Leander's Journal, 1: 2 September 1786.

70. Ibid., 2, 20 September 1786.

71. Ibid., 4 September 1786; Lorenzo's Journal, 1 September 1786.

72. Leander's Journal, 1: 7, 8, 20 September 1786.

73. Ibid., 5, 7, 8 September 1786.

74. Ibid., 27 September, 5 October 1786.

75. Ibid., 7, 30 September, 5 October 1786.

76. Ibid., 27 May 1786; Leander's Journal, 2: 26 December 1786.

77. Deborah Norris to Sally Fisher, n.d., Corbit-Higgins-Spruance Papers, Historical Society of Delaware; transcribed in John A. H. Sweeney, ed., "The Norris-Fisher Correspondence: A Circle of Friends, 1779–82," *Delaware History* 6 (1955): 215, 217. According to the *Oxford English Dictionary*, this use of the word "platonic" first appears in the seventeenth century.

78. Leander's Journal, 2: 31 January 1787.

79. Ibid., 23, 24, 28 February 1787.

80. Ibid., 5, 19, 22, 24 March 1787.

81. Ibid., 2, 10, 14 March 1787. Susan Scott Parrish argues that eighteenth-century male naturalists, whose letters were filled with "love and longing" for one another, did all they could to disassociate their naturalist endeavors from the "impure love of women." See Susan Scott Parrish, *American Curiosity: Cultures of Natural History in the Colonial British Atlantic World* (Chapel Hill: University of North Carolina Press, 2006), 166–68. Yet as Mifflin's courtship of Maria shows, the intertwining of botanical and romantic interests could manifest itself in the courtship of women as well as in male friendships.

82. Leander's Journal, 2: 19, 20 March 1787.

83. Ibid., 19 March 1787.

84. Ibid., 27 February 1787. Other relatives and friends who nurtured Mifflin's loving relationships with young men also saw no reason why these should not be compatible with romantic attachments to young women. Mifflin wrote that during one of his visits to New York, the Thomsons, who actively encouraged his close friendship with Isaac Norris, "wish[ed] to mark the progress of my attachments" and "asked after dinner" if there was any "jeune demoiselle" by whose "charms" he was currently smitten (Leander's Journal, 1: 14 August 1786).

85. Leander's Journal, 2: 14 March, 13 April 1787.

86. Ibid., 14, 17, 29 March 1787.

87. See Godbeer, *Sexual Revolution in Early America*, chap. 7.

88. Leander's Journal, 2: 26 February, 12, 13 April 1787.

89. Ibid., 31 January 1787.

90. John Mifflin to Anne Penn, 10 November 1789, John Mifflin's Letter Book, 1788–1802, Penn Collection, HSP. It is true that one of the reasons for Mifflin's failure to join Norris in Europe was that his father (a shadowy figure in his son's journal and letters) refused to endorse the plan, but there could have been any number of reasons for this. Following Isaac's return from Europe, dark rumors about Isaac (the precise nature of which Mifflin did not specify in his

journal) spread throughout the city, much to the distress of Isaac's family and friends (see Leander's Journal, 2: 26 December 1786, 4, 24 January 1787). But it seems much more likely that they were inspired by his newfound Catholic faith than that they related to his close friendship with Mifflin, particularly given the lack of comments expressing concern about that friendship in family correspondence.

Chapter Two: "A Settled Portion of My Happiness"

1. Daniel Webster to George Herbert, 20 December 1798, in *The Writings and Speeches of Daniel Webster*, 18 vols., ed. J. W. McIntyre (Boston: Little, Brown, 1903), 17:71.

2. Daniel Webster to George Herbert, 20 December 1798, in McIntyre, *Writings and Speeches of Daniel Webster*, 17:71; Webster to James Bingham, 11 February 1800, 14 June, 26 October 1801, 18 May, 22 July, 21 December 1802, 22 February, 23 December 1803, 7 December 1805, in ibid., 80, 82, 90, 97, 107, 112, 119, 128, 132, 153–54, 219.

3. Daniel Webster to James Bingham, 28 December 1800, 17 January, 26 October, 8 December 1801, 3 April 1804, 2 January 1805, in McIntyre, *Writings and Speeches of Daniel Webster*, 17: 84, 87, 95, 100, 164, 198. In *The Converse of the Pen: Acts of Intimacy in the Eighteenth-Century Familiar Letter* (Chicago: University of Chicago Press, 1986), Bruce Redford describes the letter writer as "a magician-actor who works on his audience by sustaining the illusion of physical presence" (7).

4. Daniel Webster to Thomas Merrill, 1 May 1804, 14 May 1805, in McIntyre, *Writings and Speeches of Daniel Webster*, 17: 166–67, 208.

5. E. Anthony Rotundo argues in *American Manhood: Transformations in Masculinity from the Revolution to the Modern Era* (New York: Basic Books, 1993) that close male friendships in the early national period were mostly limited to early adulthood; for studies that emphasize the potential for such friendships to last much longer, see Drew Gilpin Faust, *A Sacred Circle: The Dilemma of the Intellectual in the Old South, 1840–1860* (Baltimore: Johns Hopkins University Press, 1977), esp. 15–17, 42–44; Donald Yacovone, "Abolitionists and the 'Language of Fraternal Love,'" in *Meanings for Manhood: Constructions of Masculinity in Victorian America*, ed. Mark C. Carnes and Clyde Griffen (Chicago: University of Chicago Press, 1990), 85–95; Samuel J. Watson, "Flexible Gender Roles during the Market Revolution: Family, Friendship, Marriage, and Masculinity among U.S. Army Officers, 1815–1846," *Journal of Social History* 29 (1995): esp. 89–91; and Anya Jabour, "Male Friendship and Masculinity in the Early National South: William Wirt and His Friends," *Journal of the Early Republic* 20 (2000):

83–111. Carroll Smith-Rosenberg argues that many female friendships "lasted with undiminished, indeed often increased, intensity throughout the women's lives" in "The Female World of Love and Ritual: Relations between Women in Nineteenth-Century America," in *Disorderly Conduct: Visions of Gender in Victorian America* (New York: Knopf, 1985), 73; see also 53, 56, 68.

6. See Smith-Rosenberg, "The Female World of Love and Ritual," 66–67. Francis J. Bremer stresses the importance of friendships formed at college in his examination of the affectionate ties that bound Puritans together in *Congregational Communion: Clerical Friendship in the Anglo-American Puritan Community, 1610–1692* (Boston: Northeastern University Press, 1994): "Then as now, the university was a turning point for young lives, a place where men formulated their ideals, set their goals, and made friendships to last a lifetime" (40).

7. William Livingston to Noah Welles, 13 October 1744, 24 July 1745, 10 February 1746, 28 September 1751, Johnson Family Papers, Yale University Library. Livingston would later purchase a country estate in New Jersey, whence he retired from legal affairs in 1772. After serving in the continental congresses and as commander-in-chief of the state militia, he became New Jersey's governor, a position he held until his death in 1790. Welles continued as pastor in Stamford until his death in 1776. Both men married, and both had thirteen children. For biographical information about Livingston and Welles, see Franklin Bowditch Dexter, *Biographical Sketches of the Graduates of Yale College, with Annals of the College History, October 1701–May 1745* (New York: Henry Holt, 1885), 682–86, 693–95.

8. William Livingston to Noah Welles, 9 December 1745, 17 November 1746, 14 February 1750, Johnson Family Papers, Yale University Library.

9. Israel Cheever to Robert Treat Paine, 27 July 1749, in *The Papers of Robert Treat Paine,* 3 vols., ed. Stephen T. Riley and Edward Hanson (Boston: Massachusetts Historical Society, 1992), 1:57–58; Ellis Gray to Benjamin Dolbeare, 3 September 1763, 16 April, 3 May 1764, Dolbeare Family Papers, Massachusetts Historical Society.

10. William Smith Shaw to Arthur Maynard Walter, 4 February, 2 March, 20 April, n.d., 2, 11 June 1803, Boston Athenaeum.

11. Joseph Stevens Buckminster to William Smith Shaw, 22 February 1807, and Shaw to Buckminster, 13 May 1807, quoted in Josiah Quincy, *The History of the Boston Athenaeum* (Cambridge, Mass., 1851), 18–19.

12. Thomas Wait to George Thatcher, 14 March, 15 April 1789, 28 May 1809, 26 October 1812, Thomas B. Wait Papers, Massachusetts Historical Society.

13. Daniel Webster to Thomas Merrill, 1 May 1804, in McIntyre, *Writings and Speeches of Daniel Webster,* 17:166; William Wirt to William Pope, 5 August 1803, Wirt Papers, Maryland Historical Society; Wirt to Dabney Carr, 1 April

1810, ibid; Wirt to Carr, 10 June 1814, Library of Virginia. Anya Jabour discusses Wirt's friendships in "Male Friendship and Masculinity."

14. Ezekiel Dodge to Robert Treat Paine, 5 May 1747, in Riley and Hanson, *Papers of Robert Treat Paine*, 1:12–13.

15. John Randolph to Henry Rutledge, quoted in William Cabell Bruce, *John Randolph of Roanoke, 1773–1833*, 2 vols. (New York: G. P. Putnam's Sons, 1922), 1: 127, 135.

16. Leander's Journal, 1: 6 October 1786; Israel Cheever to Robert Treat Paine, 27 July 1749, in Riley and Hanson, *Papers of Robert Treat Paine*, 1:58; William Wirt to Dabney Carr, 19 March 1802, Wirt Papers, Maryland Historical Society. William Benemann castigates Anya Jabour for holding back from the conclusion that the language used in letters written by William Wirt and his male friends "impl[ies] actual sexual relations" (*Male-Male Intimacy in Early America: Beyond Romantic Friendships* [New York: Haworth Press, 2006], 16). Jabour does acknowledge that a few of these early nineteenth-century letters "contained erotic overtones," but as she points out, the letters between these men "give no indication that their prized reunions included sexual intimacy" (Jabour, "Male Friendship and Masculinity," 93). Benemann goes on to declare that Jabour's "reticence stems from a reluctance to make definitive statements about the past which are unsupported by surviving evidence," and that "proper interpretation of ambiguous language" is the only alternative to leaving the subject of male-male intimacy "unexplored" (*Male-Male Intimacy in Early America*, 16). Many historians will be deeply disturbed by the notion that one should feel justified in making "definitive statements about the past which are unsupported by surviving evidence." It is surely disingenuous to claim that we face a stark choice between doing so and leaving topics such as this "unexplored." There is a middle way that involves unabashed but circumspect presentation of evidence. Acknowledging that the language used by Wirt might perhaps indicate sexual attraction on his part is one thing, but to conclude that this "impl[ies] actual sexual relations" is quite another.

17. Virgil Maxcy to William Blanding, 1 January 1800, Blanding Family Papers, Massachusetts Historical Society.

18. Thomas Wait to George Thatcher, 5 January 1810, 20, 22 December 1813, 20 March 1821, Thomas B. Wait Papers, Massachusetts Historical Society.

19. *The New Universal Letter-Writer, or, Complete Art of Polite Correspondence* (Philadelphia, 1800), 192; Thomas Wait to George Thatcher, 14 March, 15 April, 16 July 1789, 17 June, 20 November 1811, Thomas B. Wait Papers, Massachusetts Historical Society.

20. William Wirt to Dabney Carr, 8 June 1804, 1 April 1810, Wirt Papers,

Maryland Historical Society; Wirt to Carr, 9 September 1824, Library of Virginia.

21. William Wirt to Dabney Carr, 7 April 1816, Wirt Papers, Maryland Historical Society; Wirt to Carr, 25 December 1833, Wirt Letters and Papers, Southern Historical Collection, Wilson Library, University of North Carolina at Chapel Hill.

22. William Wirt to Dabney Carr, 16 January 1804, Wirt Papers, Maryland Historical Society; William Wirt to Littleton Tazewell, 23 September 1811, Tazewell Papers, Library of Virginia.

23. William Wirt to Peachy Gilmer, 17 January 1804, Wirt Papers, Maryland Historical Society; Wirt to Benjamin Edwards, 2 July 1808, ibid.; Wirt to William Pope, 18 January 1818, ibid.; Wirt to St. George Tucker, 18 January 1820, ibid.

24. William Wirt to Dabney Carr, 9 September 1824, Library of Virginia; Wirt to Carr, n.d., enclosed in letter dated 31 March 1813, Wirt Papers, Maryland Historical Society.

25. William Wirt to Dabney Carr, 9 October 1830, Library of Virginia; Wirt to Carr, 16 January 1804, 23 August 1813, 15 February 1814, Wirt Papers, Maryland Historical Society.

26. William Wirt to Dabney Carr, 15 January 1814, Library of Virginia; Wirt to Carr, 6 May 1818, 25 December 1833, Wirt Letters and Papers, Southern Historical Collection, Wilson Library, University of North Carolina, Chapel Hill; Wirt to Carr, 10 August 1822, 23 March 1831; Wirt to Peachy Gilmer, 3 September 1832, Wirt Papers, Maryland Historical Society.

27. William Smith Shaw to Arthur Maynard Walter, 4 February, 2 March 1803, Boston Atheneum; Daniel Webster to George Herbert, 20 December 1798, in McIntyre, *Writings and Speeches of Daniel Webster,* 17:71–72; Jeremy Belknap's Commonplace Books, vol. A, 20, Belknap Papers, Massachusetts Historical Society; William Wirt to Dabney Carr, 8 June 1804, Wirt Papers, Maryland Historical Society; Wirt to Carr, 25 May 1819, Wirt Letters and Papers, Southern Historical Collection, Wilson Library, University of North Carolina at Chapel Hill; Wirt to Carr, 9 September 1824, Library of Virginia.

28. *Cicero's Epistles to Atticus,* trans. William Guthrie (London, 1752), 1:ii–iii. I am grateful to Benemann, *Male-Male Intimacy in Early America,* 26, for drawing my attention to this passage. For depictions of friendship in late eighteenth-century and early nineteenth-century school texts, see also Cynthia Koch, "The Virtuous Curriculum: School Books and American Culture, 1785–1830" (PhD diss., University of Pennsylvania, 1991), esp. 98.

29. William Livingston to Noah Welles, 24 January 1746, 16 December 1751, Johnson Family Papers, Yale University Library.

30. Ibid., 6 October 1745, 13, 24 January, 26 May 1746.

31. Ibid., 14 November 1743, 9 December 1745, 13 January 1746, 14 October 1748.

32. See Laurel Thatcher Ulrich, *Good Wives: Image and Reality in the Lives of Women in Northern New England, 1650–1750* (New York: Knopf, 1982).

33. Robert Treat Paine to [Richard Cranch?], 4 November 1756, in Riley and Hanson, *Papers of Robert Treat Paine*, 1:372–73. The lament paraphrased by Paine is to be found in 2 Samuel 1:19–27.

34. Ezekiel Dodge to Robert Treat Paine, 5 May 1747, 15 January 1749, in Riley and Hanson, *Papers of Robert Treat Paine*, 1: 12–13, 40–41. (The sentence beginning "O my fellow disciple . . ." was written in Latin: "O utinam! Condiscipule mihi semper amande quod animae nostrae amore Christiano ac amissica semper conjungantur et in precibus ardentibus pro gratia ac cognitione alius pro alio uniantur.") It was not only from religious instructors and publications that young men heard about biblical role models: *The New Universal Letter-Writer*, for example, described "the story of David and Jonathan" as "a fine example" of friendship (191).

35. Joseph Hooper to Benjamin Dolbeare, 8 August, 4 September 1763, Dolbeare Family Papers, Massachusetts Historical Society; Ellis Gray to Dolbeare, 3 October 1763, 31 January 1764, ibid.

36. See Richard Godbeer, *Sexual Revolution in Early America* (Baltimore: Johns Hopkins University Press, 2002), chap. 9; and Clare A. Lyons, *Sex among the Rabble: An Intimate History of Gender and Power in the Age of Revolution, Philadelphia, 1730–1830* (Chapel Hill: University of North Carolina Press, 2006).

37. Leander's Journal, 1: 20 October 1786.

38. See Godbeer, *Sexual Revolution*, chap. 8; and Rodney Hessinger, *Seduced, Abandoned, and Reborn: Visions of Youth in Middle-Class America, 1780–1850* (Philadelphia: University of Pennsylvania Press, 2005).

39. Leander's Journal, 1: 18 June, 12 August 1786; 2: 25 December 1786, 24 February, 9 April 1787; Lorenzo's Journal, 29 July 1786. The Norris family may have welcomed the prospect of John Mifflin joining Isaac in Europe in part because of John's moral fastidiousness. Isaac's cousin Charles Thomson had warned him that there lay ahead "the rough ascent of virtue on the one hand, and the flowery path of pleasure on the other." He hoped that Isaac would make the right choice (Charles Thomson to Isaac Norris, 19 June 1784, quoted in Lewis R. Harley, *The Life of Charles Thomson* [Philadelphia: George W. Jacobs, 1900], 200). Mrs. Norris wrote to Isaac in Europe that she was "greatly obliged" to John for the attention he paid to Charles, her youngest son, who apparently lacked "steadiness" and had already given her "a great deal of pains." John had "endeavored to engage his attention and friendship," though Charles was proving resistant. One of the reasons that Mrs. Norris wanted Isaac home as soon as possible

was that Charles "professe[d] a greater regard" for him "than anyone else," and so she wanted Isaac's help in "stead[ying]" him (Mary Parker Norris to Isaac Norris, 17 June, 9 September 1785, Norris Papers, Family Letters, vol. 1, HSP).

40. Leander's Journal, 1: 14 September 1786; 2: 23 January, 1 March 1787.

41. Leander's Journal, 1: 12 August 1786; 2: 19 December 1786.

42. Leander's Journal, 2: 20 January 1787.

43. Ibid., 25 December 1786.

44. Jeremy Belknap to Ebenezer Hazard, 28 August 1780, 18 March 1784, in *Collections of the Massachusetts Historical Society,* 5th ser., 2: 69, 320; Hazard to Belknap, 20 January 1787, 2 October 1788, 13 October 1789, ibid., 3: 69, 195, 449.

45. "On the Difference between Romantic and Sentimental Characters," *The Universal Magazine* 77 (December 1785): 288–89; William Smith Shaw to Arthur Maynard Walter, 4 February 1803, Boston Athenaeum. Adam Smith, whose work on sentiment is discussed below in chap. 5, acknowledged that "a man of sensibility may sometimes feel great uneasiness lest he should have yielded too much even to what may be called an honourable passion," but Smith insisted that sensibility balanced with reason and conscience would lead in the right direction; see Adam Smith, *Theory of Moral Sentiments* (1759; Oxford: Clarendon Press, 1976), 122, 137; and Mary Kelley, *Learning to Stand and Speak: Women, Education, and Public Life in America's Republic* (Chapel Hill: University of North Carolina Press, 2006), 17–19. For the eighteenth-century culture of sympathy and sensibility, see Nicole Eustace, *Passion Is the Gale: Emotion, Power, and the Coming of the American Revolution* (Chapel Hill: University of North Carolina Press, 2008); G. J. Barker-Benfield, *The Culture of Sensibility: Sex and Society in Eighteenth-Century Britain* (Chicago: University of Chicago Press, 1992); John Mullan, *Sentiment and Sociability: The Language of Feeling in the Eighteenth Century* (Oxford: Clarendon Press, 1988); and Janet Todd, *Sensibility: An Introduction* (New York: Methuen, 1986). For "men of feeling" in eighteenth-century American seduction tales, see Hessinger, *Seduced, Abandoned, and Reborn,* 24, 29–32, 36–38. Caleb Crain presents the relationship that evolved between John Mifflin, James Gibson, and Isaac Norris in late eighteenth-century Philadelphia as "a story of affection between American men at a crucial moment: at the acme of the culture of sentiment and sensibility, when individuals first considered following the unruly impulse of sympathy as far as it would go." Crain's argument that these young men used the language of sensibility to express their feelings for one another constitutes an important step toward understanding the articulation of male love in the late eighteenth century; Caleb Crain, "Leander, Lorenzo, and Castalio: An Early American Romance," *Early American Literature* 33 (1998): 6. Eustace points out that "Quaker belief and practice" had

long emphasized "shared feeling" (*Passion Is the Gale,* 241–42). In the social circle that Mifflin, Gibson, and Norris moved in, this would presumably have had an impact that complemented the modish culture of sensibility.

46. *Cumberland Gazette,* 9 November 1789; *Massachusetts Spy, or, the Worcester Gazette,* 25 July 1793.

47. *Providence Gazette and Country Journal,* 20 February 1773; *New-Hampshire Gazette, or, State Journal and General Advertiser,* 25 February 1786.

48. John Carroll, ed., *Selected Letters of Samuel Richardson* (Oxford: Clarendon Press, 1964), 65.

49. *The Complete Letter-Writer, or, Young Secretary's Instructor* (New York, 1794), 2. Konstantin Dierks examines this transformation in letter-writing style in "The Feminization of Letter Writing in Early America," paper presented to 2nd Annual Conference of the Omohundro Institute for Early American History and Culture, Boulder, Colo., 31 May–2 June 1996. See also Jurgen Habermas, *The Structural Transformation of the Public Sphere: An Inquiry into a Category of Bourgeois Society,* trans. Thomas Burger (Cambridge, Mass.: Harvard University Press, 1996): "Letters were to be written in the heart's blood, they practically were to be wept" (49). Letter-writing manuals often contained sample letters written from one friend to another or on the subject of friendship; these were notable for their affective language.

50. Ezekiel Dodge to Robert Treat Paine, 8 June 1747, in Riley and Hanson, *Papers of Robert Treat Paine,* 1:15; Israel Cheever to Paine, 27 July 1749, ibid., 1:58. Jay Fliegelman points out in *Declaring Independence: Jefferson, Natural Language, and the Culture of Performance* (Stanford, Calif.: Stanford University Press, 1993) that eighteenth-century oratory sought to convey the experience of thoughts and feelings as much as the thoughts and feelings themselves; it focused on "emotional credibility" and sought a "natural language" through which to communicate sincerity of feeling, even though "the quest for a natural language led paradoxically to a greater theatricalization of public speaking, to a new social dramaturgy, and to a performative understanding of selfhood" (2).

51. John Custis to Peter Collinson, [25 March 1735?], [summer 1741?], quoted in Susan Scott Parrish, *American Curiosity: Cultures of Natural History in the Colonial British Atlantic World* (Chapel Hill: University of North Carolina Press, 2006), 167.

52. William Livingston to Noah Welles, 13 October 1744, 24 July 1745, Johnson Family Papers, Yale University Library.

53. Malicious gossip, for example, was thought of in feminine terms, regardless of whether the culprit was male or female. Jane Kamensky points out that men accused of witchcraft, a primarily female-identified crime, were often described as having a vicious tongue; see Jane Kamensky, *Governing the Tongue:*

The Politics of Speech in Early New England (New York: Oxford University Press, 1997), 159. For a more detailed discussion of gender flexibility in early modern Anglo-American culture, see Godbeer, "Performing Patriarchy: Gendered Roles and Hierarchies in Early Modern England and Seventeenth-Century New England," in *The World of John Winthrop: Essays on England and New England, 1588–1649*, ed. Francis J. Bremer and Lynn A. Botelho (Boston: Massachusetts Historical Society, 2005), 290–333.

54. *Cumberland Gazette*, 26 March 1789. For "men of feeling" who embraced "womanly qualities of tenderness and susceptibility" in eighteenth-century fiction, see Todd, *Sensibility*, chap. 6; and Hessinger, *Seduced, Abandoned, and Reborn*, chap. 1. Susan Scott Parrish argues that the love expressed by eighteenth-century naturalists in their letters to each other would have posed a problem for those involved unless their feelings were mediated by a feminized nature. This assumes a more rigid conception of love, gender, and sexuality than was yet in place. When Cadwallader Colden wrote to fellow naturalist Peter Collinson and apologized if his effusive enthusiasm made him "become like a fond lover who by too earnest a desire of pleasing his mistress becomes intolerable to her," he went on to hope that his friend would help him to "curb" his excessive passion, but he did not express any concern about positioning Collinson in the role of a woman engaged with him in a romantic dalliance of some sort; Parrish assumes otherwise, for which see *American Curiosity*, 166–68.

55. Leander's Journal, 1: 5 October 1786; William Wirt to Dabney Carr, 23 March 1803, 15 February 1814, 20 August 1815, 10 August 1822, Wirt Papers, Maryland Historical Society; Wirt to St. George Tucker, 18 January 1820, ibid; Wirt to William Pope, 18 January 1818. For other expressions of uneasiness about the assumption of feminine-identified traits, see Andrew Burstein, *Sentimental Democracy: The Evolution of America's Romantic Self-Image* (New York: Hill and Wang, 1999), 344n34.

56. Deborah Norris to Sarah Wister, 18 April 1778, 2 August 1779, Sally Wister Papers, correspondence 1777–1779, HSP; Mary Dickinson to Deborah Norris Logan, 11 August 1788, Robert R. Logan Collection, box 12, folder 10, HSP.

57. Deborah Norris to Sally Wister, 2 August 1779, in Kathryn Zabelle Derounian, "A Dear Dear Friend: Six Letters from Deborah Norris to Sally Wister, 1778–1779," *Pennsylvania Magazine of History and Biography* 108 (1984): 513; Norris to Sally Fisher, 16 November 1779, Corbit-Higgins-Spruance Papers, Historical Society of Delaware, transcribed in John A. H. Sweeney, ed., "The Norris-Fisher Correspondence: A Circle of Friends, 1779–82," *Delaware History* 6 (1955): 197. Carroll Smith-Rosenberg has argued that the realm of female friendship was "a world in which men made but a shadowy appearance." But as Caleb Crain has pointed out, the border between communities of female and male

friendship may have been "more porous than Smith-Rosenberg estimated." See Smith-Rosenberg, "The Female World of Love and Ritual," 53, and Caleb Crain, *American Sympathy: Men, Friendship, and Literature in the New Nation* (New Haven, Conn.: Yale University Press, 2001), 32.

58. Leander's Journal, 1: 12 October 1786.

59. Dabney Carr to William Wirt, 16 October 1802, and Wirt to Carr, 19 March 1802, Wirt Papers, Maryland Historical Society.

60. William Wirt to Dabney Carr, 13 February, 6 June 1803, Wirt Papers, Maryland Historical Society. For a subtle and insightful examination of the marriage between William and Elizabeth Wirt, see Anya Jabour, *Marriage in the Early Republic: Elizabeth and William Wirt and the Companionate Ideal* (Baltimore: Johns Hopkins University Press, 1998).

61. William Wirt to Dabney Carr, 16 January 1804, Wirt Papers, Maryland Historical Society; Wirt to Carr, 15 January 1814, Library of Virginia.

62. William Wirt to Dabney Carr, 16 January 1804, Wirt Papers, Maryland Historical Society. For references to his sharing Carr's letters with his wife (and his expectation that Carr would do the same), see Wirt to Carr, 10 June 1814, 9 September 1824, Library of Virginia.

63. William Wirt to Dabney Carr, 25 May 1819, Wirt Letters and Papers, Southern Historical Collection, Wilson Library, University of North Carolina, Chapel Hill. See also Jabour, "Male Friendship and Masculinity," 103.

64. William Livingston to Noah Welles, 5 February 1750, Johnson Family Papers, Yale University Library.

65. "Letter to a Young Lady with Directions Concerning Her Future Conduct," *American Magazine*, April 1745; William Livingston to Noah Welles, 14 November 1743, 24 July 1745, 28 September 1751, Johnson Family Papers, Yale University Library.

66. Ebenezer Hazard to Jeremy Belknap, 21 May 1783, in *Collections of the Massachusetts Historical Society*, 5th ser., 2:211; Belknap to Hazard, 18 July, 12 September 1783, 4 July 1784, ibid., 2: 233, 247, 376. Belknap's and Hazard's subsequent letters to each other incorporated their spouses into expressions of affection and love. "Mrs. B's love, with mine, to you and yours," declared Belknap (Belknap to Hazard, 8 December 1787, ibid., 2:499). "Mrs. H joins me in love to Mrs. B and yourself," wrote Hazard (Hazard to Belknap, 9 September 1788, ibid., 3:63).

67. Jeremy Belknap to Ebenezer Hazard, 28 December 1779, 18 March 1784, in *Collections of the Massachusetts Historical Society*, 5th ser., 2: 26, 320; Hazard to Belknap, 18 February 1780, ibid., 31.

68. Daniel Webster to James Bingham, 22 February 1803, 3 April 1804, in McIntyre, *Writings and Speeches of Daniel Webster*, 17: 132, 164; William Liv-

ingston to Noah Welles, 7 November 1747, Johnson Family Papers, Yale University Library.

69. Daniel Webster to Mr. McGaw, 12 January 1807, in McIntyre, *Writings and Speeches of Daniel Webster*, 17:223–24.

70. Daniel Webster to James Bingham, 8 December 1801, 25 February 1802, 19 January 1806, in McIntyre, *Writings and Speeches of Daniel Webster*, 17: 101, 103, 221. For Webster's subsequent marriage, see Irving Bartlett, *Daniel Webster* (New York: Norton, 1978), 90–95.

71. Ezekiel Dodge to Robert Treat Paine, 8 June 1747, in Riley and Hanson, *Papers of Robert Treat Paine*, 1:16; William Wirt to Benjamin Edwards, 2 July 1808, Wirt Papers, Maryland Historical Society.

72. William Wirt to Dabney Carr, 27 September 1824, Library of Virginia; Wirt to William Pope, 29 August 1821, Wirt Papers, Maryland Historical Society. Peachy Gilmer was Wirt's brother-in-law, so when Wirt wrote to Peachy as "friend and brother," he used the latter word at least in part to denote their legal kinship; see, for example, Wirt to Peachy Gilmer, 9 August 1802, 9 February 1804, Wirt Papers, Library of Congress.

73. Daniel Webster to James Bingham, 11 February 1800, in McIntyre, *Writings and Speeches of Daniel Webster*, 17:82; William Livingston to Noah Welles, 24, 26 July 1745, Johnson Family Papers, Yale University Library.

74. William Livingston to Noah Welles, 13 January 1746, Johnson Family Papers.

Chapter Three: "The Best Blessing We Know"

1. Stith Mead, Letter Book, 1792–95, Virginia Historical Society, 10, 47, 68, 125, 132, 142, 156.

2. Ibid., 66, 95, 123.

3. The connections that I have drawn between religious sensibility, friendship, and social identity were first inspired by my reading of Michael Warner's essay, "New English Sodom," in *Queering the Renaissance*, ed. Jonathan Goldberg (Durham, N.C.: Duke University Press, 1994), 330–58; and Christine Leigh Heyrman's *Southern Cross: The Beginnings of the Bible Belt* (New York: Knopf, 1997).

4. John Winthrop to Sir William Spring, 8 February 1630, in *Winthrop Papers*, 6 vols., ed. Worthington C. Ford, Stewart Mitchell, Allyn Bailey Forbes, and Malcolm Freiberg (Boston: Massachusetts Historical Society, 1929–92), 2: 203, 205–6.

5. John Winthrop to Sir William Spring, 8 February 1630, in Ford et al., *Winthrop Papers*, 2:206; John Winthrop, "Experiencia," ibid., 1: 166, 202–4.

6. John Cotton, *The Way of the Churches of Christ in New-England* (London,

1645), 4, and *The Fountain of Life* (London, 1651), 36–37. For a more detailed discussion of gender flexibility in colonial New England, see Richard Godbeer, "Performing Patriarchy: Gendered Roles and Hierarchies in Early Modern England and Seventeenth-Century New England," in *The World of John Winthrop: Essays on England and New England, 1588-1649,* ed. Francis J. Bremer and Lynn A. Botelho (Boston: Massachusetts Historical Society, 2005), 290–333.

7. John Winthrop, "Experiencia," in Ford et al., *Winthrop Papers*, 1:202–3; Robert C. Winthrop, ed., *The Life and Letters of John Winthrop*, 2 vols. (Boston: Ticknor and Fields, 1864–67), 1:193.

8. John Winthrop to Sir William Spring, 8 February 1630, in Ford et al., *Winthrop Papers*, 2:205–6; Spring to Winthrop, n.d. March 1637, ibid., 3:365.

9. John Winthrop, "A Model of Christian Charity," ibid., 2: 284, 288–90.

10. Ibid., 2:290–94. Winthrop noted that "other instances might be brought to show the nature of this affection, as of Ruth and Naomi and many others, but this truth is cleared enough" (291). Back in England, Puritan minister Thomas Brooks also referred to the bond between Ruth and Naomi as a model for the kind of relationship that should bind the saints; see Thomas Brooks, *Heaven on Earth* (1654; Carlisle, Pa.: Banner of Truth Trust, 1961), 251. For a more detailed analysis of Winthrop's sermon, see Francis J. Bremer, *John Winthrop: America's Forgotten Founding Father* (New York: Oxford University Press, 2003), 173–84.

11. Richard Sibbes, John Cotton, and George Gifford, quoted in Francis Bremer, *Congregational Communion: Clerical Friendship in the Anglo-American Puritan Community, 1610-1692* (Boston: Northeastern University Press, 1994), 6, 15. This paragraph is much indebted to Bremer's discussion of Puritan friendship in ibid., esp. 3–15, and also Bremer, *John Winthrop*, 180, as well as Stephen Foster's conception of loving communion among Puritans as "a kind of socialized Eucharist" in *Their Solitary Way: The Puritan Social Ethic in the First Century of Settlement in New England* (New Haven, Conn.: Yale University Press, 1971), 44; see also Donald Yacovone, "'Surpassing the Love of Women': Victorian Manhood and the Language of Fraternal Love," in *A Shared Experience: Men, Women, and the History of Gender,* ed. Laura McCall and Donald Yacovone (New York: New York University Press, 1998), 197.

12. Ford et al., *Winthrop Papers*, 4: 20, 36–37.

13. Nathaniel Bernardiston to John Winthrop, 19 March 1647, ibid., 5:145; Thomas Jenner to John Winthrop, 6 April 1646, ibid., 5:76; Benjamin Wadsworth, *Mutual Love and Peace among Christians* (Boston, 1701), 13.

14. "John Winthrop to the Elders of the Massachusetts Churches," 14 October 1642, in Ford et al., *Winthrop Papers*, 4:360–61.

15. John Allin, "A Brief History of the Church of Christ at Dedham," in *Puritans in the New World: A Critical Anthology,* ed. David D. Hall (Princeton, N.J.:

Princeton University Press, 2004), 55–57, 61; see also Bremer, *Congregational Communion*, 256.

16. Francis Kirby to John Winthrop Jr., 26 March, 18 June 1633, in Ford et al., *Winthrop Papers*, 3: 117, 129; Nathaniel Barnardiston to John Winthrop, 15 March 1640, ibid., 4:218; John Humfrey to Winthrop Jr., 3 December 1632, ibid., 3:104; William Coddington to Winthrop Jr., 14 October 1648, ibid., 5:269; William Bradford to Winthrop, 12 March 1647, ibid., 5:139.

17. Ezekiel Rogers to John Winthrop, 3 November 1639, ibid., 4:149–50; Nehemiah Bourne to Winthrop, 12 August 1648, ibid., 5:245; Thomas Jenner to Winthrop, 26 April 1641, ibid., 4:331–32; Thomas Harrison to Winthrop, 14 January 1648, ibid., 5:199; Samuel Newman to John Winthrop Jr., n.d. October 1654, ibid., 6:464.

18. Hugh Peter to John Winthrop Jr., 30 September 1638, ibid., 4:63; 23 June 1645, 15 March 1649, ibid., 5: 30, 319.

19. Ibid., ca. April 1647, 15 March 1649, 5: 146, 319–20.

20. Edward Howes to John Winthrop Jr., 9 November 1631, 7, 26 March 1632, ibid., 3: 54, 66, 72; 25 February 1640, ibid., 4:203.

21. John Wilson to Thomas Weld and John Eliot, n.d. ca. September 1642, ibid., 4:353; Thomas Thacher to Wilson et al., 27 February 1654, ibid., 6:364; John Humfrey to Isaac Johnson, 23 December 1630, ibid., 2:340–41; George Jenney to John Winthrop, 18 February 1640, ibid., 4:196–97.

22. Edward Howes to John Winthrop Jr., 9 November 1631, ibid., 3:54; for examples of letters pledging "offices of love" or "service of love," see Samuel Whiting and Thomas Cobbett to John Winthrop, 10 July 1643, ibid., 4:397; Theophilus Eaton to Winthrop, 6 August 1646, ibid., 5:96, Eaton to Winthrop Jr., 21 July 1648, ibid., 5:239; and Ralph Partridge to Winthrop Jr., 14 August 1650, ibid., 6:56.

23. George Fenwick to John Winthrop, 7 October 1639, 6 May 1641, ibid., 4: 141–42, 339.

24. Stephen Goodyear to John Winthrop Jr., 17 June 1651, ibid., 6:109; Thomas Stanton to Winthrop Jr., 1 May 1650, ibid., 6:40; William Lord to Winthrop Jr., 11 June 1654, ibid., 6:388.

25. John Winthrop Jr.'s 1650 letter quoted in Bremer, *Congregational Communion*, 9; Thomas Arkisden to Winthrop Jr., 20 March 1632, in Ford et al., *Winthrop Papers*, 3:71; John Hull to James Richards, 6 July 1654, ibid., 6:400; Edward Winslow to John Winthrop, 28 March 1645, ibid., 5:16; Thomas Harrison to Winthrop, 10 April 1648, ibid., 5:212; Ezekiel Culverwell to Winthrop, n.d. 1618, ibid., 1:229.

26. Throughout the second half of the seventeenth century, New England ministers faced the challenge of evangelizing to new generations of young people

who had not chosen to live in a Puritan society. Their initial response to this generational challenge was to invoke the threat of God's wrath if New England forsook its spiritual mission. But in the closing decades of the century, they adopted a more positive message, reaffirming and intensifying their depiction of union with Christ as a loving and passionate marriage. Samuel Willard, one of John Cotton's successors in the Boston pulpit, declared that the redeemed would "lie in Christ's bosom, and be ravished with his dearest love, and most intimate embraces." Edward Taylor, the pastor at Westfield, Massachusetts, envisaged Christ as "a spotless male in prime," yearned for "such love raptures" as only his savior could provide, and hoped that they would conceive together "the babe of grace" (Samuel Willard, *The High Esteem Which God Hath of the Death of His Saints* [Boston, 1683], 15; Donald E. Stanford, ed., *The Poems of Edward Taylor* [New Haven: Yale University Press, 1960], 212, 295, 448). See Emory Elliott, *Power and the Pulpit in Puritan New England* (Princeton, N.J.: Princeton University Press, 1975), and Richard Godbeer, *Sexual Revolution in Early America* (Baltimore: Johns Hopkins University Press, 2002), esp. 73–74.

27. For recent studies of the Great Awakening and its impact, see Alan Heimert, *Religion and the American Mind: From the Great Awakening to the Revolution* (Cambridge, Mass.: Harvard University Press, 1966); Rhys Isaac, *The Transformation of Virginia, 1740–1790* (Chapel Hill: University of North Carolina Press, 1982); Patricia U. Bonomi, *Under the Cope of Heaven: Religion, Society, and Politics in Colonial America* (New York: Oxford University Press, 1986); Nathan O. Hatch, *The Democratization of American Christianity* (New Haven, Conn.: Yale University Press, 1989); Jon Butler, *Awash in a Sea of Faith: Christianizing the American People* (Cambridge, Mass.: Harvard University Press, 1990); Michael J. Crawford, *Seasons of Grace: Colonial New England's Revival Tradition in Its British Context* (New York: Oxford University Press, 1991); Harry S. Stout, *The Divine Dramatist: George Whitefield and the Rise of Modern Evangelicalism* (Grand Rapids, Mich.: Eerdmans, 1991); Frank Lambert, *"Pedlar in Divinity": George Whitefield and the Transatlantic Revivals, 1737–1770* (Princeton, N.J.: Princeton University Press, 1994); Lambert, *Inventing the "Great Awakening"* (Princeton, N.J.: Princeton University Press, 1999); and Thomas S. Kidd, *The Great Awakening: The Roots of Evangelical Christianity in Colonial America* (New Haven, Conn.: Yale University Press, 2007).

28. Gilbert Tennent, *Brotherly Love Recommended* (Philadelphia, 1748), 3.

29. Jonathan Edwards, "Sinners in the Hands of an Angry God," in *The Sermons of Jonathan Edwards: A Reader,* ed. Wilson H. Kimnach, Kenneth P. Minkema, and Douglas A. Sweeney (New Haven, Conn.: Yale University Press, 1999), 57–58.

30. Jonathan Edwards, "Heaven, a World of Charity or Love," in *Charity and*

Its Fruits, ed. Tryon Edwards (1852; Carlisle, Pa.: Banner of Truth Trust, 1969), 357; and Edwards, "All True Grace in the Heart Summed Up in Charity, or Love," in ibid., 3, 4–5.

31. Edwards, "All True Grace," 5, 9, 10, 13, 21.

32. Edwards, "Heaven," 324, 326–28, 335, 348, 352.

33. Ibid., 330, 333–34, 336, 338, 343–44.

34. Ibid., 351, 366, 367–68.

35. John Gillies, ed., *A Select Collection of Letters of the Late Reverend George Whitefield,* 3 vols. (London, 1772), 1: 126, 132, 162.

36. Ibid., 1: 63, 90, 100, 114, 117, 169–70, 216.

37. Ibid., 1: 93, 129, 161–62, 214.

38. Ibid., 1: 64, 93–94, 115, 156, 186.

39. Tennent, *Brotherly Love Recommended,* 4, 16.

40. George Whitefield, "The Marriage of Cana," in *The Great Awakening: Documents on the Revival of Religion, 1740-1745,* ed. Richard L. Bushman, (Chapel Hill: University of North Carolina Press, 1989), 33–34.

41. Tennent, *Brotherly Love Recommended,* 13–17, 35.

42. Cotton Mather, *Ornaments for the Daughters of Zion* (Cambridge, Mass., 1692), 64; Jonathan Edwards, "The Church's Marriage to Her Sons, and to Her God," in *The Works of Jonathan Edwards,* vol. 25, ed. Wilson H. Kimnach (New Haven, Conn.: Yale University Press, 2006), 174, 177, 180–81, 186. See also John Webb, *Christ's Suit to the Sinner* (Boston, 1741), 30–31. Erik R. Seeman discusses lay use of sensual imagery in *Pious Persuasions: Laity and Clergy in Eighteenth-Century New England* (Baltimore: Johns Hopkins University Press, 1999), 104.

43. Michael J. Crawford, ed., "The Spiritual Travels of Nathan Cole," *William and Mary Quarterly* 33 (1976): 93, 96, 97, 104, 105, 109–10, 112, 114, 119.

44. Richard Hockley to John Watson, 29 November 1740, Letter Book of Richard Hockley, 1737–1742, Quaker Collection, Haverford College.

45. "The Testimony of the Pastors of the Churches in the Province of the Massachusetts Bay," in Bushman, *Great Awakening,* 128; Samuel Blair, "A Short and Faithful Narrative," in ibid., 73; Jonathan Parsons, "Account of the Revival at Lyme," in *The Great Awakening: Documents Illustrating the Crisis and Its Consequences,* ed. Alan Heimert and Perry Miller (Indianapolis: Bobbs-Merrill, 1967), 200; Chauncy, "A Letter from a Gentleman in Boston," in Bushman, *Great Awakening,* 117, 120; J. M. Bumsted and John E. Van de Wetering, *What Must I Do to Be Saved? The Great Awakening in Colonial America* (Hindale, Ill.: Dryden Press, 1976), 144. See also Richard J. Hooker, ed., *The Carolina Backcountry on the Eve of Revolution: The Journal and Other Writings of Charles Woodmason, Anglican Itinerant* (Chapel Hill: University of North Carolina Press, 1953), 99,

100, 102, 103. For perceptions of sexual and gendered disorder during the revivals, see Seeman, *Pious Persuasions,* chap. 5; and Susan Juster, *Disorderly Women: Sexual Politics and Evangelicalism in Revolutionary New England* (Ithaca, N.Y.: Cornell University Press, 1994).

46. Jonathan Edwards, "The Distinguishing Marks of a Work of the Spirit of God," in *The Great Awakening,* ed. C. C. Goen (New Haven, Conn.: Yale University Press, 1972), 256–57; Edwards, "Some Thoughts Concerning the Present Revival," ibid., 468.

47. William G. McLoughlin, ed., *The Diary of Isaac Backus,* 3 vols. (Providence, R.I.: Brown University Press, 1979), 1:35.

48. Joseph Tracy, *The Great Awakening: A History of the Revival of Religion in the Time of Edwards and Whitefield* (Boston: Charles Tappan, 1845), 143; *Boel's* Compaint *against Frelinghuysen,* trans. and ed. Joseph Anthony Loux Jr. (Rensselaer, N.Y.: Hamilton Printing, 1979), 33, 144–48; and Randall H. Balmer, *A Perfect Babel of Confusion: Dutch Religion and English Culture in the Middle Colonies* (New York: Oxford University Press, 1989), 112–13.

49. Richard Hockley to John Watson, 29 November 1740, Letter Book of Richard Hockley, 1737–1742, Quaker Collection, Haverford College.

50. Gillies, *Letters,* 1: 148, 158, 194; Stout, *Divine Dramatist,* 161.

51. Gillies, *Letters,* 1: 159, 160–61.

52. Ibid., 1:363; Stout, *Divine Dramatist,* 171.

53. See Godbeer, *Sexual Revolution,* chap. 2; Henry Abelove, *The Evangelist of Desire: John Wesley and the Methodists* (Stanford, Calif.: Stanford University Press, 1990), esp. chap. 5.

54. Elmer C. Clark, J. Manning Potts, and Jacob Payton, eds., *The Journal and Letters of Francis Asbury,* 3 vols. (Nashville, Tenn.: Abingdon Press, 1958), 2:474, 3:19; Dee E. Andrews, *The Methodists and Revolutionary America, 1760-1800: The Shaping of an Evangelical Culture* (Princeton, N.J.: Princeton University Press, 2000), 110–11. My discussion of post-revolutionary evangelicals is much endebted to Heyrman, *Southern Cross,* 181–84; and Cynthia Lynn Lyerly, *Methodism and the Southern Mind, 1770-1810* (New York: Oxford University Press, 1998), 158–60.

55. Mead, Letter Book, 111–12, 114.

56. James Meacham, Journal, in the Rare Book, Manuscript, and Special Collections Library, Duke University, 22 November 1789, 25 April, 5 July, 7 August, 1790.

57. See, for examples, Andrews, *Methodists and Revolutionary America,* 218–19.

58. Jeremiah Minter, *A Brief Account of the Religious Experience, Travels, Preaching, Persecutions from Evil Men, and God's Special Helps in the Faith and*

Life, Etc. of Jeremiah Minter (Washington, D.C., 1817), 13–15. Heyrman discusses the relationship between Jones and Minter in *Southern Cross*, 132, 294n19.

59. Meacham, Journal, 2, 3, 4, 27 November 1789, 10, 18, 28 March, 3, 11 April, 6 July 1790, 22 August, 9 October 1792, 17 March 1793, 31 July 1794, 11 January 1795.

60. *The Experience and Travels of Mr. Freeborn Garrettson, Minister of the Methodist-Episcopal Church in North-America* (Philadelphia: Parry Hall, 1791), 35, 51, 134, 266–67; Edward P. Humphrey and Thomas H. Cleland, eds., *Memoirs of the Rev. Thomas Cleland, D.D.* (Cincinnati: Moore, Wilstach, Keys, 1859), 54–55.

61. David Sherman, *A History of the Revisions of the Discipline of the Methodist Episcopal Church*, 3rd ed. (New York: Hunt and Eaton, 1890), 450.

62. Meacham, Journal, 13 May 1789, 30 July 1794, 21 February 1797; John Taylor, *A History of the Baptist Churches* (Frankfort, Ky.: J. H. Holeman, 1833), 20–21.

63. Mead, Letter Book, 66, 121, 123, 136, 148–49, 162.

64. Ibid., 14, 28, 66, 69, 132. Mead's conception of Kobler as a bridegroom may have been bound up with his conviction that believers in general and preachers in particular should emulate their savior. When Mead enquired as to how his friend's evangelizing efforts were faring, he wrote that he trusted Kobler was "imitating him who bought our souls with a price and was manifested to destroy the works of the Devil" (130).

65. Ibid., 32, 48, 57, 79, 81.

66. See, for example, ibid., 83.

67. Ibid., 143–44, 161; Meacham, Journal, 26 February 1790.

68. William M. Wightman, ed., *The Life of William Capers, D.D.* (Nashville, Tenn.: Southern Methodist Publishing House, 1858), 90, 112, 114; Mead, Letter Book, 79. These nicknames were much more straightforward than the classical and literary pseudonyms used by John Mifflin and his social circle in Philadelphia, reflecting perhaps a difference in social and educational background as well as a less theatrical conception of personal relationships within the evangelical ministry (however self-consciously dramatic these preachers may have been in their public sermons).

69. William Spencer to Mary Gordon, 22 May 1796, Gordon-Hackett Family Papers, Southern Historical Collection, University of North Carolina, Chapel Hill; Wightman, *Life of William Capers*, 110–11; *Experience and Travels of Mr. Freeborn Garrettson*, 56; Sherman, *History of the Revisions*, 449.

70. *Experience and Travels of Mr. Freeborn Garrettson*, 133; Taylor, *History of the Baptist Churches*, 16; see also William Watters, *A Short Account of the*

Christian Experience and Ministereal Labours of William Watters, Drawn Up by Himself (Alexandria, Va., 1806), 127.

71. Mead, Letter Book, 66; see also Heyrman, *Southern Cross*, 145.

72. Meacham, Journal, 20 November 1789, 16, 24 April, 13 August 1790, 27 December 1794, 14 February 1795, 3 January 1797.

73. Ford et al., *Winthrop Papers*, 2:175–76.

74. Brooks, *Heaven on Earth*, 249.

75. John Winthrop, "A Model of Christian Charity," in Ford et al., *Winthrop Papers*, 2:282–83; John Cotton, *Christ the Fountain of Life* (London, 1651), 34–35.

76. "Proceedings of Excommunication against Mistress Ann Hibbens of Boston," in *Remarkable Providences: Readings on Early American History*, ed. John Demos (Boston: Northeastern University Press, 1991), 266–67; Anne S. Lombard, *Making Manhood: Growing Up Male in Colonial New England* (Cambridge, Mass.: Harvard University Press, 2003), 25–26, 148; Samuel Greene Arnold, *History of the State of Rhode Island and Providence Plantations, 1636–1700* (Providence, R.I., 1894), 148. For a helpful discussion of the New Englanders' radicalism, see David D. Hall, "The Experience of Authority in Early New England," *Journal of American and Canadian Studies* 23 (2005): 3–32.

77. Francis Asbury, quoted in *Arminian Magazine* 7 (London, 1784): 681; Hatch, *Democratization of American Christianity*, 81–93.

78. Isaac, *Transformation of Virginia*, chap. 8, esp. 173.

79. See especially Bonomi, *Under the Cope of Heaven*, 152–53. The notion of covenant figured as a central theme in the revolutionary sermons that played a key role in sacralizing the patriot cause for ordinary Americans, for which see Harry Stout, *The New England Soul: Preaching and Religious Culture in Colonial New England* (New York: Oxford University Press, 1986); and Ellis Sandoz, ed., *Political Sermons of the American Founding Era, 1730–1805*, 2 vols. (Indianapolis: Liberty Fund, 1998).

80. Heyrman's *Southern Cross* discusses the difficulties that faced evangelicals as they sought to change the tone of Southern culture and the compromises that they made in the early nineteenth century so as to placate critics and skeptics. Even some of those ministers who identified with evangelical religion were shocked by this new populist spirituality and its implications; while evangelical firebrands sought to destroy the "aristocracy" of the pulpit, their more conservative colleagues feared the triumph of vulgarity and ignorance. See Hatch, *Democratization of American Christianity*, chap. 2.

81. See especially Gordon S. Wood, *The Radicalism of the American Revolution* (New York: Knopf, 1992). Those principles became embedded in the new

republic's political and constitutional fabric not only in the form of measures designed to ensure popular representation and the accountability of elected officials, but also through the separation of church and state, which established as a fundamental precept of American democracy that religious association should take the form of a voluntary compact between people of common faith.

82. "To the Inhabitants of the British Colonies in America," *Pennsylvania Gazette*, 15 June 1774; Robert Ross, *A Sermon in Which the Union of the Colonies Is Considered and Recommended* (New York, 1776), 27.

83. *Vermont Gazette*, 25 May 1792.

Chapter Four: "A Band of Brothers"

1. Marquis de Chastellux, *Travels in North America*, 2 vols., trans. and ed. Howard C. Rice (Chapel Hill: University of North Carolina Press, 1963), 1: 101, 105–6.

2. See Arthur S. Lefkowitz, *George Washington's Indispensable Men: The 32 Aides-de-Camp Who Helped Win American Independence* (Mechanicsburg, Pa.: Stackpole Books, 2003); and Emily Stone Whitely, *Washington and His Aides-de-Camp* (New York: Macmillan, 1936).

3. See, for example, John C. Fitzpatrick, ed. *Writings of George Washington*, 39 vols. (Washington, D.C.: Government Printing Office, 1931–44), 11:65; 22:32; 26:30; 27: 232, 284.

4. *The Army Correspondence of Colonel John Laurens in the Years 1777–8* (New York: Arno Press, 1969), 96, 146, 202; Richard Meade to Alexander Hamilton, 13 January 1781, in *Papers of Alexander Hamilton*, 27 vols., ed. Harold C. Syrett et al. (New York: Columbia University Press, 1961–87) [henceforth *PAH*], 2:535; Hamilton to James Duane, 14 September 1779, ibid., 2: 173, 174; Duane to Hamilton, 23 September 1779, ibid., 2:187.

5. *Army Correspondence of Colonel John Laurens*, 93, 170, 174, 202, 205.

6. Alexander Hamilton to John Laurens, n.d. April, 22 May 1779, 8 January, 30 March 1780, *PAH*, 2: 36, 38, 52–54, 255, 304. See also Whitely, *Washington and His Aides-de-Camp*, 8: "The story of the Aides is a *journal intime* . . . they stand forever an ardent boyish group gathered together around a King of Men at the center of a great drama."

7. For discussion of military camaraderie and the language of brotherhood in other historical contexts, see Martyn Downer, "Nelson and his 'Band of Brothers': Friendship, Freemasonry, Fraternity," in *Admiral Lord Nelson: Context and Legacy*, ed. David Cannadine (New York: Palgrave Macmillan, 2005), 30–48; Ludovic H. C. Kennedy, *Nelson's Band of Brothers* (London: Odham's Press, 1951); James M. McPherson, *For Cause and Comrades: Why Men Fought in the*

Civil War (New York: Oxford University Press, 1997); Reid Mitchell, *The Vacant Chair: The Northern Soldier Leaves Home* (New York: Oxford University Press, 1993); Nina Silber, *The Romance of Reunion: Northerners and the South, 1865–1900* (Chapel Hill: University of North Carolina Press, 1993); Stuart McConnell, *Glorious Contentment: The Grand Army of the Republic, 1865–1900* (Chapel Hill: University of North Carolina Press, 1992); Sarah Cole, *Modernism, Male Friendship, and the First World War* (New York: Cambridge University Press, 2003); and Paul Fussell, *The Great War and Modern Memory* (New York: Oxford University Press, 1975), esp. chap. 8.

8. Thomas J. Fleming, ed., *Affectionately Yours, George Washington: A Self-Portrait in Letters of Friendship* (New York: Norton, 1967), 85, 116, 134–35, 143, 155–56, 164, 170, 178, 190, 229.

9. John Laurens to Richard Meade, 22 October 1781, Alexander Hamilton Papers, Library of Congress; Laurens to Alexander Hamilton, 12 December 1779, *PAH*, 2:226; Hamilton to Laurens, 16 September 1780, 4 February 1781, ibid., 2: 431, 550.

10. Alexander Hamilton to John Laurens, 22 May 1779, *PAH*, 2:52–54; Tench Tilghman to James McHenry, quoted in Bernard C. Steiner, *Life and Correspondence of James McHenry* (Cleveland: Burrows Brothers, 1907), 25–26.

11. Richard K. Showman, ed., *The Papers of General Nathaniel Greene*, vol. 4 (Chapel Hill: University of North Carolina Press, 1986), 323–24; "Letters from Ephraim Douglas to James Irvine," *Pennsylvania Magazine of History and Biography* 1 (1877): 44, 50; Isaac Sherman to Anthony Wayne, 22 August 1779, in Charles J. Stille, *Major-General Anthony Wayne and the Pennsylvania Line in the Continental Army* (1893; Port Washington, N.Y.: Kennikat Press, 1968), 408–9.

12. Worthington C. Ford, ed., *Correspondence and Journals of Samuel Blachley Webb*, 2 vols. (1893; New York: Arno Press, 1969), 2:293–94. I first became aware of the response to John André's execution through reading Sarah Knott's superb essay, "Sensibility and the American War for Independence," *American Historical Review* (2004): 19–40.

13. Henry B. Dawson, ed., *Papers Concerning the Capture and Detention of Major John André* (Yonkers, N.Y.: printed "for private circulation" in 26 copies, 1866), 108; Alexander Hamilton to John Laurens, *PAH*, 2:466–68; Richard K. Showman, ed., *The Papers of General Nathaniel Greene*, vol. 6 (Chapel Hill: University of North Carolina Press, 1991), 366; Patrick J. Furlong, ed., "An Execution Sermon for Major John André," *New York History* 51 (1970): 68–69; James Thacher, *A Military Journal during the American Revolutionary War* (Boston, 1823), 275.

14. Winthrop Sargent, *The Life and Career of Major John André* (Boston, 1861), 348; *Pennsylvania Packet*, 6 September 1781.

15. Fleming, *Affectionately Yours*, 144; Alexander Hamilton to John Laurens, 30 June 1780, *PAH*, 2:347–48.

16. Alexander Hamilton to John Laurens, 30 June, 12, 16 September 1780, *PAH*, 2: 347, 427, 431.

17. Alexander Hamilton to John Laurens, 30 June, 12 September 1780, *PAH*, 2: 347–48, 427–28; Laurens to Hamilton, 14 July 1779, n.d. July 1782, *PAH*, 2:102–3, 3:121.

18. Alexander Hamilton to John Laurens, n.d. April 1779, *PAH*, 2: 34–35, 38.

19. For a discussion of this genre, see Richard Godbeer, *Sexual Revolution in Early America* (Baltimore: Johns Hopkins University Press, 2002), chap. 8.

20. Alexander Hamilton to John Laurens, n.d. April 1779, *PAH*, 2:35; for the tomcat, see Willard Sterne Randall, *Alexander Hamilton: A Life* (New York: Harper Collins, 2003), 124; for seduction of young men into a life of libertinism by male friends, see Godbeer, *Sexual Revolution*, 286.

21. Alexander Hamilton to John Laurens, n.d. April, 11 September 1779, *PAH*, 2: 35, 165.

22. See, for example, Gregory D. Massey, *John Laurens and the American Revolution* (Columbia: University of South Carolina Press, 2000), 79.

23. Alexander Hamilton to John Laurens, n.d. April 1779, *PAH*, 2:36.

24. Ibid., 2:37–38.

25. Ibid., 2:34–38.

26. Alexander Hamilton to John Laurens, 30 June, 16 September 1780, *PAH*, 2: 348, 431.

27. Alexander Hamilton to Catharine Livingston, 11 April 1777, *PAH*, 1:225–27.

28. Ibid., n.d. May 1777, *PAH*, 1:259.

29. Alexander Hamilton to Elizabeth Schuyler, 2–4 July, 5 October 1780, *PAH*, 2: 351, 455; Alexander Hamilton to Margarita Schuyler, n.d. February 1780, *PAH*, 2:270.

30. Alexander Hamilton to Elizabeth Schuyler, 17 March, n.d. August, 5 October 1780, *PAH*, 2: 287, 397, 455.

31. Ibid., 17 March, 2–4 July, n.d. August, 27 October 1780, *PAH*, 2: 287, 351, 397, 493.

32. Alexander Hamilton to John Laurens, 16 September 1780, *PAH*, 2: 431.

33. Alexander Hamilton to Elizabeth Schuyler, n.d. August, 5 October 1780, *PAH*, 2: 397, 455.

34. Alexander Hamilton to Elizabeth Schuyler, 6 September 1781, *PAH*, 2:675; Hamilton to Richard Meade, n.d. March 1782, *PAH*, 3:69–70; John Laurens to Hamilton, n.d. July 1782, *PAH*, 3:120–21.

35. Alexander Hamilton to John Laurens, 30 March, 12 September 1780, *PAH*, 2: 304, 427–28.

36. Ibid., 15 August 1782, *PAH*, 3:145. Hamilton used this parting phrase— "Yours for ever"—in writing to his wife as well as to Laurens (see, for example, *PAH*, 3:572, 9:87), but to no one else.

37. Alexander Hamilton to Nathaniel Greene, 12 October 1782, *PAH*, 3:183–84; Robert Hayne, speaking in Congress on the bill for relief of the grandson of John Laurens, *Army Correspondence of Colonel John Laurens*, 46; Hamilton to the Marquis de Lafayette, 3 November 1782, *PAH*, 3:193.

38. William North to Benjamin Walker, 13 June [n.d.], case 4, box 13, Simon Gratz Collection, Historical Society of Pennsylvania. Friedrich von Steuben had flourished in the Prussian army until he was summarily discharged as the result of what he somewhat vaguely described as "an inconsiderate step and the rancor of an implacable enemy" (John McAuley Palmer, *General Von Steuben* [New Haven, Conn.: Yale University Press, 1937], 50). After eleven years as grand marshall at the court of the prince of Hohenzollern-Hechingen, he sought to revive his military career by offering his services to the American Continental army. When the new nation's representatives in Paris declined even to pay for his travel expenses, let alone a salary, he withdrew his offer and returned to Germany, but he then changed his mind when rumors that he had "taken familiarity with young boys" forced him to leave Hohenzollern-Hechingen (quoted in Palmer, *General Von Steuben*, 92). Whether these rumors had any foundation is unclear, but Steuben returned to Paris and agreed to join the Continental army with no guarantee of rank, commission, or salary. Washington lent Laurens and Hamilton to Steuben as temporary aides until Walker and North replaced them. William Benemann suggests that Steuben may have had sexual feelings for Walker and North; he also implies that the friendship between North and Walker "included sexual intimacy," though he acknowledges that "it is impossible to prove the nature of the[se] relationships" (William Benemann, *Male-Male Intimacy in Early America: Beyond Romantic Friendships* [New York: Haworth Press, 2006] chap. 4, esp. 102).

39. Benjamin Walker to William North, quoted in Palmer, *General Von Steuben*, 361; North to Walker, 28 September [n.d.], case 2, box 1, Simon Gratz Collection, Historical Society of Pennsylvania.

40. Friedrich von Steuben to William North, 24 September [n.d.], Steuben Papers, New York Historical Society.

41. Horatio Gates wrote, for example, that soldiers saw him as "their military father," and a 1783 address referred to him as a "military parent"; see Horatio Gates to Friedrich von Steuben, 6 December 1785, Steuben Papers; and New York Cantonment to Friedrich von Steuben, 9 June 1783, ibid.

42. Friedrich von Steuben, Last Will and Testament, 12 February 1794, Steuben Papers; William North, quoted in Palmer, *General Von Steuben,* 403.

43. William North to Benjamin Walker, n.d. November 1792, 28 September [n.d.], case 4, box 13, Gratz Collection.

44. William North to BenjaminWalker, n.d. November 1792, 28 September [n.d.], 12 June [n.d.], case 4, box 13, Gratz Collection.

45. William North to Benjamin Walker, 16 February 1783, case 4, box 22, Gratz Collection; North to Walker, 15 May 1796, case 4, box 13, ibid.

46. William North to Benjamin Walker, 28 November 1799, case 4, box 13, Gratz Collection; North to Walker, 30 May 1788, alpha series under North, ibid.; North to Walker, 30 September 1812, case 4, box 13, ibid.

47. William North to Friedrich von Steuben, 8 January 1789, Steuben Papers; North to Benjamin Walker, 23 November 1788, case 4, box 13, Gratz Collection.

48. William North to BenjaminWalker, n.d. November 1792, case 4, box 13, Gratz Collection.

49. William North to Benjamin Walker, 18 September 1800, case 2, box 1, Gratz Collection; North to Walker, 27 September 1804, case 4, box 13, ibid.; North to Walker, 20 February 1797, case 4, box 13, ibid.

50. William North to Benjamin Walker, 11 June 1813, case 4, box 13, Gratz Collection.

51. Ibid., 11 November 1811, 30 September 1812, 2 July 1817.

52. Cynthia A. Kierner, ed., *The Contrast: Manners, Morals, and Authority in the Early American Republic* (New York: New York University Press, 2007), 85–86.

53. For early modern England, see E. M. W. Tillyard, *The Elizabethan World Picture* (London, 1943); James Daly, *Sir Robert Filmer and English Political Thought* (Toronto: University of Toronto Press, 1979); and Susan Dwyer Amussen, *An Ordered Society: Gender and Class in Early Modern England* (New York: Blackwell, 1988). For the North American colonies, see Edmund S. Morgan, *The Puritan Family: Religion and Domestic Relations in Seventeenth-Century New England* (1944; New York: Harper and Row, 1966); John Demos, *A Little Commonwealth: Family Life in Plymouth Colony* (New York: Oxford University Press, 1970); Gordon J. Schochet, *Patriarchalism in Political Thought: The Authoritarian Family and Political Speculation and Attitudes, Especially in Seventeenth-Century New England* (New York: Basic Books, 1975); and Mary Beth Norton, *Founding Mothers and Fathers: Gendered Power and the Forming of American Society* (New York: Knopf, 1996).

54. *Pennsylvania Packet,* 1 April 1778; [John Dickinson], *Letters from a Farmer in Pennsylvania to the Inhabitants of the British Colonies* (Philadelphia,

1768), Letter XII; "Observations on the Port Bill," *Memoir of the Life of Josiah Quincy, Jr., of Massachusetts: By His Son, Josiah Quincy* (Boston, 1825), 375.

55. This was not the only eighteenth-century context in which revolutionaries reimagined the family as a social and political trope: in the aftermath of 1789, the French eradicated their "political parents," the king and queen, envisaging "a different kind of family" in which parents were "effaced" and brotherhood took center stage; see Lynn Hunt, *The Family Romance of the French Revolution* (Berkeley: University of California Press, 1992), xiv.

56. *Providence Gazette*, 11 May 1765; "Freeborn American," Supplement to the *Boston Gazette*, 9 February 1767; James Otis, quoted in Clifford K. Shipton, ed., *Sibley's Harvard Graduates* 11 [the classes of 1741–45] (Boston: Massachusetts Historical Society, 1960), 270.

57. See Brendon McConville, *The King's Three Faces: The Rise and Fall of Royal America, 1688-1776* (Chapel Hill: University of North Carolina Press, 2006), esp. 204–5.

58. John Adams to Hezekiah Niles, 13 February 1818, in *Works of John Adams*, ed. Charles Francis Adams (Boston: Little, Brown, 1850–56), 10:282–83; see also William Shakespeare, *Macbeth*, 1.7.

59. [Dickinson], *Letters from a Farmer*, Letter V; John Adams to William Tudor, 21 August 1818, in C. F. Adams, *Works of John Adams*, 10:350.

60. *South Carolina Gazette*, 17 July 1769.

61. "Hyperion," *Boston Gazette*, 19 September 1768.

62. See Gordon Wood, *The Radicalism of the American Revolution* (New York: Knopf, 1992), 160.

63. Thomas Hutchinson, "Essay on Colonial Rights" (1765), quoted in Edmund S. Morgan, "Thomas Hutchinson and the Stamp Act," *New England Quarterly* 21 (1948): 489; "Nedham's Remembrancer, No. I," *Boston Gazette*, 20 December 1773; James Otis, *Brief Remarks on the Defence of the Halifax Libel* (Boston, 1765), 11.

64. Peter Shaw describes these ritual processions in *American Patriots and the Rituals of Revolution* (Cambridge, Mass.: Harvard University Press, 1981).

65. "Observations on the Port Bill," 307, 310, 375.

66. Thomas Paine, *Common Sense*, ed. Isaac Kramnick (1776; New York: Penguin Classics, 1986), 76, 78, 79, 81, 84, 92.

67. Lynn Hunt writes that "[t]he killing of the king was the most important political act" of the French Revolution and "the central drama in the revolutionary family romance" (*Family Romance of the French Revolution*, 2). This is no less true of the American Revolution, even though the patriots' murder of George III took metaphorical form.

68. *London Chronicle,* 18:523 (28–30 November 1765); article penned by "William Pym" for the *London General Evening Post,* 20 August 1765, reprinted in the *Newport Mercury,* 28 October 1765.

69. Thus, a contractual (or, to use early modern language, covenantal) conception of relationships intrinsic to the Puritan ethos that informed settlement in early New England now became common currency throughout British North America; see David Zaret, *The Heavenly Contract: Ideology and Organization in Pre-Revolutionary Puritanism* (Chicago: University of Chicago Press, 1985). For the shift from status to contract as the basis for legitimate authority, see Holly Brewer, *By Birth or Consent: Children, Law, and the Anglo-American Revolution in Authority* (Chapel Hill: University of North Carolina Press, 2005); Wood, *Radicalism of the American Revolution,* esp. 162–66; J. R. Pole, *The Pursuit of Equality in American History* (Berkeley: University of California Press, 1993), xiv; Edmund S. Morgan, *Inventing the People: The Rise of Popular Sovereignty in England and America* (New York: Norton: 1988); and Jay Fliegelman, *Prodigals and Pilgrims: The American Revolution against Patriarchal Authority* (New York: Cambridge University Press, 1982).

70. James Otis, *A Vindication of the British Colonies against the Aspersions of the Halifax Gentleman* (Boston, 1765), 11. Locke himself denied an equivalency between parental and political authority, but because eighteenth-century Americans continued to use familial language to articulate political relationships, his reevaluation of parental authority had a profound impact on political relations. Indeed, Locke's principal contribution on this subject, *Some Thoughts on Education,* first published in London in 1693, may have had more influence on political life than his famous *Second Treatise of Government* (1690).

71. For an overview of this transformation, see Wood, *Radicalism of the American Revolution,* chap. 9.

72. Samuel Thornely, ed., *Journal of Nicholas Cresswell* (New York: Dial Press, 1924), 270; Jack P. Greene, ed., *The Diary of Colonel Landon Carter of Sabine Hall, 1752–1778,* 2 vols. (Charlottesville, Va.: University Press of Virginia, 1965), 2:1004; Nicholas Collin, "Remarkable Occurrences Concerning Marriage," 29 July 1797, 15 July 1805, in "The Records of Gloria Dei Church," Historical Society of Pennsylvania.

73. John Adams to Thomas B. Adams, 17 October 1799, quoted in Page Smith, *John Adams* (New York, 1962), 2:1016–17. Philip Greven links the experience of childhood to political behavior during the revolutionary period in *The Protestant Temperament: Patterns of Child-Rearing, Religious Experience, and the Self in Early America* (New York: Knopf, 1977), 339–41.

74. See Francois Furstenberg, *In the Name of the Father: Washington's Legacy, Slavery, and the Making of a Nation* (New York: Penguin, 2006), esp. chap. 1.

Jan Lewis emphasizes the anti-patriarchal tone of stories and essays published in late eighteenth-century ephemeral literature, for which see Jan Lewis, "The Republican Wife: Virtue and Seduction in the Early Republic," *William and Mary Quarterly* 44 (1987): 689–721.

75. Paine, *Common Sense*, 63–64, 85, 99–100, 122, and Paine, *The American Crisis*, no. 1 (Philadelphia, 1776), 8, 10. Robert A. Ferguson also argues that *Common Sense* envisaged "a new family" in *Reading the Early Republic* (Cambridge, Mass.: Harvard University Press, 2004), 98. In passages that urged American males to rise up and protect their families against the cruelty of the British troops, Paine invoked a more traditional conception of men as husbands, fathers, and household heads, but he depicted them as roused by natural affection for their dependents and their future well-being rather than by a desire to defend their own patriarchal prerogatives against British intrusion. See also Nicole Eustace's insightful reading of *Common Sense* in *Passion Is the Gale: Emotion, Power, and the Coming of the American Revolution* (Chapel Hill: University of North Carolina Press, 2008), 439–79. Eustace sees Paine's essay as a canny response to a shift in attitudes toward emotion during the mid third of the eighteenth century, away from a paradigm that used the articulation of emotion as an important marker of gender, class, ethnicity, and race to a more egalitarian ethos that emphasized the universality of emotions. This shift had its limits, however, as Eustace acknowledges (259–66) and as I argue in chapter 5.

76. "Observations on the Port Bill," 375; Julian P. Boyd, ed., *The Papers of Thomas Jefferson*, vol. 1 (Princeton, N.J.: Princeton University Press, 1950), 135, 170, 171, 199, 420–22; vol. 10 (Princeton, N.J.: Princeton University Press, 1954), 451. See Gary Wills, *Inventing America: Jefferson's Declaration of Independence* (New York: Doubleday, 1978), part 4, for a thoughtful and compelling portrayal of Jefferson as an apostle of sensibility.

77. John Adams to Hezekiah Niles, 13 February 1818, *Works of John Adams*, 10:288.

78. *Pennsylvana Packet*, 12 December 1783; *Pennsylvania Gazette*, 23 July 1783.

79. William Eustis, "Statement Concerning the Origin of the Cincinnati," in *Memorials of the Massachusetts Society of the Cincinnati*, ed. James M. Bugbee (Boston: Massachusetts Society, 1890), 531–32; feature on a meeting of the Cincinnati in Philadelphia, *New-Hampshire Gazette, or, State Journal and General Advertiser*, 12 June 1784. For a detailed account of the Cincinnati, see Minor Myers Jr., *Liberty without Anarchy: A History of the Society of the Cincinnati* (Charlottesville: University of Virginia Press, 1983).

80. Federalist Papers, nos. 2, 15, 51, 57; *Pennsylvania Gazette*, 26 September 1787.

Chapter Five: "The Overflowing of Friendship"

1. *Pennsylvania Gazette*, 7 May 1794.

2. George Washington, Farewell Address, 17 September 1796.

3. Merrill D. Peterson, ed., *The Portable Thomas Jefferson* (New York, 1975), 290–92.

4. For the influence of Scottish thinkers on America's version of the Enlightenment, see Henry F. May, *The Enlightenment in America* (New York: Oxford University Press, 1976), and Morton White, *The Philosophy of the American Revolution* (New York: Oxford University Press, 1978).

5. Adam Smith, *The Theory of Moral Sentiments*, ed. D. D. Raphael and A. L. Macfie (1759; Oxford: Clarendon Press, 1976), 224–25. Allan Silver considers the eighteenth-century Scottish Enlightenment and its reconception of personal relationships in "Friendship in Commercial Society: Eighteenth-Century Social Theory and Modern Sociology," *American Journal of Sociology* 95 (1990): 1474–1504. For Dr. Johnson's definition of friendship and its implications, see Lawrence Stone, *The Family, Sex, and Marriage in England 1500–1800* (New York: Harper and Row, 1977), 97; and also Randolph Trumbach, *The Rise of the Egalitarian Family: Aristocratic Kinship and Domestic Relations in Eighteenth-Century England* (New York: Academic Press, 1978), 64.

6. Francis Hutcheson, *A System of Moral Philosophy* (1755; repr. in facsimile, Hildesheim: Georg Olms Verlagsbuchhandlung, 1971), 5:281; Francis Hutcheson, *An Inquiry into the Original of Our Ideas of Beauty and Virtue* (1725; repr. in facsimile, Hildesheim: Georg Olms Verlagsbuchhandlung, 1971), 1:198–99; David Hume, *A Treatise of Human Nature*, ed. L. A. Selby-Bigge (1739–40; Oxford: Clarendon Press, 1978), 602–3.

7. R. S. Downie, ed., *Philosophical Writings of Francis Hutcheson* (London: J. M. Dent, 1994), 72; Smith, *Theory of Moral Sentiments*, 9, 10. For sympathy as an effort of the imagination, see John B. Radner, "The Art of Sympathy in Eighteenth-Century British Moral Thought," *Studies in Eighteenth-Century Culture* 9 (1979): 189–210, and Elizabeth Barnes, *States of Sympathy: Seduction and Democracy in the American Novel* (New York: Columbia University Press, 1997), chap. 1 and 21–22.

8. Smith, *Theory of Moral Sentiments*, 109, 152. John Mullan examines this culture of sympathy in *Sentiment and Sociability: The Language of Feeling in the Eighteenth Century* (New York: Oxford University Press, 1988).

9. Daniel Webster to Thomas Merrill, 1 May 1804, in *The Writings and Speeches of Daniel Webster*, 18 vols., ed. J. W. McIntyre (Boston: Little, Brown, 1903), 17:166; Leander's Journal, 1: 26 July 1786; Nathaniel Greene to Samuel Ward, n.d. April 1772, in *The Papers of General Nathaniel Greene*, vol. 1., ed.

Richard K. Showman (Chapel Hill: University of North Carolina Press, 1976), 27; Alexander Hamilton to John Laurens, 15 August 1782, in *The Papers of Alexander Hamilton*, 27 vols., ed. Harold C. Syrett et al. (New York: Columbia University Press, 1961–87) [henceforth *PAH*], 3:145; Samuel Cooper, *A Sermon Preached in Boston* (Boston, 1753), 2.

10. Thomas Paine, *Common Sense*, 1776; ed. Isaac Kramnick (New York: Penguin Classics, 1986), 65; E. B. Williston, ed., *Eloquence of the United States*, vol. 5 (Middletown, Conn., 1827), 108–9. Gordon Wood discusses the importance of social benevolence as a component of post-revolutionary social theory in *The Radicalism of the American Revolution* (New York: Knopf, 1992), chap. 12.

11. "Jefferson," writes Joyce Appleby, "integrated a program of economic development and a policy for nation building into a radical moral theory . . . Abandoning the eternal Adam of Christianity as well as the creature of passions portrayed in ancient texts, he had embraced a conception of human nature that emphasized its benign potential." Appleby, "The Social Origins of American Revolutionary Ideology," *Journal of American History* 64 (1978): 955–56. See also Appleby, "What Is Still American in the Political Philosophy of Thomas Jefferson?" *William and Mary Quarterly* 39 (1982): esp. 293–94; Appleby, *Capitalism and a New Social Order: The Republican Vision of the 1790s* (New York: New York University Press, 1984), esp. 50; and James T. Kloppenberg, "The Virtues of Liberalism: Christianity, Republicanism, and Ethics in Early American Political Discourse," *Journal of American History* 74 (1987–88): 18.

12. See David A. Copeland, *Colonial American Newspapers: Character and Content* (Newark: University of Delaware Press, 1997); and Jeffrey L. Pasley, *"The Tyranny of Printers": Newspaper Politics in the Early American Republic* (Charlottesville: University of Virginia Press, 2001).

13. *Boston Gazette and Country Journal*, 18 February 1782; *Worcester Magazine*, 16 April 1788; *Cumberland Gazette*, 22 May 1789.

14. *Massachusetts Spy*, 3 July 1799; *Dunlap's American Daily Advertiser*, 13 March 1792; *Connecticut Gazette*, 2 January 1794.

15. *Newburyport Herald*, 23 August 1799; *Massachusetts Spy*, 4 April 1793.

16. *Cumberland Gazette*, 9 November 1789; *Massachusetts Spy*, 25 July 1793; *Columbian Magazine* 1 (1786), 200; *American Museum* 3 (1788), 150; *Providence Gazette and Country Journal*, 20 February 1773; *New-Hampshire Gazette, or, State Journal and General Advertiser*, 25 February 1786.

17. *Cumberland Gazette*, 9 November 1789.

18. Pay Book of the State Company of Artillery [1777], *PAH*, 1:400; for self-comparisons by the aides-de-camp to classical heroes such as Damon and Pythias, see John C. Miller, *Alexander Hamilton: Portrait in Paradox* (New York: Harper and Brothers, 1959), 22.

19. "Disinterested Friendship," *The Worcester Magazine*, 18 November 1790.

20. Ibid.; see also Laurie Shannon, *Sovereign Amity: Figures of Friendship in Shakespearean Context* (Chicago: University of Chicago Press, 2002), esp. 8, 53; and Laurens J. Mills, *One Soul in Bodies Twain: Friendship in Tudor Literature and Stuart Drama* (Bloomington, Ind.: Principia Press, 1937), 134–46.

21. *Massachusetts Spy*, 6 September 1792, 4 April 1793, 3 July 1799; *New-Hampshire Gazette, or, State Journal and General Advertiser*, 25 February 1786; *New-York Daily Gazette*, 1 June 1790; *New York Magazine* 2 (1792): 406.

22. *Columbian Centinel*, 20 April 1791; *Newburyport Herald*, 23 August 1799; *South Carolina State Gazette and Timothy's Daily Adviser*, 1 December 1800.

23. *New Hampshire Gazette*, 25 June 1799; *Windham Herald*, 14 January 1792; *Massachusetts Spy*, 3 September 1800.

24. *Vermont Gazette*, 25 May 1792; *New Hampshire Gazette*, 25 June 1799.

25. *Connecticut Gazette*, 2 January 1794; *State Gazette of South Carolina*, 4 March 1793; *Providence Gazette and Country Journal*, 16 February 1771; *Newburyport Herald*, 23 August 1799.

26. *Dunlap's American Daily Advertiser*, 13 March 1792.

27. See Shannon, *Sovereign Amity*, esp. 2–3.

28. *New-York Daily Gazette*, 1 June 1790; *Boston Gazette and Country Journal*, 18 February 1782; *Independent Gazetteer*, 11 October 1786; *Boston Post Boy*, 7 September 1772. See also Wood, *Radicalism of the American Revolution*, 220.

29. *Massachusetts Spy*, 6 September 1792; see also Ivy Schweitzer, *Perfecting Friendship: Politics and Affiliation in Early American Literature* (Chapel Hill: University of North Carolina Press, 2006), 2.

30. See also Nicole Eustace, *Passion Is the Gale: Emotion, Power, and the Coming of the American Revolution* (Chapel Hill: University of North Carolina Press, 2008), 259–66; and Jeanne Boydston's review of Mary Kelley, *Learning to Stand and Speak: Women, Education, and Public Life in America's Republic* (Chapel Hill: University of North Carolina Press, 2006) in *Journal of the Early Republic* 28 (2008): 47–60.

31. Benjamin Banneker, letter to Thomas Jefferson, 19 August 1791, in Carla Mulford et al., *Early American Writings* (New York: Oxford University Press, 2002), 1106; John Woolman, "Some Considerations on the Keeping of Negroes" (1754), in *The Journal and Major Essays of John Woolman*, ed. Phillips P. Moulton (New York: Oxford University Press, 1971), 200, 202; Woolman, "Considerations on Keeping Negroes, Part Second" (1762), in ibid., 226; 1779 Connecticut petitioners quoted in Gary B. Nash, *Red, White, and Black: The Peoples of Early North America*, 4th ed., (Upper Saddle River, N.J.: Prentice-Hall, 2000), 273.

32. For paternalism and slavery, see Francois Furstenberg, *In the Name of the*

Father: Washington's Legacy, Slavery, and the Making of a Nation (New York: Penguin, 2006), esp. 92–101; Eugene D. Genovese, *Roll, Jordan, Roll: The World the Slaves Made* (New York: Vintage, 1976); and Drew Gilpin Faust, *James Henry Hammond and the Old South: A Design for Mastery* (Baton Rouge: Louisiana State University Press, 1982); see also Elizabeth Fox-Genovese, *Within the Plantation Household: Black and White Women of the Old South* (Chapel Hill: University of North Carolina Press, 1988).

33. *Boston Post Boy*, 12 October 1772; *Providence Gazette and Country Journal*, 16 February 1771; *Dunlap's American Daily Advertiser*, 13 March 1792; *Cumberland Gazette*, 22 May 1789.

34. *Cumberland Gazette*, 22 May 1789; *Newport Mercury*, 27 June 1774; *Pennsylvania Gazette*, 20 October 1784; *Federal Gazette and Baltimore Daily Advertiser*, 25 January 1798; *Dunlap's American Daily Advertiser*, 13 March 1792.

35. Gordon Wood reads this declaration as supporting his argument that civic republicanism asked Americans to subordinate self-interest in favor of the general good. But Elizabeth Barnes points out that it actually asked them "to reinvest the common good with the properties of personal attachment": Americans would bind themselves to one another through "an understanding of the feeling self as the foundation of democratic society." See *Continental Journal*, 9 April 1778; Gordon Wood, *The Creation of the American Republic, 1776–1787* (New York: Norton, 1972), 60; and Barnes, *States of Sympathy*, 17–18.

36. *Pennsylvania Gazette*, 9 March 1796, 5 March 1800; *New Jersey Journal*, 6 February 1798.

37. "Review of the Boarding School," *Columbian Phoenix and Boston Review*, May 1800, 278; *Connecticut Courant*, 18 August 1788.

38. *Continental Journal*, 26 January 1786; *New Jersey Journal*, 23 August 1786; Hamilton to Catherine Livingston, 11 April 1777, *PAH*, 1:227.

39. *Independent Gazetteer*, 6 April 1789; *Windham Herald*, 25 July 1799; "On the Pleasures Arising from a Union between the Sexes," *Columbia Magazine*, January 1787, 244. Jan Lewis discusses post-revolutionary depictions of marriages as friendships in "The Republican Wife: Virtue and Seduction in the Early Republic," *William and Mary Quarterly* 44 (1987), 689–721.

40. *Massachusetts Spy*, 10 November 1785; *Dunlap's American Daily Advertiser*, 13 March 1792; *Continental Journal*, 14 July 1785, 26 January 1786.

41. "An Address to the Ladies," *American Magazine* 1 (March 1788): 246; "On the Virtues of Women," *Gentleman and Lady's Town and Country Magazine* 1 (December 1784), 337. Mary Kelley uses the term "civil society" to describe activities and settings that transcended the domestic and yet were not formally political. For women's engagement and influence in "civil society," see Kelley, *Learning to Stand and Speak*, esp. 5 and 50; and also Catherine Allgor, *Parlor Politics:*

In Which the Ladies of Washington Help Build a City and a Government (Charlottesville: University of Virginia Press, 2000). Some Americans did argue that women should become actively involved in formal politics, for which see Rosemarie Zagarri, *Revolutionary Backlash: Women and Politics in the Early American Republic* (Philadelphia: University of Pennsylvania Press, 2007).

42. "Female Character," *New York Magazine,* May 1792; *Continental Journal,* 14 July 1785, 26 January 1786. Rosemarie Zagarri has pointed out that Scottish Enlightenment thinkers saw the family as a crucial venue in which citizens could acquire virtue and that these thinkers accorded women a central role as wives and mothers in creating and nurturing sympathetic as well as virtuous citizens. Jan Lewis has shown that essays and short stories published in postrevolutionary magazines depicted republican wives as loving friends. See Zagarri, "Morals, Manners, and the Republican Mother," *American Quarterly* 44 (1992): 192–215, and Lewis, "Republican Wife." For women's role as exemplars of virtue, see Ruth Bloch, "American Feminine Ideals in Transition: The Rise of the Moral Mother, 1785–1815," *Feminist Studies* 4 (1978): 101–26; Bloch, "The Gendered Meanings of Virtue in Revolutionary America," *Signs* 13 (1987): 37–58; Linda Kerber, *Women of the Republic: Intellect and Ideology in Revolutionary America* (Chapel Hill: University of North Carolina Press, 1980); Mary Beth Norton, *Liberty's Daughters: The Revolutionary Experience of American Women, 1750–1800* (Boston: Little, Brown, 1980); Laurel Thatcher Ulrich, "Daughters of Liberty: Religious Women in Revolutionary New England," in Ronald Hoffman and Peter J. Albert, eds., *Women in the Age of the American Revolution* (Charlottesville: University Press of Virginia, 1989); and Richard Godbeer, *Sexual Revolution in Early America* (Baltimore: Johns Hopkins University Press, 2002), chap. 8.

43. "Reflections on Marriage Unions," *New York Magazine,* October 1790, 561; "On Marriage," *General Magazine and Review,* July 1798, 42.

44. *Connecticut Courant,* 18 August 1788; *Vermont Gazette,* 21 February 1791; *Independent Journal,* 17 March 1787.

45. *Vermont Gazette,* 21 February 1791; *Lady's Magazine and Musical Repository,* November 1801, 245.

46. *Pennsylvania Magazine* 2 (1776): 176–77. The culture of sensibility clearly had a profound effect on the ways in which women expressed and perceived themselves; For the influence of sensibility on female conversation, see David S. Shields, *Civil Tongues and Polite Letters in British America* (Chapel Hill: University of North Carolina Press, 1997), 126–40.

47. Quoted in Sarah Knott, "Sensibility and the American War for Independence," *American Historical Review* 109 (2004): 27–28.

48. See William Benemann, *Male-Male Intimacy in Early America: Beyond*

Romantic Friendships (New York: Haworth Press, 2006), 25. As Benemann points out, Jefferson was "familiar with a broad range of the world's literature, a literature rich in the words of men mourning the loss of the women they loved," and yet at this moment of grief reached out to an evocation of "love between two men" that he would have encountered as a boy, which says much about "the impact of those early images on developing imaginations."

49. *Cumberland Gazette*, 22 May 1789.

50. Some of the newspaper items on sentimental friendship and its social implications did not specify the gender of those involved; others either focused explicitly on relationships between men or discussed friendship in the context of marriage between a man and a woman; a modest number were comparative.

51. Catherine Allgor notes that the contributions made by women to the development of political culture in Washington City were depicted as "family work," for which see Allgor, *Parlor Politics*, 241. Joseph Ellis points out that President Jefferson's style of governance was modeled on a sentimental and consensual conception of the family; see Joseph Ellis, *American Sphinx: The Character of Thomas Jefferson* (New York: Knopf, 1997), 190.

52. *New Jersey Journal*, 23 August 1786; *New-York Daily Gazette*, 1 June 1790. "Society still appeared as the family writ large," writes Jan Lewis, but eighteenth-century "anti-patriarchalists" shifted emphasis "from the parent-child nexus to the husband-wife bond," which they depicted as an affectionate and companionate relationship, "a friendship of equals" characterized, at least rhetorically, by a spirit of reciprocity; see Lewis, "Republican Wife," esp. 699 and 707. I wish not to challenge this argument, but to add that at the same time fraternal love became a crucial component within republican ideology.

53. *New-York Daily Gazette*, 21 February 1789; "Reflections on Gallantry," *Pennsylvania Gazette*, 11 November 1772.

54. Janet Todd points out that men of feeling acquired "the womanly qualities of tenderness and susceptibility," but did not share the vulnerability of women to seduction and abandonment; see Janet Todd, *Sensibility: An Introduction* (New York: Methuen, 1986), chap. 6 (quotation, 89). Though it is true that men who were lured into a life of dissipation by rakish friends did not risk unmarried pregnancy and the attendant consequences, they could end up losing their worthier friends and perhaps falling prey to venereal disease, which was rampant and often fatal in the early republic. They risked, in other words, social and even literal death.

55. *Windham Herald*, 14 January 1792.

56. Cathy N. Davidson discusses this function of seduction literature in *Revolution and the Word: The Rise of the Novel in America* (New York: Oxford University Press, 1986), 113.

57. Cynthia A. Kierner, ed., *The Contrast* (New York: New York University Press, 2007), 43, 44, 47, 48, 51, 53, 54, 56, 69, 78, 82, 98.

58. "Reflections on Gallantry," *Pennsylvania Gazette*, 11 November 1772. Cathy N. Davidson discusses the novel as a form of education for young women in *Revolution of the Word: The Rise of the Novel in America* (New York: Oxford University Press, 1986).

59. *South Carolina Gazette*, 26 April 1773; *New-York Daily Gazette*, 21 February 1789. See also Godbeer, *Sexual Revolution*, chap. 8.

60. Smith-Carter Family Papers, 1669–1880, reel 1, Massachusetts Historical Society; "The Order of the Young Men's Meeting," in "Ebenezer Parkman's Book for Sundry Collections, 1718," Ebenezer Parkman Papers, box 2, folder 4, American Antiquarian Society, Worcester, Massachusetts; *Publications of the Colonial Society of Massachusetts*, 24 (Boston: Colonial Society of Massachusetts, 1923): 310; see also ibid., 12 (Boston: Colonial Society of Massachusetts, 1911): 228; *The Autobiography of Benjamin Franklin*, ed. Kenneth Silverman (New York: Penguin Classics, 1986), 59. See also "Autobiography of the Reverend John Barnard," *Collections of the Massachusetts Historical Society*, 3rd ser., 5 (1836): 186. Not all male societies were devoted to the cultivation of loving friendship, virtue, and harmony: the Tuesday Club of Annapolis, for example, was exuberantly contentious and competitive, priding itself on its rowdy and smutty proceedings; see Robert Micklus, ed., *The History of the Ancient and Honorable Tuesday Club, by Dr. Alexander Hamilton*, 3 vols. (Chapel Hill: University of North Carolina Press, 1990), and Wilson Somerville, *The Tuesday Club of Annapolis (1745–1756) as Cultural Performance* (Athens: University of Georgia Press, 1996).

61. Smith-Carter Family Papers, 1669–1880, reel 1; "The Order of the Young Men's Meeting," *Publications of the Colonial Society of Massachusetts*, 24 (Boston: Colonial Society of Massachusetts, 1923): 310. See also Anne S. Lombard, *Making Manhood: Growing up Male in Colonial New England* (Cambridge, Mass.: Harvard University Press, 2003), 81; and Mary Macmanus Ramsbottom, "Religious Society and the Family in Charlestown, Massachusetts, 1630–1740" (PhD diss., Yale University, 1987), chap. 6, esp. 237. Ramsbottom goes so far as to argue that the Charlestown group "supplanted the family as the critical arena of religious nurture for these boys during their adolescence" (264).

62. William Smith, *A Sermon Preached in Christ Church, Philadelphia, before the Provincial Grand Master and General Communication of Free and Accepted Masons* (Philadelphia, 1755), 9, 24; Thomas Pollen, *Universal Love* (Boston, 1758), 12–13; William Brogden, *Freedom and Love* (Annapolis, Md., 1750), 15; Michael Smith, *A Sermon Preached in Christ Church, New Bern, in North Carolina* (New Bern, N.C., 1756), 11. For an overview of early American freemasonry, see Steven C. Bullock, *Revolutionary Brotherhood: Freemasonry and the Trans-*

formation of the American Social Order, 1730–1840 (Chapel Hill: University of North Carolina Press, 1996); see in particular 56–59 for representations of masonry as an antidote to divisions within colonial society. For freemasonry and friendship in a French context, see Kenneth Loiselle, "'New but True Friends': Freemasonry and the Culture of Male Friendship in Eighteenth-Century France" (PhD diss., Yale University, 2007).

63. *Boston Evening Post*, 7 January 1751; Joseph Green, *Entertainment for a Winter's Evening* (Boston, 1750), 14, and Green, *The Grand Arcanum Detected* (Boston, 1755), 9. As Thomas A. Foster notes in *Sex and the Eighteenth-Century Man: Massachusetts and the History of Sexuality in America* (Boston: Beacon, 2006), "Treenails (commonly used in eighteenth-century shipbuilding) effectively joined timbers because they swell when wet," which would have given the metaphor "an added emphasis on sexual arousal" (171).

64. These comments are much endebted to Foster, "Antimasonic Satire, Sodomy, and Eighteenth-Century Masculinity in the *Boston Evening Post*," *William and Mary Quarterly* 60 (2003): 171–84; see also Clare A. Lyons, "Mapping an Atlantic Sexual Culture: Homoeroticism in Eighteenth-Century Philadelphia," *William and Mary Quarterly* 60 (2003): 152.

65. Bullock, *Revolutionary Brotherhood*, 137.

66. Samuel Seabury, *A Discourse on Brotherly Love* (New York, 1777), 14–15; Joshua L. Lyte, ed., *Reprint of the Minutes of the Grand Lodge of Free and Accepted Masons of Pennsylvania*, 12 vols. (Philadelphia, 1895–1907), 1:267.

67. Zabdiel Adams, *Brotherly Love and Compassion* (Worcester, Mass., 1778), 15; William Bentley, *A Discourse Delivered in Roxbury, October 12, 5796, before the Grand Lodge of Free and Accepted Masons* (Boston, 1797), 5–6; De Witt Clinton, *An Address Delivered before Holland Lodge* (New York, 1794), 10; and Benjamin Gleason, *An Oration* (Boston, 1812), 13. See also Bullock, *Revolutionary Brotherhood*, 74–76.

68. See chapter 4 above, and also Bullock, *Revolutionary Brotherhood*, 122, 124.

69. Bulkley Olcott, *Brotherly Love and Friendship* (Westminster, Vt., 1782), 4; Gleason, *Oration*, 5; Adams, *Brotherly Love and Compassion*, 17; Bentley, *Discourse Delivered in Roxbury*, 15.

70. Gleason, *Oration*, 6; Thaddeus Mason Harris, *A Discourse Delivered at Bridgewater, November 3, 1797, at the Request of the Members of Fellowship Lodge* (Boston, 1797), 12–13; Walter Monteath, *Brotherly Love* (New Brunswick, N.J., 1789), 4, 11, 14.

71. William Dix, *A Salutatory Address on the Social Influence and Merit of Free Masonry* (Boston, 1797), 6–7; Gleason, *Oration*, 6; [Abigail Lyon], *Observations on Freemasonry; With a Masonic Vision, Addressed by a Lady in Worcester*

to Her Female Friend (Worcester, Mass., 1798), 5. Some women still worried about the impact of Masonic membership on their husbands' "moral and religious sentiments," though Hannah Crocker wrote that when a number of Bostonian matrons voiced their concerns to her, she was "soon" able to reassure them "respecting the value of the institution." This latter incident appears to have taken place in the 1790s; [Hannah Martha Crocker], *A Series of Letters on Freemasonry* (Boston, 1815), 7.

72. De Witt Clinton, *An Address Delivered before Holland Lodge* (New York, 1794), 4; Seabury, *Discourse on Brotherly Love*, 5; Gleason, *Oration*, 12; Bentley, *Discourse Delivered in Roxbury*, 17–18; Hector Orr, *An Oration* (Boston, 1797), 9; Dix, *Salutatory Address*, 3–4.

73. Seabury, *Discourse on Brotherly Love*, 13–15.

74. Simeon Howard, *A Sermon on Brotherly Love* (Boston, 1779), 13; Orr, *Oration*, 10; Gleason, *Oration*, 11.

75. Seabury, *Discourse on Brotherly Love*, 14, 17; Dix, *Salutatory Address*, 3–4.

76. Adams, *Brotherly Love and Compassion*, 10, 13–15.

77. See Bullock, *Revolutionary Brotherhood*, chap. 6.

78. Monteath, *Brotherly Love*, 3, 4; Adams, *Brotherly Love and Compassion*, 13; Howard, *Sermon on Brotherly Love*, 7; Orr, *Oration*, 4; Harris, *Discourse Delivered at Bridgewater*, 20.

79. R. S. Crane argues that the sermons and writings of Anglican latitudinarian ministers in the late seventeenth and early eighteenth centuries provided an important source of inspiration for the culture of sensibility and its promotion of social benevolence; Crane, "Suggestions Toward A Genealogy of the 'Man of Feeling,'" *Journal of English Literary History* 1 (1934): 205–30.

80. Monteath, *Brotherly Love*, 11, 14; Adams, *Brotherly Love and Compassion*, 10–11, 15–16, 19.

81. *Massachusetts Spy*, 1 June 1796; *Washington Spy*, 22 June 1796; *Windham Herald*, 14 January 1792; *New-York Daily Gazette*, 1 June 1790.

82. George Washington, Farewell Address, 17 September 1796; *Vermont Journal and Universal Advertiser*, 24 July 1792; *Vermont Gazette*, 25 May 1792.

83. Ministers also played a crucial role in popularizing the patriot cause by translating political and constitutional arguments, which some ordinary folk may have found difficult to grasp and perhaps of limited relevance to their own lives, into a vivid spiritual drama that had compelling precedents in scripture and recent experience. From this perspective, the exodus of colonists from the empire reenacted the departure of Israel from Egypt, of Puritans from England, and of evangelicals from congregations that refused to embrace their version of spirituality; see Ellis Sandoz, ed., *Political Sermons of the American Founding*

Era, 1730–1805, 2 vols. (Indianapolis: Liberty Fund, 1998); and Harry S. Stout, *The New England Soul: Preaching and Religious Culture in Colonial New England* (New York: Oxford University Press, 1986), esp. chaps. 13 and 14.

84. John Woolman, *Considerations on the True Harmony of Mankind* (Philadelphia, 1770), 4, 9, 13, 14, 17, 18, 28; *The Works of John Woolman* (Philadelphia, 1774), 386, 389, 391, 396. Woolman himself died several years before the Declaration of Independence, in 1772.

85. Adams, *Brotherly Love and Compassion*, 10–11; Olcott, *Brotherly Love and Friendship*, 5, 6, 8.

Epilogue

1. Joseph Hooper to Benjamin Dolbeare, 8 August 1763, Dolbeare Family Papers, Massachusetts Historical Society.

2. The most famous of these commentaries was and remains Alexis de Tocqueville's *On Democracy in America* (originally published in two volumes as *De la démocratie en Amérique*, the first in 1835 and the second in 1840), with its subtle but nonetheless trenchant discussion of American "individualisme." For the rise of this atomistic individualism, see Gordon S. Wood, *The Radicalism of the American Revolution* (New York: Knopf, 1992), part 3, esp. chap. 17, and James T. Kloppenberg's thoughtful analysis in "The Virtues of Liberalism: Christianity, Republicanism, and Ethics in Early American Political Discourse," *Journal of American History* 74 (1987–88): 9–33. See also Elizabeth Barnes, *States of Sympathy: Seduction and Democracy in the American Novel* (New York: Columbia University Press, 1997), 13–14: "The myth of classic American literature—the idea that an autonomous individualism (and a specifically male individualism) represents the hallmark of the American novel and American identity—breaks down in the face of early American culture's prevailing concern for promoting sympathetic relations between individuals."

3. See Mary Kelley, *Learning to Stand and Speak: Women, Education, and Public Life in America's Republic* (Chapel Hill: University of North Carolina Press, 2006), esp. 19; Rodney Hessinger, *Seduced, Abandoned, and Reborn: Visions of Youth in Middle-Class America, 1780–1850* (Philadelphia: University of Pennsylvania Press, 2005), 113; and Andrew Burstein, *Sentimental Democracy: The Evolution of America's Romantic Self-Image* (New York: Hill and Wang, 1999), 308–19.

4. *Pennsylvania Gazette*, 9 March 1796. See also Kelley, *Learning to Stand and Speak*, 26, 52–54; Hessinger, *Seduced, Abandoned, and Reborn*, 160–63; and Ann Douglas, *The Feminization of American Culture* (New York: Knopf, 1977).

5. My discussion of changes in the late nineteenth century is much indebted to Donald Yacovone, "'Surpassing the Love of Women': Victorian Manhood and the Language of Fraternal Love," in *A Shared Experience: Men, Women, and the History of Gender*, ed. Laura McCall and Donald Yacovone (New York: New York University Press, 1998), esp. 213–15.

classical role models, 7–8, 18, 62–63, 147, 165–66, 168, 176, 177
Cleland, Thomas, 107–8
Clinton, Henry, 123
Coke, Thomas, 108
Colchester, Conn., 52
Cole, Nathan, 101–2
college life, 1, 24–42, 44, 49–54, 56, 63–64, 66–68, 81, 126, 182–83
Common Sense (Thomas Paine), 147–48, 151–52, 160
Complaint and the Consolation, The, or, Night Thoughts (Edward Young), 25
Concord, Mass., 148
Congress of the United States, 55, 58, 142, 153
Connecticut, colonial assembly of, 90
Constitution of the United States, 153–54, 167
Continental Army, 118–43, 152–53, 165, 178
Continental Congress, 126, 137, 212n7
Contrast, The (Royall Tyler), 142–43, 179–80
correspondence. *See* letters and letter-writing
Cotton, John, 86, 89, 114, 223n26
courtship of women, 42–48, 76–78, 131–35
Crocker, Hannah, 244n71
Culverwell, Ezekiel, 94
Custis, John, 73

Dartmouth College, 49–51
Darwin, Charles, 196
David and Jonathan, 7, 55, 65–66, 82, 84, 85, 88–89, 90, 99, 176, 191
death and mourning, 47, 53, 54–55, 60, 65–66, 76, 77, 85–86, 92, 98, 110, 137–38, 141–42
Declaration of Independence, the, 13, 16, 118, 144, 148, 150
Dedham, Mass., 91
De la Démocratie en Amerique (Alexis de Tocqueville), 245n2
Delamotte, Elizabeth, 104
dependency, 160–61, 194
depression. *See* melancholy
Devil, the, 106, 111, 141, 146–47, 150, 226n64

Dickinson, John, 143, 145
Dickinson, Mary, 20, 75
disinterestedness, 157, 168, 170
Dodge, Ezekiel, 56, 66, 72, 81
Dolbeare, Benjamin, 1, 54, 67, 193
Douglas, Ephraim, 123
Douglas, William, 102
dreams, 21, 39–40, 129
Duane, James, 120
Duanesburg, N.Y., 140
Dutch Reformed Church, 103

Edwards, Benjamin, 60, 81
Edwards, Jonathan, 95–97, 100–101, 102, 116
effeminacy, 6, 73–75, 159. *See also* gendered attributes and roles
egalitarianism and fraternal love, 12, 15–16, 82, 84, 113–18, 121, 143–44, 151–56, 160–62, 170, 178, 182–83, 185, 190–92
elective kinship. *See* kinship
Eliot, John, 92
Eliza. *See* Rhoads, Elizabeth
emotion. *See* feeling
England, 3, 5, 6–9, 13, 18, 25, 62, 68, 70, 84–86, 89–90, 92, 94, 104, 113, 123, 125, 126, 129, 143–49, 151–52, 169, 183, 191, 200n10, 244n83
Enlightenment, the, 94, 118, 149, 156–62, 166, 190, 193–94, 240n42. *See also* moral philosophy
ephemeral literature, 7, 10, 13–14, 21, 58, 62, 70, 71, 74, 75, 118, 130, 153–56, 162–69, 171–82, 184, 185, 189–90, 193, 195, 235n74
Episcopalianism. *See* Church of England
Eugenius (the pseudonym of one of John Mifflin's friends, his real name unknown), 76
Europe, 3, 5, 6, 10, 12, 17, 19, 22–23, 24–25, 30, 33, 40, 41, 43, 44, 54, 138, 156–60, 195, 200n10, 210n90, 215n39, 231n38. *See also* England; France
Eustis, William, 141, 153
evangelicals, 8, 9, 16, 83–84, 94–113, 116–118, 190. *See also* Great Awakening, the

Eve. *See* Adam and Eve

exclusivity of fraternal love, 14, 169–71, 184–85, 194

faction and social division, 11, 90–91, 155–56, 159–60, 167–68, 183–84, 187, 194–95

Fairlie, James, 139

familial imagery, 8, 9, 12, 14–16, 50, 81–82, 84–122, 125–26, 132, 136, 139–140, 142–56, 162, 166, 170–72, 178, 182–92

father figures. *See* paternal authority; paternal imagery

Federalist Papers, 153–54

feeling, as a facet of manhood and male friendship, 10–13

femininity. *See* gendered attributes and roles

Fenwick, George, 93

Fisher, Sally, 76

France, 20–21, 30, 119, 129, 131, 135, 147, 155, 233n55, 233n67

Franklin, Benjamin, 182

fraternal imagery, 8, 12, 14–16, 50, 81–82, 84–85, 87, 89–95, 97–102, 105–6, 108–118, 120–22, 125–26, 139–40, 142, 143–44, 151–56, 162, 166, 170–72, 178, 182–92

fraternal love: exclusivity of, 14, 169–71, 184–85, 194; political implications of, 9–10, 82, 121–22, 151–62, 167–75, 177–79, 182–96; religious faith and, 83–118, 182–92; social implications of, 9–10, 82, 155–78, 182–96. *See also* familial imagery; fraternal imagery

fraternal societies, 182–83. *See also* Freemasons

Freemasons, 7, 12, 182–89, 191–92

Frelinghuysen, Theodorus Jacobus, 103

Freud, Sigmund, 197

friendships between men: among aides-de-camp in Continental Army, 118–42, 165, 178; changing attitudes toward, in late nineteenth and twentieth centuries, 196–97; compared to marriage, 78–80, 172–78; definitions of, 9–10, 156–57, 163; and egalitarianism, 12, 15–16, 82, 84, 113–18, 121, 143–44, 151–56, 160–62, 170, 178, 182–83, 185, 190–92; envisioned as a marriage, 87, 109–10; and evangelicals, 9, 16, 83–84, 94–113, 116–18, 190; and the fostering of knowledge, 30, 61–64, 66–70, 79, 182, 183; and the fostering of virtue, 61–70, 77–78, 92, 118, 120, 122, 124, 155, 157, 159, 161, 163, 166–68, 171–92, 194, 215n39; and Freemasons, 7, 12, 182–89, 191–92; and implications of for civic life, 2, 12–16, 48, 82, 84, 118, 121–22, 151–62, 167–75, 177–79, 182–96; implications for social harmony, 9–10, 48, 82, 155–78, 182–96; longevity of, 15, 51–52, 58–61, 76–81, 138–43, 153, 163; and moral philosophy, 12, 156–62, 169–70; and physical affection, 2, 5–7, 18, 25, 28, 36, 38–40, 55–58, 63, 70–73, 83–87, 90–92, 94, 102–3, 110–12, 117, 120–21, 127, 139, 142, 164, 193; and Puritans, 16, 84–94, 99, 105, 113–18, 144, 154, 194, 204n16; relatives and encouragement of, 2, 9, 13, 17–20, 23, 24, 26, 40, 46, 48; seen as compatible with marriage to a woman, 42–48, 76–78, 81, 172–78; seen as competitive with marriage to a woman, 78–81, 141; seen as inferior to marriage with a woman, 175–76; and sexual intimacy, 2–7, 38–40, 56–58, 63, 102–3, 127–31, 139, 184–85, 197, 231n38. *See also* fraternal imagery; friendships between women

friendships between women, 6, 10–11, 197, 201n11, 212n5; as a model for male friendships, 11, 75–76

gardening, 44–45

gardens, 22, 24, 25–26, 27, 41, 44–45, 96, 164, 193

Garrettson, Freeborn, 107, 112

gendered attributes and roles, 2, 4, 6–7, 10–13, 48, 52, 73–75, 127–29, 130, 159, 177, 179, 187, 195–97, 203n14, 205n26

George III, 144–48, 151

Gibbs, Caleb, 119, 121

Gibson, James, 1, 24–43, 44, 46, 47–48, 52, 57, 59, 67–70, 74, 75–76, 129, 164, 193, 216n45. *See also* Lorenzo

Gibson, John (James's father), 24

Gibson, Mrs. (James's mother), 24, 26, 29, 36–37, 43, 44, 46, 47, 69

Gifford, George, 90

Gilmer, Peachy, 77, 220n72

Goodyear, Stephen, 93

Gray, Ellis, 54, 67

Great Awakening, the, 16, 94–105, 107, 113, 116–18, 190

Greene, Nathaniel, 123, 137, 159

Guy Fawkes Day, 146

Hamilton, Alexander, 119, 120, 121, 122, 124–38, 153–54, 159, 161, 165, 173, 179; and relationship with John Laurens, 122, 125–31, 133–38, 178, 200n9; and relationship with Catherine Livingston, 131–32, 134; and relationship with Elizabeth Schuyler, 131–36, 178, 231n36

Hamilton, Elizabeth. *See* Schuyler, Elizabeth

Harris, Nathaniel, 110

Harrison, Robert, 121, 122

Harrison, Thomas, 92

Harvard College, 1, 53, 54, 66, 67, 81, 182–83

Hayne, Robert, 138

Hazard, Ebenezer, 70, 78–79

Herbert, George, 49

Hibbens, William, 115

homosexuality, 3–5, 197. *See also* sexual orientation; sodomy

Hooper, Joseph, 1, 66, 193

Howard, Simeon, 188

Howe, Robert, 153

Howes, Edward, 92

Hull, John, 94

Hume, David, 156, 158

Humfrey, John, 92

Hutcheson, Francis, 156, 157

Hutchinson, Thomas, 146

individualism, 160, 194–95

interdependence, 160, 194–95

James, Elizabeth, 104–5

jealousy: of other friends, 40–42, 61, 85; of wives, 80, 85

Jefferson, Thomas, 152, 156, 161, 177

Jenner, Thomas, 92

Jenney, George, 92

Jesuits, 91, 148

Jesus Christ, 4, 8, 83–115, 117, 189, 191, 196; as a friend, 99, 108; as a spouse, 4, 8, 84, 85–87, 92, 94, 96–97, 99–101, 105, 107–8, 109–10, 223n26

Johnson, Isaac, 92

Johnson, Samuel, 157

Johnson [first name unknown], friend of John Rhea Smith, 39

Jonathan and David. *See* David and Jonathan

Jones, Patty, 43

Jones, Sarah, 106

journals and journal-writing, 1, 5, 13, 15, 17–18, 20–47, 52, 67–70, 74, 106–8, 111–13, 197

King's College (now Columbia University), 126

kinship, elective and biological, 8–9, 20, 77, 81–82, 84–118, 140, 185, 193, 205n26

knowledge, fostered by friendship, 30, 61–64, 66–70, 79, 182, 183

Knox, Mrs. (owner of boarding house in Princeton), 30–36

Kobler, John, 83–84, 109–10, 112

La Fayette, Marquis de, 119, 124, 138

Lancaster, Mass., 188

Laurens, Henry, 120–21

Laurens, John, 120–21; and relationship with Alexander Hamilton, 122, 125–31, 133–38, 178, 200n9; and relationship with Martha Manning, 129

Laurens, Martha. *See* Manning, Martha

lawyers, 1, 19, 38, 50, 56, 57, 60–61, 69–70, 126, 129

Leander, as a pseudonym, 18. *See also* Mifflin, John; pseudonyms

Leonora. *See* Rhoads, Leonora

letters and letter-writing, 1–2, 5, 10–11, 13–15, 19–22, 24, 26–30, 32–34, 41,

50–67, 70–81, 83–87, 91–94, 97–99, 103–6, 109–12, 120–123, 125–42, 197, 215n34

libertines, 67–68, 77–78, 127–29, 178–82

Livingston, Catherine, 131–32, 134

Livingston, William, 52–53, 63–65, 67, 73, 77, 78, 79, 81, 131

Locke, John, 149, 205n22

London (England), 6, 7, 54, 70, 113, 126, 129, 144, 146

longevity of friendships between men, 15, 51–52, 58–61, 76–81, 138–43, 153, 163

Lord, William, 93

Lorenzo, as a pseudonym, 25. *See also* James Gibson; pseudonyms

love. *See* friendships between men; friendships between women; marriage

loving friendships. *See* friendships; marriage

Lutherans, 150

Lyme, Conn., 102

Macbeth (William Shakespeare), 145

Machiavelli, Niccolo, 91

magazines. *See* ephemeral literature

Manning, Martha, 129

Marblehead, Mass., 1

Maria. *See* Rhoads, Mary

marriage, 2–4, 8–9, 12, 15, 18, 20, 42–48, 57, 76–82, 84–87, 92, 103–6, 109–10, 115, 129–31, 135–37, 140–42, 172–81, 231n36; avoided by evangelical ministers, 9, 105–6; compared to friendship, 172–78; as a distraction from public service, 136–37; as a distraction from religious ministry, 103–6; as a form of friendship, 173; friendship between men envisioned as, 87, 109–10; as a rival to friendship, 78–81, 141; seen as compatible with male friendship, 42–48, 76–78, 81, 172–78; seen as superior to friendship, 175–76; and a wife's duty to foster virtue in her husband, 172–81. *See also* Jesus Christ

masculinity. *See* gendered attributes and roles

Massachusetts Historical Society, 62

Maxcy, Virgil, 57–58

McHenry, James, 121, 122–23

Meacham, James, 106–7, 108, 111, 112–13

Mead, Stith, 83–84, 105–6, 109–11, 112

Meade, Richard, 120, 121, 122, 124, 134–35, 136

melancholy, 20–21, 23–34, 42, 46, 49–51, 53–55, 58–60, 67–68, 85, 98, 123, 125–27, 138, 140–42. *See also* death and mourning

Merrill, Thomas, 51, 55

Metcalf, John, 110

Methodists, 83, 105, 107, 108, 112, 117

Middlebury, Mass., 51

Mifflin, John, 1, 17–48, 52, 57, 59, 67–70, 74, 75–76, 129, 159, 164, 193, 216n45, 226n68. *See also* Leander

military camaraderie. *See* aides-de-camp

Minter, Jeremiah, 106

Mitchell, Edward, 110

monarchy, 8, 12, 144–51, 166, 167

moral corruption, thwarted by virtuous friendship, 12–13, 67–68, 77–78, 161, 178–82

morality. *See* virtue

moral philosophy, 12, 156–62, 169–70

Nassau Hall, Princeton University, 25, 26, 30–31, 33, 35, 37, 38–39, 41

neglect: accusations of, 29–30, 32–34, 59–60, 125–26, 128–29; guilt about, 41–42

Nest, Joris Van, 103

Newman, Samuel, 92

newspapers. *See* ephemeral literature

New York City, 17, 20–21, 29, 30, 34, 52, 64, 67, 126, 143, 152

Norris, Charles (Isaac's brother), 215n39

Norris, Deborah (Isaac's sister), 19, 22, 43, 75–76

Norris, Isaac, 17–24, 25, 26, 30, 33, 36, 39, 40–48, 74, 75, 76, 164, 193, 216n45. *See also* Castalio

Norris, Joseph (Isaac's brother), 23

Norris, Mary (Isaac's mother), 17–21, 23, 24, 26, 36, 37, 43, 44, 45, 215n39

North, Polly, 140–41

North, William, 138–42

Northampton, Mass., 95

Oliver, Andrew, 146
Orphan, The, or, The Unhappy Marriage (Thomas Otway), 18
Otis, James, 146, 149
Otway, Thomas, 18

Paine, Robert Treat, 53–54, 56, 57, 65–66, 72
Paine, Thomas, 147–48, 151–52, 160
Pamela (Samuel Richardson), 158
parenthood, conceptions of, 148–49
Parsons, Jonathan, 102–3
paternal authority, 12, 15, 113, 115, 118, 143–51, 171, 191
paternal imagery, 8, 12, 109, 112, 113, 115, 118, 120–21, 139, 143–51, 156, 166, 171, 178, 183, 189, 191. *See also* familial imagery; paternal authority
Pemberton, Mrs., 44, 45, 47
Peter, Hugh, 92
Philadelphia, 1, 17–31, 35–37, 38, 40–48, 67–69, 76, 103, 125, 126, 135, 150, 153, 155, 164, 182, 191, 226n68
physical affection between friends, 2, 5–7, 18, 25, 28, 36, 38–40, 55–58, 63, 70–73, 83–87, 90–92, 94, 102–3, 110–12, 117, 120–21, 127, 139, 142, 164, 193
"platonic" friendship, 5, 43
Pope, Alexander, 1
Pope, William, 60, 75, 81
Portland, Maine, 55
Princeton University, 24–42, 68
Providence, R.I., 116
pseudonyms, 18, 25, 111–12
Puritans, 3, 4, 16, 84–94, 99, 105, 113–118, 144, 154, 194, 204n16, 222n26, 234n69, 244n83

Quakers, 23, 170, 190–91, 216n45
Quincy, Josiah, 147, 152

rakes. *See* libertines
Randolph, John, 56
reason, in relation to emotion and feeling, 70, 95–97, 173, 195–96
refinement, as a prerequisite for sensibility and sympathy, 14, 70, 118, 123–24, 164, 168, 169–70
Rehoboth, Mass., 57

relatives and encouragement of male friendships, 2, 9, 13, 17–20, 23, 24, 26, 40, 46, 48
religious faith: fostered by friendship, 61–67, 70, 82, 87–91, 98, 109, 188–92; and Freemasons, 188–89, 191–92; friendship among the faithful, 83–118; images of loving friendship in heaven, 87, 96–99; reunion of friends after death, 55, 58, 61, 85, 98; and social affection in the new republic, 82, 118, 188–92. *See also* Baptists; biblical models; Catholics; Church of England; David and Jonathan; Dutch Reformed Church; evangelicals; Great Awakening, the; Jesuits; Jesus Christ; Lutherans; Methodists; Puritans; Quakers; virtue
republican ideology, 2, 12–16, 52, 82, 84, 118, 153–96
revivalists. *See* evangelicals; Great Awakening, the
rhetoric, 6, 14–15, 71–73, 121,
Rhoads, Elizabeth (known as Eliza), 42, 43
Rhoads, Leonora, 42, 43, 47
Rhoads, Mary (known as Maria), 43–47
Rhoads, Sarah (mother of above), 43, 45, 47
Richards, James, 94
Richardson, Samuel, 71, 158, 159
Roderick Random (Tobias Smollett), 7
Rogers, Ezekiel, 91
romantic friendship. *See* friendships between men; friendships between women
Ross, Clementina, 47
Rush, Benjamin, 47
Rutledge, Henry, 56

Satan. *See* Devil, the
Schuurman, Jacobus, 103
Schuyler, Elizabeth, 131–36, 178, 231n36
Schuyler, Margarita, 133
Schuyler, Philip, 131, 134
Scottish Enlightenment. *See* Enlightenment; moral philosophy
seduction and abandonment, 47, 68, 77–78, 127–29, 130, 179

self-improvement societies. *See* fraternal societies
self-love, 64, 88, 168–69, 186
sensibility, 10, 14, 70–76, 82, 123–24, 128, 151–54, 158–59, 164, 173–81, 186, 190, 193–96. *See also* moral philosophy; sympathy
sentimental friendship. *See* friendships; sensibility
separation from friends, xii, 13, 17–35, 37, 40–41, 43, 49–62, 71–72, 80, 83–87, 92–94, 98, 109–10, 125–31, 134–35, 138–42, 153, 164
sexual intimacy between male friends, 2–7, 38–40, 56–58, 63, 102–3, 127–31, 139, 184, 197, 231n38
sexuality. *See* sexual orientation
sexual orientation, 3–5, 197
shared feeling. *See* sympathy
Shaw, William, 54–55, 61, 70
Sheridan, Richard, 34
Sherman, Isaac, 123
Sibbes, Richard, 89
slavery, 118, 170–71, 191, 195, 196
sleeping together, 33, 35–39, 57–58, 79, 103, 111–12, 139
Smibert, Nathaniel, 65
Smith, Adam, 156–59, 161, 166, 216n45
Smith, John Rhea, 30, 37, 38–39
Smithfield, R. I., 57
Smollett, Tobias, 7
social division. *See* faction and social division
social harmony, fostered by friendship, 9–10, 48, 82, 118, 155–78, 182–96. *See also* fraternal love
sodomy, 3, 7, 102–3, 184, 231n38. *See also* homosexuality
Song of Solomon, 85–86, 100–101, 107–8
Sons of Liberty, 145, 146
Spencer, William, 112
Spring, Sir William, 85–86, 87, 93
Stamford, Conn., 53
Stanton, Thomas, 93
Steuben, Friedrich von, 138–41
support groups. *See* fraternal societies
sympathy, 10, 13, 14, 19, 52, 70–76, 78, 88, 97, 109, 123–26, 129–30, 143, 152–53, 157–64, 166–73, 175, 177–78,

182, 190–91, 193–96. *See also* moral philosophy; sensibility

Tallmadge, Benjamin, 123–24
Tantalus, 53
Tappan, N.Y., 123, 139
Taylor, Edward, 223n26
Taylor, John, 108, 112
Tazewell, Littleton, 60
Tennent, Gilbert, 99, 100, 104
Thacher, James, 124
Thacher, Thomas, 92
Thatcher, George, 55, 58–59
Theory of Moral Sentiments (Adam Smith), 158
Thomson, Charles, 210n84, 215n39
Thomson, Hannah, 20, 27, 210n84
Tilghman, Tench, 119, 122, 130
Tocqueville, Alexis de, 245n2
Totowa Falls, N.J., 119
Treatise of Nature (David Hume), 158
Tucker, George, 60
Tuesday Club of Annapolis, 242n60
Tufts, Cotton, 81
Tyler, Royall, 142, 179–80
Tyndal, Margaret, 87

University of Pennsylvania, 44

virtue, personal and civic, 61–70, 67, 77–78, 92, 118, 120, 122, 124, 155, 157, 159, 161, 163, 166–68, 171–92, 194, 215n39

Wait, Thomas, 55, 58–59
Walker, Benjamin, 138–42
Walker, Molly, 140, 142
Walter, Arthur, 54–55
Washington, George, 119–26, 128, 138, 139, 143, 144, 151, 152–53, 155–56, 166, 171, 178, 185, 190
Washington, Martha, 121, 128
Waterhouse, Jacob, 93
Webster, Daniel, 49–51, 55, 62, 79–81, 159
Weld, Thomas, 92
Welles, Noah, 52–53, 63–65, 73, 77, 78, 81, 131
Wesley, John, 105

Westfield, Mass., 223n26
Wharton, Mrs., 69
Whitefield, George, 95, 97–105, 116
Willard, Samuel, 223n26
Wilson, John, 92
Winthrop, John, Jr., 92–94
Winthrop, John, Sr., 84–94, 113, 114, 115
Winthrop, Margaret. *See* Tyndal, Margaret
Wirt, Elizabeth, 9, 77, 219n60
Wirt, William, 1–2, 9, 56, 57, 59–61, 62, 74–75, 76–77, 81

Wister, Sally, 75
wives: as friends to their husbands, 172–78, 181–82; and their responsibility to foster virtue in their husbands, 12, 172–81, 187
Woolman, John, 170, 191
Worcester, Mass., 187
women. *See* friendships between women; marriage; wives
Wrentham, Mass., 57

Yale College, 52
Young, Edward, 25